Network+ Countdown Calendar

The lines after the countdown number enable you to add the actual calendar days for reference.

31 _____
Network Devices

30 _____
Network Serv[...]
and Applicatio[...]

[29] _____
[...]Technologies

28 _____
Cable Installation

27 _____
Network Topologies and Infrastructure

26 _____
Implement IPv4 Addressing

25 _____
Implement IPv6 Addressing

24 _____
Routing Concepts

23 _____
Unified Communications, Virtualization, and Cloud

22 _____
Network Design and Documentation

21 _____
Network Monitoring and Metrics

20 _____
Network Segmentation, Patches, and Updates

19 _____
Switch Configuration

18 _____
STP, VLANs, Trunking, and VTP

17 _____
WLAN Implementation

16 _____
Risks, Threats, and Vulnerabilities

15 _____
Hardening Devices

14 _____
Physical Security, Firewalls, Access Control, and Forensics

13 _____
Network Models

12 _____
Network Theory

11 _____
Wired and Wireless Standards

10 _____
Implement Policies, Procedures, and Safety Practices

9 _____
Best Practices and Change Management

8 _____
Implement Ports and Protocols

7 _____
Troubleshooting Methodology

6 _____
Troubleshooting Tools

5 _____
Troubleshoot Wireless Issues

4 _____
Troubleshoot Copper and Fiber Cabling Issues

3 _____
Troubleshoot Network Issues

2 _____
Troubleshoot Security Issues

1 _____
Troubleshoot WAN Issues

EXAM DAY

Time
_____

Location
_____

Exam Checklist

Network+ Checklist Days 31–24

✔	Date	Objective
		Schedule to take the Network+ Exam at http://www.pearsonvue.com/comptia.
		Take at least one practice Network+ exam.
		Create a network model using a collection of network devices.
		Describe the difference between site-to-site and client-to-site VPNs.
		Explain to a friend how a computer can automatically get on the network without user intervention. Include DHCP, DNS, and NAT.
		List and summarize the major WAN technologies.
		Get a networking cable and explain to a friend how data travels across the pins. Point out the transmit and receive pairs.
		Explain when the three major types of cables are used: coax, twisted-pair, and fiber.
		Draw an example of each type of network topology. Explain situations in which each are appropriate.
		Describe the structure and operation of IPv4. List and describe the uses for the various types of IPv4 addresses.
		Develop several VLSM addressing schemes with various host requirements and implement them in a lab or simulator.
		Describe the structure and operation of IPv6. List and describe the uses for the various types of IPv6 addresses.
		Describe the various methods that a router can use to learn about and share knowledge of remote networks.
		Read and review Days 31–24 in this book.

Network+ Checklist Days 23–17

✔	Date	Objective
		Take an additional Network+ practice exam.
		Describe the impact of network evolution, including unified communications, virtualization, and cloud computing.
		Come up with a scenario for a network implementation that would include wired and wireless devices. Create a topology and list of requirements to install the network.
		List and describe the types of metrics that are used in monitoring networks.
		Describe the operation of SNMP. Compare the versions that are available.
		List and describe the various reasons to segment networks.
		Design a set of requirements to configure a basic switched network, including AAA and link aggregation.

✔	Date	Objective
		List and describe the uses for various types of VLANs.
		Describe the purpose of VTP.
		Design a set of requirements to configure a three-switch network with trunking and VLANs.
		Describe the three main 802.11 WLAN topologies.
		Configure a wireless router, including administrative access, DHCP settings, and wireless access for clients.
		Read and review Days 23–17 in this book.

Network+ Checklist Days 16–8

✔	Date	Objective
		Take an additional Network+ practice exam.
		Describe basic security threats and the methods used to mitigate them.
		Describe the methodologies and techniques used to harden devices from security vulnerabilities.
		Draw the OSI and TCP/IP models side by side. Compare and contrast the layer structures.
		List the major functions of each layer of the OSI model.
		Describe the details of sending an email from source to destination. Use a topology with several routers and switches.
		Describe the CSMA/CD process to someone who knows nothing about networking.
		Describe the major policies, procedures, and safety and best practices that impact a network technician's job.
		List and describe each of the major protocols. Include their associated port numbers.
		Read and review days 16–8 in this book.

Network+ Checklist Days 7–1

✔	Date	Objective
		For each of the troubleshooting days, have a friend introduce a few errors in your previous designs. Then use your troubleshooting skills to isolate and resolve the problem. If you are working solo, make a list of potential issues and the steps you would take to resolve each one.
		Take an additional Network+ practice exam.
		Read and review Days 7–1 in this book.
		Visit the testing center and talk with the proctor at least two days before the exam.
		Eat a decent meal, watch a good movie, and get a good night's rest before the exam.

31 Days Before Your
CompTIA Network+
Certification Exam

Allan Johnson

PEARSON IT
CERTIFICATION • 800 East 96th Street • Indianapolis, Indiana 46240 USA

31 Days Before Your CompTIA Network+ Certification Exam

ISBN-13: 978-0-7897-5647-3
ISBN-10: 0-7897-5647-1

Library of Congress Control Number: 2015957629

Printed in the United States of America

First Printing: February 2016

Trademarks

All terms mentioned in this book that are known to be trademarks or service marks have been appropriately capitalized. Pearson IT Certification cannot attest to the accuracy of this information. Use of a term in this book should not be regarded as affecting the validity of any trademark or service mark.

Warning and Disclaimer

Every effort has been made to make this book as complete and as accurate as possible, but no warranty or fitness is implied. The information provided is on an "as is" basis. The author and the publisher shall have neither liability nor responsibility to any person or entity with respect to any loss or damages arising from the information contained in this book.

Special Sales

For information about buying this title in bulk quantities, or for special sales opportunities (which may include electronic versions; custom cover designs; and content particular to your business, training goals, marketing focus, or branding interests), please contact our corporate sales department at corpsales@pearsoned.com or (800) 382-3419.

For government sales inquiries, please contact governmentsales@pearsoned.com.

For questions about sales outside the U.S., please contact intlcs@pearson.com.

Associate Publisher	Dave Dusthimer
Executive Editor	Mary Beth Ray
Development Editor	Andrew Cupp
Managing Editor	Sandra Schroeder
Senior Project Editor	Tonya Simpson
Copy Editor	Bart Reed
Indexer	Lisa Stumpf
Proofreader	Laura Hernandez
Technical Editor	Chris Crayton
Publishing Coordinator	Vanessa Evans
Cover Designer	Mark Shirar
Compositor	Studio Galou

Contents at a Glance

Contents

About the Author

Allan Johnson entered the academic world in 1999 after 10 years as a business owner/operator to dedicate his efforts to his passion for teaching. He holds both an MBA and an M.Ed in Occupational Training and Development. He taught CCNA courses at the high school level for 7 years and has taught both CCNA and CCNP courses at Del Mar College in Corpus Christi, Texas. In 2003, Allan began to commit much of his time and energy to the CCNA Instructional Support Team, providing services to Networking Academy instructors worldwide and creating training materials. He now works full time for Cisco Networking Academy as a Learning Systems Developer.

About the Technical Reviewer

Chris Crayton (MCSE) is an author, technical consultant, and trainer. He has worked as a computer technology and networking instructor, information security director, network administrator, network engineer, and PC specialist. Chris has authored several print and online books on PC repair, CompTIA A+, CompTIA Security+, and Microsoft Windows. He has also served as technical editor and content contributor on numerous technical titles for several of the leading publishing companies. He holds numerous industry certifications, has been recognized with many professional teaching awards, and has served as a state-level SkillsUSA competition judge.

Dedication

For my wife, Becky. You continue to travel with me through those "thin times" when projects like these need to be nurtured. Without your constant vigilance and loving support, this work would not have come to fruition.

Acknowledgments

This book is a concise summary of networking concepts and draws upon the work of several Pearson authors. Thank you to Keith Barker, Emmett Dulaney, Anthony Sequeira, and Kevin Wallace for blazing a trail in the Network+ domain by authoring some outstanding resources for the reader.

Thank you to my technical editor, Chris Crayton, who is a tough task master and excellent subject matter expert. This book was made much better by his attentive guidance.

The Digital Study Guide version of this book includes activities, videos, and quizzes for each day.

I am grateful to Dan Alberghetti for agreeing to do the videos. Students of Cisco Network Academy will be familiar with his work. But you can also find Dan's work at his website, http://danscourses.com, and his YouTube channel, http://youtube.com/danscourses.

For writing outstanding quiz items to challenge our readers, we called on Troy McMillan. Thank you, Troy, for your attention to detail and assessment-authoring skill.

Lisa Matthews took my activity designs and Troy's quiz questions and made them interactive—a task that requires creativity, talent, and skill. Thank you, Lisa, for taking the final steps to make activities and quizzes available on PCs, tablets, and mobile devices.

Thank you to Drew Cupp, development editor, and Tonya Simpson, project editor, for juggling all the many pieces that must be managed to bring this product to our students, both in a book format and as a digital study guide.

A project like this goes through many review cycles. One of the very last reviews is for grammar and style. It always amazes me how much of an impact a copy editor can have on the final readability of a product. Thank you, Bart Reed, for making me look good.

And, finally, thank you to my editor, Mary Beth Ray, for bringing me this project when I said, "Okay, what's next?" You continue to challenge me to grow and expand my horizons.

Command Syntax Conventions

The conventions used to present command syntax in this book are the same conventions used in the IOS Command Reference. The Command Reference describes these conventions as follows:

- **Boldface** indicates commands and keywords that are entered literally as shown. In actual configuration examples and output (not general command syntax), boldface indicates commands that are manually input by the user (such as a **show** command).

- *Italic* indicates arguments for which you supply actual values.

- Vertical bars (|) separate alternative, mutually exclusive elements.

- Square brackets ([ ]) indicate an optional element.

- Braces ({ }) indicate a required choice.

- Braces within brackets ([{ }]) indicate a required choice within an optional element.

We Want to Hear from You!

As the reader of this book, *you* are our most important critic and commentator. We value your opinion and want to know what we're doing right, what we could do better, what areas you'd like to see us publish in, and any other words of wisdom you're willing to pass our way.

We welcome your comments. You can email or write to let us know what you did or didn't like about this book—as well as what we can do to make our books better.

Please note that we cannot help you with technical problems related to the topic of this book.

When you write, please be sure to include this book's title and author as well as your name and email address. We will carefully review your comments and share them with the author and editors who worked on the book.

Email: feedback@pearsonitcertification.com

Mail: Pearson IT Certification
         ATTN: Reader Feedback
         800 East 96th Street
         Indianapolis, IN 46240 USA

Reader Services

Register your copy of *31 Days Before Your CompTIA Network+ Certification Exam* at www.pearsonitcertification.com for convenient access to downloads, updates, and corrections as they become available. To start the registration process, go to www.pearsonitcertification.com/register and log in or create an account*. Enter the product ISBN 9780789756473 and click Submit. When the process is complete, you will find any available bonus content under Registered Products.

Be sure to check the box that you would like to hear from us to receive exclusive discounts on future editions of this product.

Introduction

You are almost there! If you're reading this Introduction, you've probably already spent a considerable amount of time and energy pursuing your CompTIA Network+ certification. Regardless of how you got to this point in your travels through your networking studies, *31 Days Before Your CompTIA Network+ Certification Exam* most likely represents the last leg of your journey on your way to the destination: to become Network+ certified.

However, if you're like me, you might be reading this book at the *beginning* of your studies. If such is the case, then this book provides you with an excellent overview of the material you must now spend a great deal of time studying and practicing. However, I must warn you: unless you are extremely well-versed in networking technologies and have considerable experience as a network technician or administrator, this book will not serve you well as the sole resource for Network+ exam preparation. I know this first hand. I recently took the Network+ exam and was impressed with both the breadth and depth of knowledge required to pass. I have been teaching, writing about, and implementing networks for more than a decade, and yet there was a moment during the Network+ exam where I thought, "Wow, this is really a tough exam!"

You see, CompTIA states that the Network+ exam "covers the configuration, management, and troubleshooting of common wired and wireless network devices." You simply cannot just study this content. You must practice it. Although I have a solid understanding of networking concepts and technologies, I also have extensive experience implementing and troubleshooting networks. That's why I was able to easily pass the exam. There really is no other way to correctly answer the many scenario-based questions a candidate will receive during the exam than to have experienced the same or similar scenarios in the real-world or a lab simulation.

Now that I've sufficiently challenged you, let me spend some time discussing my recommendations for study resources.

Study Resources

Pearson IT Certification offers an abundance of books and resources to serve you well as you learn how to configure, manage, and troubleshoot wired and wireless networks. Most of the resources can be purchased in book form or as e-books for your tablet reader by visiting www.pearsonitcertification.com.

Safari Books Online

All the resources I reference in the book are available with a subscription to Safari Books Online (https://www.safaribooksonline.com). If you don't have an account, you can try it free for 10 days.

Primary Resources

First on the list must be Keith Barker and Kevin Wallace's book *CompTIA Network+ N10-006 Cert Guide* (ISBN: 9780789754080). These two Cisco Certified Internetwork Experts (CCIE) do an outstanding job of gathering together and organizing all the material you need to study for the Network+ certification exam. If you get the premium edition bundle, you'll also receive an e-book version, more practice exams, a free copy of the CompTIA Network+ Simulator Lite software, and more than 60 minutes of video mentoring from the author. The practice exams and study materials on the DVD in the back of the book are worth the price of the book. There is no better resource on the market for a Network+ candidate.

Kevin Wallace also recorded more than 17 hours of video in his *CompTIA Network+ N10-006 Complete Video Course* (ISBN: 9780789754721), which is available free with your Safari Books Online account. You can also purchase it separately at pearsonitcertification.com. Kevin walks you through the full range of topics on the CompTIA Network+ exam using a variety of presentation styles, including live instructor whiteboarding, real-world demonstrations, animations of network activity, dynamic KeyNote presentations, and doodle videos. He also demonstrates hands-on router and switch CLI configuration and troubleshooting in real lab environments, enabling you to learn both the concepts and the hands-on application.

Next on the list must be Emmett Dulaney and Mike Harwood's *CompTIA Network+ N10-006 Exam Cram, Fifth Edition* (ISBN: 9780789754103). This dense Exam Cram book is jam packed with essential content for the Network+ exam. It also includes a handy, pullout exam cram sheet and a CD with practice exams.

At the end of each day in *31 Days Before Your CompTIA Network+ Certification Exam*, you will find a handy reference of what topics to look at in these three resources. They are referred to as "Certification Guide," "Video Course," and "Exam Cram," respectively.

Supplemental Resources

In addition to the book you hold in your hands, there are two more supplemental resources I recommend to augment your final 31 days of review and preparation.

Michael Taylor's *CompTIA Network+ N10-006 Hands-on Lab Simulator* (ISBN: 9780789755179) helps you gain hands-on experience with the concepts presented on the Network+ exam. Using the labs in this software, you will be able to experience realistic operating system and network device configuration and troubleshooting. The three types of labs in the software present you with progressively more difficult real-world challenges. Drag-and-drop labs demonstrate network design concepts and allow you to manipulate physical network cables. Matching labs help reinforce key networking concepts. Operating system and Cisco router and switch command-line interface (CLI) simulator labs present real-world configuration and troubleshooting scenarios for you to solve.

Anthony Sequeira is a CCIE and well-respected networking technologies author. His *CompTIA Network+ N10-006 Flash Cards and Exam Practice Pack* (ISBN: 9780789754646) is a compilation of more than 700 flash cards, practice questions, and quick reference sheets to help you prepare for the Network+ exam. Go through the printed flash cards or install the flash card software on your computer. The CD also includes the practice test software as well as 40 performance-based question exercises, including drag-and-drop and command-line interface questions that mimic the kinds of hands-on questions you will face on the actual exam.

So which resources should you buy? That question is largely up to how deep your pockets are or how much you like books. If you're like me, you want it all—online access for mobile and tablet reading, as well as hard copies for intensive study sessions with a pencil in hand. I admit it: My bookcase is a testament to my "geekness." However, that's not practical for most students. So if you are on a budget, then choose one of the primary study resources and one of the supplemental resources, such as the Cert Guide and the Lab Simulator. Whatever you choose, you will be in good hands. Any or all of these authors will serve you well.

Digital Study Guide

Pearson offers this book in an online digital format that includes enhancements such as video, activities, and Check Your Understanding questions:

- Read the complete text of the book on any web browser that supports HTML5, including mobile.

- Watch dozens of unique embedded videos that demonstrate configurations, explain important topics, and visually describe key Network+ exam objectives.

- Reinforce key network concepts with more than 30 dynamic and interactive hands-on exercises, and see the results with the click of a button.

- Test your understanding of the material at the end of each day with more than 300 fully interactive online quiz questions.

31 Days Before Your CompTIA Network+ Certification Exam Digital Study Guide is available at a discount for anyone who purchases this book. You can find details about redeeming this offer in the back of the book.

Throughout this book you'll see references to the Digital Study Guide enhancements that look like this:

Video: Data Encapsulation Summary

Refer to the Digital Study Guide to view this video.

Activity: Identify the Encapsulation Layer

Refer to the Digital Study Guide to complete this activity.

Check Your Understanding

Refer to the Digital Study Guide to take a 10-question quiz covering the content of this day.

When you are at these points in the Digital Study Guide, you can start the enhancement.

Goals and Methods

The main goal of this book is to provide you with a clear and succinct review of the Network+ exam objectives. Each day's exam topics are grouped into a common conceptual framework and uses the following format:

- A title for the day that concisely states the overall topic

- A list of one or more CompTIA Network+ N10-006 exam topics to be reviewed

- A "Key Topics" section to introduce the review material and quickly orient you to the day's focus

- An extensive review section consisting of short paragraphs, lists, tables, examples, and graphics

- A "Study Resources" section to provide you a quick reference for locating more in-depth treatment of the day's topics

The book counts down starting with Day 31 and continues through the exam day to provide post-test information. You will also find a calendar and checklist that you can tear out and use during your exam preparation inside the book.

Use the calendar to enter each actual date beside the countdown day and the exact day, time, and location of your Network+ exam. The calendar provides a visual for the time that you can dedicate to each Network+ exam topic.

The checklist highlights important tasks and deadlines leading up to your exam. Use it to help you map out your studies.

Who Should Read This?

The audience for this guide is anyone finishing his or her preparation for taking the CompTIA Network+ N10-006 exam. A secondary audience is anyone needing a refresher review of Network+ exam topics—possibly before attempting to recertify.

Getting to Know the CompTIA Network+ N10-006 Exam

CompTIA launched the newest version of the Network+ exam, numbered N10-006, in February 2015. The exam covers the configuration, management, and troubleshooting of common wired and wireless network devices. Also included are emerging technologies such as unified communications, mobile, cloud, and virtualization technologies. CompTIA recommends that you are A+ certified and have at least 9 months of networking experience.

Currently for the Network+ exam, you are allowed 90 minutes to answer a maximum of 90 questions. A passing score is 720 on a scale of 100 to 900. If you've never taken a certification exam before with Pearson VUE, there is a 2-minute 45-second video titled "What to expect in a Pearson VUE test center" that nicely summarizes the experience. You will find it under "Related Links" at http://www.pearsonvue.com/comptia, or you can search for it on YouTube.

When you get to the testing center and check in, the proctor verifies your identity, gives you some general instructions, and then takes you into a quiet room containing a PC. When you're at the PC, you have a few things to do before the timer starts on your exam. For instance, you can take the tutorial to get accustomed to the PC and the testing engine. Every time I sit for an exam, I go through the tutorial even though I know how the test engine works. It helps me settle my nerves and get focused. Anyone who has user-level skills in getting around a PC should have no problems with the testing environment.

What Topics Are Covered on the Network+ Exam

Table I-1 summarizes the five domains of the Network+ exam.

Table I-1   Network+ Domains and Weightings

Domain	% of Examination
1.0 Network architecture	22%
2.0 Network operations	20%
3.0 Network security	18%
4.0 Troubleshooting	24%
5.0 Industry standards, practices, and network theory	16%
Total	100%

Registering for the Network+ N10-006 Exam

If you are starting your *31 Days Before Your CompTIA Network+ Certification Exam* today, register for the exam right now. In my testing experience, there is no better motivator than a scheduled test date staring me in the face. I'm willing to bet it's the same for you. Don't worry about unforeseen circumstances. You can cancel your exam registration for a full refund up to 24 hours before taking the exam. So if you're ready, then you should gather the following information and register right now:

- Legal name
- Social Security or passport number
- Company name
- Valid email address
- Method of payment

You can schedule your exam at any time by visiting http://www.pearsonvue.com/comptia/. I recommend you schedule it for 31 days from now. The process and available test times will vary based on the local testing center you choose.

Network Devices

CompTIA Network+ N10-006 Exam Topics

- 1.1 Explain the functions and applications of various network devices

Key Topics

Today's review focuses on the network device functions, including common devices and specialty devices.

Common Network Devices

Designing, installing, administering, and troubleshooting a network requires the ability to recognize various network components and their functions. Table 31-1 lists several common network components and their functions.

Table 31-1   Common Network Device Functions

Device	Description
Client	Any device, such as a workstation, laptop, tablet, or smartphone, that is used to access a network.
Server	Provides resources to network users, including email, web pages, or files.
Hub	A Layer 1 device that does not perform any inspection of traffic. A hub simply receives traffic in a port and repeats that traffic out of all the other ports.
Switch	A Layer 2 device that makes its forwarding decisions based on the destination Media Access Control (MAC) address. A switch learns which devices reside off which ports by examining the source MAC address. The switch then forwards traffic only to the appropriate port, and not to all the other ports.
Router	A Layer 3 device that makes forwarding decisions based on Internet Protocol (IP) addressing. Based on the routing table, the router intelligently forwards the traffic out of the appropriate interface.
Multilayer switch	Can operate at both Layer 2 and Layer 3. Also called a Layer 3 switch, a multilayer switch is a high-performance device that can switch traffic within the LAN and forward packets between subnets.
Media	Media can be copper cabling, fiber-optic cabling, or radio waves. Media varies in its cost, bandwidth capacity, and distance limitation.
Analog modem	Modem is short for modulator/demodulator. An analog modem converts the digital signals generated by a computer into analog signals that can travel over conventional phone lines.

Device	Description
Broadband modem	A digital modem used with high-speed DSL or cable Internet service. Both operate in a similar manner to the analog modem, but use higher broadband frequencies and transmission speeds.
Access point (AP)	A network device with a built-in antenna, transmitter, and adapter that provides a connection point between WLANs and a wired Ethernet LAN. APs usually have several wired RJ-45 ports to support LAN clients. Most small office or home office (SOHO) routers integrate an AP.

Some of the devices listed in Table 31-1 are shown in Figure 31-1.

Figure 31-1   Common Network Components

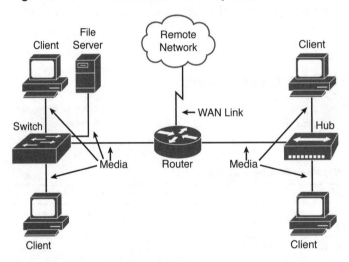

Specialty Devices

Although common network devices make up the backbone of a network, many networks integrate various specialized network devices.

Firewalls

A firewall is a networking device, either hardware or software based, that controls access to your organization's network. This controlled access is designed to protect data and resources from outside threats.

Organizations implement software firewalls through network operating systems (NOS) such as Linux/UNIX, Windows servers, and Mac OS X servers. The firewall is configured on the server to allow or block certain types of network traffic. Hardware firewalls are often dedicated network devices that can be implemented with little configuration.

A basic firewall is shown in Figure 31-2.

Figure 31-2   The Function of a Firewall

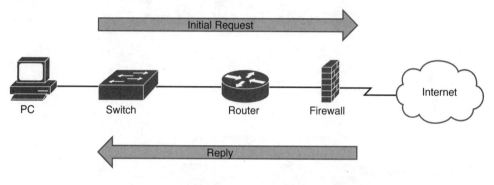

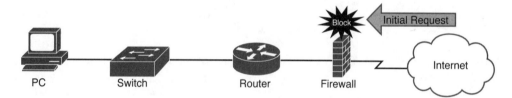

IDS and IPS

Both intrusion detection systems (IDS) and intrusion prevention systems (IPS) can recognize network attacks; they differ primarily in their network placement. An IDS device receives a copy of traffic to be analyzed. An IPS device is placed in line with the traffic, as shown in Figure 31-3.

Figure 31-3   IPS and IDS Comparison

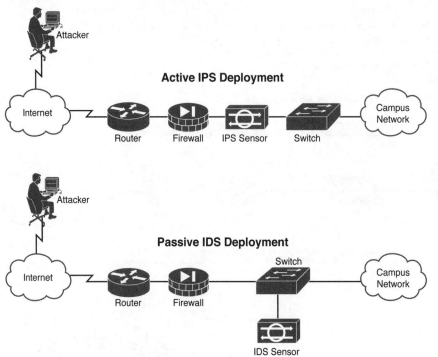

An IDS is a passive detection system. It can detect the presence of an attack, log the information, and send an alert.

Following are several variations on IDSs:

- **Behavior-based IDSs** look for variations in behavior so they can recognize potential threats and quickly log the information as well as send an alert.

- **Signature-based IDSs** evaluate attacks based on attack signatures and audit trails. This type of IDS uses an extensive database to determine the signature of the traffic.

- **Network-based IDSs (NIDS)** examine all network traffic to and from network systems.

- **Host-based IDSs (HIDS)** include applications such as spyware and virus applications that are installed on individual network systems.

An intrusion prevention system (IPS) includes the functionality of an IDS. However, an IPS is an active device that continually scans the network, looking for inappropriate activity. It can shut down any potential threats. The IPS looks for any known signatures of common attacks and automatically tries to prevent those attacks.

Proxy Server

A proxy server is a computer that provides a computer network service allowing clients to make indirect network connections to other network services. A proxy server can effectively hide the IP addresses of a trusted network because all requests going out to the Internet are sourced from the proxy server's IP address, as shown in Figure 31-4.

Figure 31-4   Proxy Server Operation

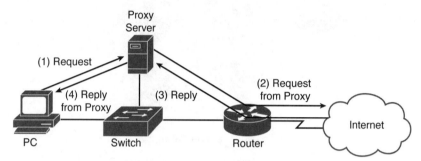

Reverse proxy is used when a proxy server protects another server (normally a web server) that responds to requests from users on the other side of the proxy server. Proxy servers can also conserve expensive WAN bandwidth by performing content caching. In addition, proxy servers can provide content filtering services.

Content Caching

When the user first visits a website, the proxy server will store the website for a configurable amount of time. When another user requests the website, the proxy server will check to see if the website has changed. If not, the proxy server can locally serve up the content. Proxy servers can also serve as content filters.

Content Filter

A content filter is software that usually controls what websites a user is allowed to access. An employer can block access to specific types of sites for all users, some users, or even just an individual user. The filter can be applied as software on client machines, on a proxy server on the network, at the Internet service provider (ISP), or even within the search engine itself. The latter is most commonly used on home machines or SOHO routers, and an example is Content Advisor in Internet Explorer.

Load Balancer

For companies with a large Internet presence, a single server could be overwhelmed with requests flooding in from the Internet. To alleviate the burden placed on a single server, a load balancer distributes incoming requests across mirrored servers, as shown in Figure 31-5.

Figure 31-5   Load Balancer Scenario

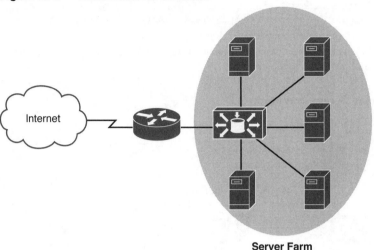

Server Farm

Load balancers allow a server farm to scale. As demand increases, new servers can be added. Maintenance is also easier because a failed server can be replaced with little or no impact to the service level experienced by users.

Packet Shaper

Traffic shaping establishes priorities for data traveling to and from the Internet and within the network. A packet shaper essentially performs two key functions: monitoring and shaping. Monitoring includes identifying where usage is high and the time of day. After that information is obtained, administrators can customize or shape bandwidth usage for the best needs of the network.

VPN Concentrator

A virtual private network (VPN) provides a cost-effective way to create a secure connection, or tunnel, through an untrusted network such as the Internet. Although several router models can terminate a VPN circuit, a VPN concentrator can be used instead to perform the processor-intensive processes required to terminate multiple VPN tunnels. Figure 31-6 shows a sample VPN topology, with a VPN concentrator at each corporate location.

Figure 31-6   VPN Concentrator Scenario

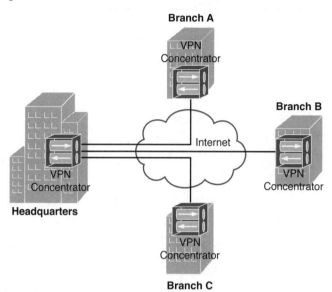

Video: Network Devices – Function and Application

Refer to the Digital Study Guide to view this video.

Video: Proxy Servers

Refer to the Digital Study Guide to view this video.

Activity: Compare Network Devices

Refer to the Digital Study Guide to complete this activity.

Study Resources

For today's exam topics, refer to the following resources for more study.

Resource	Location	Topic
Primary Resources		
Certification Guide	1	Defining a Network
	12	Intrusion Detection and Prevention
Exam Cram	4	Common Network Devices
Video Course	2	Network Devices and Theory

Resource	Location	Topic
Supplemental Resources		
Lab Simulator	2	Network Application Protocols
Flash Cards	1	Network Devices and Services
Quick Reference	1	Network Devices and Services

 Check Your Understanding

Refer to the Digital Study Guide to take a 10-question quiz covering the content of this day.

Network Services and Applications

CompTIA Network+ N10-006 Exam Topics

- 1.2 Compare and contrast the use of networking services and applications

- 1.3 Install and configure the following networking services/applications

Key Topics

Today's review focuses on several important network services and applications, including VPNs, AAA, DHCP, DNS, and NAT.

VPN

Virtual private networks (VPNs) support secure communication between two sites over an untrusted network, typically the Internet. VPNs are an important tool for remote or telecommuting users to securely access corporate headquarters. VPNs provide a low-cost, efficient method for branch locations to securely connect to corporate headquarters.

Types

The two primary types of VPNs are site-to-site and client-to-site VPNs:

- **Site-to-site VPNs** provide a low-cost, efficient method for branch locations to securely connect to corporate headquarters. Site-to-site VPNs are usually faster and cost less than leased lines. Figure 30-1 shows an example of a site-to-site VPN.

Figure 30-1   Site-to-Site VPN

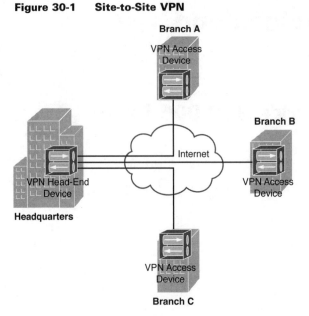

■ **Client-to-site VPNs** (or remote-access VPNs) are an important tool for remote or telecommuting users to securely access corporate headquarters. Client-to-site VPNs are faster and cost less than traditional dial-up or ISDN connections. Figure 30-2 shows an example of a client-to-site VPN.

Figure 30-2   Client-to-Site VPN

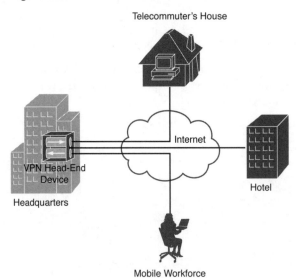

IPsec and IKE

Internet Protocol Security (IPsec) is a suite of protocols used to create a VPN. IPsec is composed of two separate protocols. Authentication Header (AH) provides the authentication and integrity checking for data packets, and Encapsulating Security Payload (ESP) provides encryption services.

IPsec provides three key security services:

- **Data confidentiality** ensures that the data sent between the two parties is unreadable by a third party.

- **Data integrity** ensures that data is not modified in transit.

- **Authentication** verifies that the party on the other side of the tunnel is the party they claim to be.

Internet Key Exchange (IKE) is the key negotiation and management protocol that is most commonly used to provide dynamically negotiated and updated keying material for IPsec. Specifically, IPsec can use IKE to provide encryption between authenticated peers.

The process of establishing, maintaining, and tearing down an IPsec site-to-site VPN uses IKE and consists of five primary steps, as shown in Figure 30-3:

Figure 30-3   Site-to-site IPsec VPN Steps

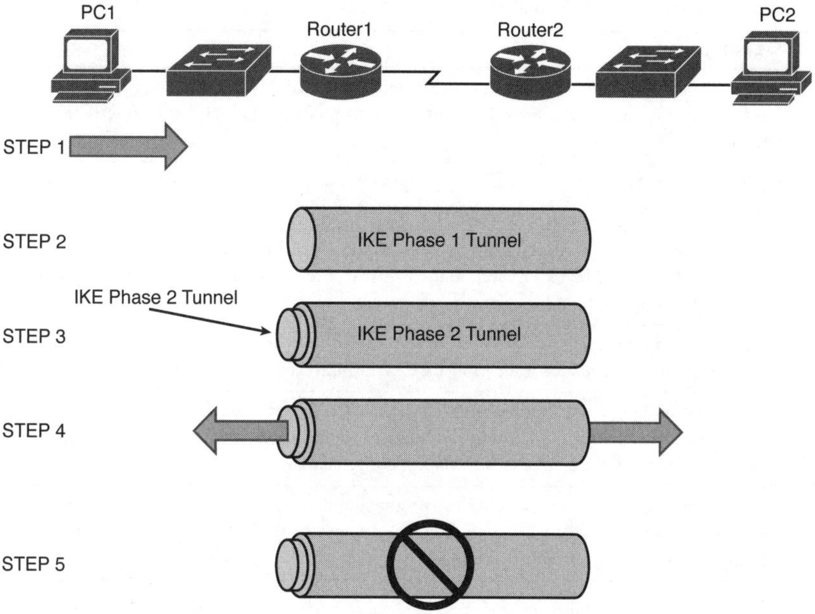

Step 1. PC1 sends traffic destined for PC2. Router1 classifies the traffic as "interesting" traffic (usually classified as interesting by an ACL), which initiates the creation of an IPsec tunnel.

Step 2. Router1 and Router2 negotiate a security association (SA) used to form an IKE Phase 1 tunnel, which is also known as an Internet Security Association and Key Management Protocol (ISAKMP) tunnel.

Step 3.   Within the protection of the IKE Phase 1 tunnel, an IKE Phase 2 tunnel is negotiated and set up. An IKE Phase 2 tunnel is also known as an IPsec tunnel.

Step 4.   After the IPsec tunnel is established, interesting traffic flows through the protected IPsec tunnel. Note that traffic not deemed interesting can still be sent between PC1 and PC2. However, the non-interesting traffic is neither authenticated nor encrypted.

Step 5.   After no interesting traffic is seen for a specified amount of time, the IPsec tunnel is torn down and the IPsec SA is deleted.

 Video: Types of VPNs

Refer to the Digital Study Guide to view this video.

 Activity: Order the Steps for Site-to-Site VPNs

Refer to the Digital Study Guide to complete this activity.

Other VPN Technologies

Although IPsec VPNs are popular for securely interconnecting sites or connecting a remote client to a site, you need to be aware of other VPN protocols for the exam, examples of which are provided in Table 30-1.

Table 30-1   Examples of VPN Protocols

Protocol	Description
SSL	Secure Sockets Layer (SSL) provides cryptography and reliability for the upper layers (Layers 5–7) of the OSI model. SSL provides secure web browsing via Hypertext Transfer Protocol Secure (HTTPS).
TLS	Transport Layer Security (TLS) has largely replaced SSL. For example, when you securely connect to a website using HTTPS, you are probably using TLS.
L2TP	Layer 2 Tunneling Protocol (L2TP) is a VPN protocol that lacks security features, such as encryption. However, L2TP can still be used for a secure VPN connection if it is combined with another protocol that does provide encryption.
L2F	Layer 2 Forwarding (L2F) is a VPN protocol designed (by Cisco Systems) with the intent of providing a tunneling protocol for PPP. Like L2TP, L2F lacks native security features.
PPTP	Point-to-Point Tunneling Protocol (PPTP) is an older VPN protocol and lacks native security features. However, Microsoft's versions of PPTP bundled with various versions of Microsoft Windows were enhanced to offer security features.
GRE	Generic Routing Encapsulation (GRE) is a tunneling protocol developed by Cisco Systems that can encapsulate a wide variety of network layer protocols. It is particularly useful for sending routing updates across secure links.

Remote Access Services

Remote access services include any combination of hardware or software that allows a user to remotely access another device on the network. For the Network+ exam, you need to be able to compare and contrast RADIUS, TACACS+, and Microsoft's RAS.

AAA Services

Authentication, authorization, and accounting (AAA) services allow an administrator to create and manage one repository for all user credentials. Functionally, AAA works as follows:

- **Authentication**—Users must prove that they are who they say they are.

- **Authorization**—Authorization services determine which resources the user can access and which operations the user is allowed to perform.

- **Accounting**—Accounting keeps track of how network resources are used.

RADIUS and TACACS+ are protocols commonly used to communicate with a AAA server:

- **Remote Authentication Dial-In User Service** (RADIUS) is a UDP-based protocol used to communicate with a AAA server. Unlike TACACS+, RADIUS does not encrypt an entire authentication packet, but only the password. However, RADIUS does offer more robust accounting features than TACACS+. Also, RADIUS is a standards-based protocol, whereas TACACS+ is a Cisco proprietary protocol.

- **Terminal Access Controller Access-Control System Plus** (TACACS+) is a TCP-based protocol used to communicate with a AAA server. Unlike RADIUS, TACACS+ encrypts an entire authentication packet, rather than just the password. TACACS+ does offer accounting features, but they are not as robust as the accounting features found in RADIUS. Also, unlike RADIUS, TACACS+ is a Cisco proprietary protocol.

Table 30-2 compares RADIUS and TACACS+.

Table 30-2   RADIUS and TACACS+ Comparison

Characteristic	RADIUS	TACACS+
Functionality	Combines authentication and authorization but separates accounting	Separates AAA according to the AAA architecture, allowing modularity of the security server implementation
Standard	Open/RFC standard	Mostly Cisco supported
Transport Protocol	UDP	TCP
Challenge Handshake Protocol (CHAP)	Unidirectional challenge and response from the RADIUS security server to the RADIUS client	Bidirectional challenge and response, as used in CHAP
Confidentiality	Password encrypted	Entire packet encrypted
Customization	Has no option to authorize router commands on a per-user or per-group basis	Provides authorization of router commands on a per-user or per-group basis
Accounting	Extensive	Limited

Microsoft's RAS

Remote access service (RAS) is a remote-access solution included with Windows Server products. Although the system is called RAS, the underlying technologies that enable the RAS process are dial-up protocols such as the Point-to-Point Protocol (PPP). Any system that supports dial-up protocols can connect to a RAS server.

RAS supports remote connectivity from all the major client operating systems available today, including all newer Windows operating systems:

- Windows Server products

- Windows Home–based clients

- Windows Professional–based clients

- Windows Enterprise–based clients

- UNIX-based/Linux clients

- Mac OS X–based clients

Other Remote Access Services

Other remote access services include the following:

- **RDP**—Remote Desktop Protocol (RDP) is a Microsoft protocol that allows a user to view and control the desktop of a remote computer.

- **ICA**—Independent Computing Architecture (ICA) is a Citrix Systems proprietary protocol that allows an application running on one platform (for example, Microsoft Windows) to be seen and controlled from a remote client, independent of the client platform (for example, UNIX/Linux).

- **SSH**—Secure Shell is a protocol used to securely connect to a remote host (typically via a terminal emulator).

- **Telnet**—Telnet is an unsecure protocol used to connect to a remote host. All traffic, including username and password, is sent in clear text. Telnet should not be used.

Unified Communications

Unified communications (UC), referred to as unified voice services in the Network+ exam topics, combine data, voice, and video all on the same network. UC networks implement Voice over IP (VoIP) to digitize the voice traffic into packets to be transmitted across a data network. Figure 30-4 shows a sample VoIP network topology.

Figure 30-4   VoIP Network Topology

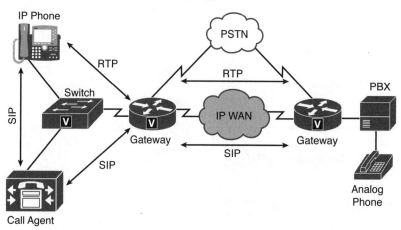

Table 30-3 defines the VoIP devices and protocols shown in Figure 30-4.

Table 30-3   VoIP Network Elements

Protocol/Device	Description
IP phone	An IP phone digitizes the spoken voice, packetizes it, and sends it out over a data network (via the IP phone's Ethernet port).
Call agent	When a user dials a number from an IP phone, the call agent analyzes the dialed digits and determines how to route the call toward the destination.
Gateway	A gateway in a VoIP network acts as a translator between two different telephony signaling environments. In Figure 30-4, both gateways interconnect a VoIP network with the Public Switched Telephone Network (PSTN). The gateway on the right interconnects a traditional PBX with a VoIP network.
PBX	A Private Branch Exchange (PBX) is a privately owned telephone switch traditionally used in corporate telephony systems. Although a PBX is not typically considered a VoIP device, it can connect into a VoIP network through a gateway, as shown in Figure 30-4.
Analog phone	An analog phone is a traditional telephone, which can connect into a VoIP network via a PBX, which is connected to a VoIP network.
SIP	Session Initiation Protocol (SIP) is a VoIP signaling protocol used to set up, maintain, and tear down VoIP phone calls.
RTP	Real-time Transport Protocol (RTP) is a protocol that carries voice (and interactive video). Notice in Figure 30-4 that the bidirectional RTP stream does not flow through the call agent.

DHCP

You could manually assign IP address information to every device on the network. However, static address assignment is time consuming and prone to error. A much more efficient method is to have IP address information assigned dynamically. The most common approach for this auto-assignment of IP addresses is to use Dynamic Host Configuration Protocol (DHCP). Not only does DHCP assign an IP address to a network device, it can assign a wide variety of other IP parameters, such as a subnet mask, a default gateway, and the IP address of a DNS server.

Figure 30-5 illustrates the DHCP process.

Figure 30-5   DHCP Process

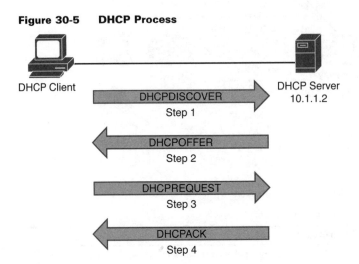

Use the mnemonic DORA to remember the steps in the DHCP process: **D**iscover, **O**ffer, **R**equest, and **A**cknowledge.

Step 1.   DHCPDISCOVER messages are broadcasted by the client when it initially boots to discover DHCP servers.

Step 2.   DHCPOFFER messages are replies from DHCP servers.

Step 3.   DHCPREQUEST messages are sent by the client request to a particular server's offer.

Step 4.   DHCPACK messages are sent by the DHCP server acknowledging the DHCP client and providing a collection of IP configuration parameters.

DHCP enables ranges of IP addresses, known as scopes, to be defined on a system running a DHCP server application. When another system configured as a DHCP client is initialized, it asks the server for an address. If all things are as they should be, the server assigns an address from the scope to the client for a predetermined amount of time, known as the lease.

At various points during the lease (normally the 50 percent and 85 percent points), the client attempts to renew the lease from the server. If the server cannot perform a renewal, the lease expires at 100 percent, and the client stops using the address.

Some devices on the network, such as servers and printers, may require a consistent IP address. In such cases, the network administrator can configure the DHCP server to reserve specific IP addresses for these clients.

DHCP servers can also be configured to provide clients with other parameters such as DNS servers, domain names, and WINS servers.

If there are no DHCP servers on the same LAN as the client, then the gateway router must be configured to relay DHCP requests to a DHCP server. This is because DHCPDISCOVER messages are broadcasted. By default, broadcast messages are not forwarded by routers.

 Activity: Order the Steps in the DHCPv4 Operation

Refer to the Digital Study Guide to complete this activity.

DNS

A Domain Name System (DNS) server performs the task of resolving a domain name to an IP address. As shown in Figure 30-6, an end user who wants to navigate to the www.ciscopress.com website enters that fully qualified domain name (FQDN) into the web browser. The end user's computer sends a DNS request to the DNS server asking for the IP address that corresponds to www.ciscopress.com. The DNS server responds with 192.168.1.11, and now the end user's computer can send packets to the destination.

Figure 30-6   DNS Operation

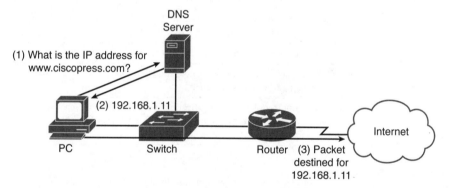

A DNS server maintains a database of local FQDNs and their corresponding IP addresses, in addition to pointers to other servers that can resolve IP addresses for other domains. DNS servers are arranged in a hierarchy, as shown in Figure 30-7.

Figure 30-7   DNS Hierarchy

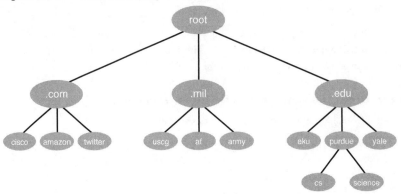

In addition to FQDNs, a DNS server contains other common DNS record types, as shown in Table 30-4.

Table 30-4   Common DNS Record Types

Record Type	Description
A	Maps a hostname to an IPv4 address.
AAAA	Maps a hostname to an IPv6 address.
CNAME	A canonical name record is an alias of an existing record, thus allowing multiple DNS records to map to the same IP address.
MX	A mail exchange record maps a domain name to an email server for that domain.
PTR	A pointer record points to a canonical name. A PTR record is commonly used when performing a reverse DNS lookup.
SOA	A start of authority record provides information about a DNS zone, such as email contact information for the zone's administrator, the zone's primary name server, and various refresh timers.

What happens if the IP address used by a server changes dynamically? In such a situation, the DNS records would need to be updated. Dynamic DNS providers supply software that monitors the IP address changes and reports any change to the DNS servers.

NAT

Private IPv4 addresses within an organization's network must be translated to a public IPv4 address before packets can be sent to the public Internet. Network Address Translation (NAT) provides this service. Figure 30-8 summarizes basic NAT operation.

Figure 30-8   NAT Operation

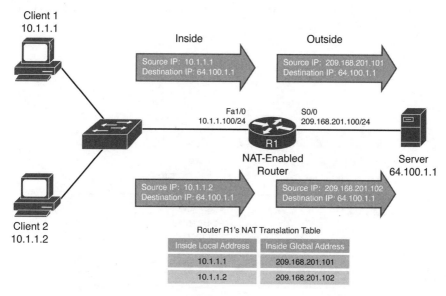

In Figure 30-8, packets from the two client PCs are translated at the NAT-enabled router, R1. The inside local addresses are translated to inside global addresses. Table 30-5 reviews the terminology used when describing the various IP addresses involved in a translation.

Table 30-5   NAT Terminology

NAT Term	Definition
Inside local	A private IP address referencing an inside device
Inside global	A public IP address referencing an inside device
Outside local	A private IP address referencing an outside device
Outside global	A public IP address referencing an outside device

Sometimes, you want to statically configure the inside global address assigned to a specific device inside your network, such as a web server or email server. This approach to NAT is referred to as Static NAT (SNAT).

The addresses in Figure 30-8 were dynamically assigned to the clients from a pool of available addresses. This is called dynamic NAT. However, this one-to-one dynamic mapping of one private IP address to one public IP address is far less common than another variety of NAT called Port Address Translation (PAT).

NOTE: Dynamic NAT should not be confused with destination NAT (DNAT). DNAT, more commonly referred to as port forwarding, is used to change the destination IP address on a packet. Typically, the packet is coming from an outside network, such as the Internet, and is destined for an inside device, such as a server or gaming console.

PAT allows multiple inside local addresses to share a single inside global address. PAT does this by tracking source and destination port numbers as well as the inside local and inside global addresses. Figure 30-9 summarizes PAT operation.

Figure 30-9   PAT Operation

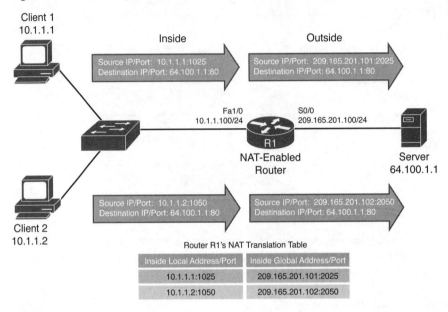

Video: NAT Terminology

Refer to the Digital Study Guide to view this video.

Study Resources

For today's exam topics, refer to the following resources for more study.

Resource	Location	Topic
Primary Resources		
Certification Guide	3	Specialized Network Devices
		Voice over IP Protocols and Components
	5	Assigning IPv4 Addresses
	6	Address Translation
	12	Virtual Private Networks
		Remote-Access Security

Resource	Location	Topic
Exam Cram	2	Dynamic Host Configuration Protocol (DHCP)
		Domain Name Service (DNS)
	3	NAT, PAT, SNAT, and DNAT
	11	Tunneling, Encryption, and Access Control
Video Course	4	All
Supplemental Resources		
Lab Simulator	2	DHCP Technology
	3	Details of DHCP Client Address Configuration Process
		Configuring Static Hostname Resolution on a Workstation
Flash Cards	2	Configuring Network Services
Quick Reference	2	Configuring Network Services

 Check Your Understanding

Refer to the Digital Study Guide to take a 10-question quiz covering the content of this day.

WAN Technologies

CompTIA Network+ N10-006 Exam Topics

- 1.4 Explain the characteristics and benefits of various WAN technologies

Key Topics

First today, we review packet switching and circuit switching. Then we review all the various ways networks are connected together through WAN technologies.

Packet Switching and Circuit Switching

The switching function provides communication pathways between two endpoints and manages how data flows between them. The two most common switching methods are circuit switching and packet switching.

Integrated Service Digital Network (ISDN), shown in Figure 29-1, is an example of a circuit-switched network.

Figure 29-1   Circuit Switching ISDN Topology

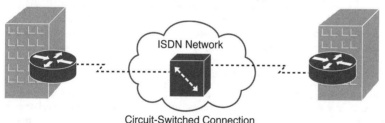

Circuit-Switched Connection

Circuit switching requires a dedicated physical connection between the sending and receiving devices. For example, parties involved in a phone call have a dedicated link between them for the duration of the conversation. When either party disconnects, the circuit is broken, and the data path is lost. This is an accurate representation of how circuit switching works with network and data transmissions. The sending system establishes a physical connection, and the data is transmitted between the two. When the transmission is complete, the channel is closed.

A Frame Relay network, shown in Figure 29-2, is an example of a packet-switched network.

Figure 29-2   Packet Switching Frame Relay Topology

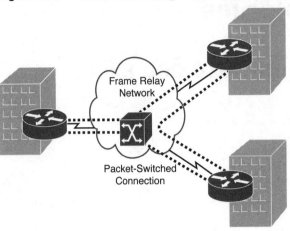

In packet switching, messages are broken into smaller pieces called packets. Each packet is assigned source and destination addresses. Packets are required to have this information because they do not always use the same path or route to get to their intended destination. Packets can take an alternative route if a particular route is unavailable for some reason.

Table 29-1 compares circuit switching and packet switching.

Table 29-1   Circuit Switching and Packet Switching Comparison

Switching Method	Pros	Cons	Key Features
Circuit switching	Offers a dedicated transmission channel that is reserved until it is disconnected.	Dedicated channels can cause delays because a channel is unavailable until one side disconnects. Uses a dedicated physical link between the sending and receiving devices.	Offers the capability of storing messages temporarily to reduce network congestion.
Packet switching	Packets can be routed around network congestion. Packet switching makes efficient use of network bandwidth.	Packets can become lost while taking alternative routes to the destination. Messages are divided into packets that contain source and destination information.	The two types of packet switching are datagram and virtual circuit. Datagram packets are independently sent and can take different paths throughout the network. Virtual circuit uses a logical connection between the source and destination device.

WAN Link Options

A variety of different methods can be used to link networks together. To select an appropriate WAN technology, you need the ability to compare one WAN technology to another.

Home and Small Office

Home and small office networks can connect to other networks and the Internet through a variety of methods.

Dialup

Dialup connectivity is done through the Public Switched Telephone Network (PSTN), which is composed of multiple telephone carriers from around the world. Although the bandwidth available on the PSTN is limited, it is more likely to be available in a given location than other wired WAN solutions. A dialup connection can be used to access the Internet by connecting a computer to a modem, connecting the modem to an analog phone line, and dialing in to a service provider. The service provider can then connect to the Internet, as shown in Figure 29-3. Modems in the United States and Canada are limited to 53.3Kbps download and 48.0Kbps upload.

Figure 29-3   PSTN Dialup Topology

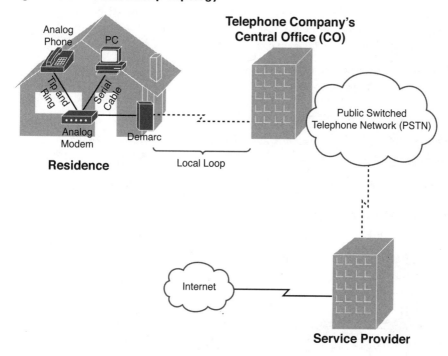

Table 29-2 describes some of the common terminology used to describe PSTNs.

Table 29-2   Common PSTN Terms

Term	Definition
Telco	Abbreviation for telephone company.
Local loop	A local loop is a connection between a customer's premises and his local telephone central office (CO).

Term	Definition
Central office (CO)	A building containing a telephone company's telephone switching equipment is referred to a central office (CO).
Tip and ring	The tip and ring wires are the red and green wires found in an RJ-11 wall jack, which carry voice, ringing voltage, and signaling information between an analog device and a telephone's wall jack.
Demarc	A demarc, short for demarcation point, is the point in a telephone network where the maintenance responsibility passes from a telephone company to the subscriber.
Smart jack	A smart jack is a type of network interface device that adds features such as converting between framing formats on digital circuits, supporting remote diagnostics, and regenerating a digital signal.

ISDN

ISDN connections are considerably faster than regular modem connections. ISDN is a digital technology that supports multiple 64Kbps channels on a single connection. ISDN circuits are classified as either a basic rate interface (BRI) circuit or a primary rate interface (PRI) circuit:

- **BRI**—A BRI circuit consists of two 64Kbps bearer (B) channels and one 16Kbps delta (D) channel. The B channels carry voice, video, and data. They can carry two separate voice conversations or they can be combined using PPP multilink. The D channel carries Layer 2 (Q.921) and Layer 3 (Q.931) signaling.

- **PRI**—A PRI circuit is equivalent to a 1.544Mbps T1 circuit. Therefore, it consists of 23 B channels and one 64Kbps D channel.

The components of an ISDN network are shown in Figure 29-4.

Figure 29-4   ISDN Topology

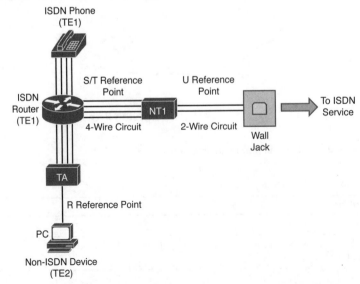

Table 29-3 lists a brief description of the ISDN components shown in Figure 29-4.

Table 29-3   ISDN Components

Term	Definition
R reference point	The R reference point resides between a non-ISDN device and a terminal adapter (TA).
S/T reference point	The S/T reference point resides between a network termination 1 (NT1) and a terminal endpoint 1 (TE1).
U reference point	The U reference point resides between a network termination 1 (NT1) and the wall jack connecting back to an ISDN service provider.
Terminal adapter (TA)	A TA performs protocol conversion between a non-ISDN device and a terminal endpoint 1 (TE1) device.
Terminal endpoint 1 (TE1)	A TE1 is a device (such as an ISDN phone) that natively supports ISDN.
Terminal endpoint 2 (TE2)	A TE2 is a device (such as a PC) that does not natively support ISDN.
Network termination 1 (NT1)	An NT1 is a device that interconnects a four-wire ISDN circuit and a two-wire ISDN circuit.

DSL

Digital Subscriber Line (DSL) is a group of technologies that provide high-speed data transmission over existing telephone wiring. There are many different varieties of DSL. Together, all these variations are referred to as xDSL. Popular variants include the following:

- **Asymmetric DSL (ADSL)**—ADSL is the most popular variant. It include a channel for analog voice conversations, a channel for uploads, and a channel for downloads. It is called asymmetrical because the download channel is faster than the upload channel.

- **Symmetric DSL (SDSL)**—SDSL is more suited to business applications because it offers the same speeds for uploads and downloads.

- **Very High Bit-Rate DSL (VDSL)**—VDSL is a variant of ADSL that provides data speeds of up to 13Mbps.

Table 29-4 summarizes the maximum speeds for all the DSL variants.

Table 29-4   DSL Speeds

DSL Variation	Upload Speed	Download Speed
ADSL	1Mbps	3Mbps
ADSL2	1.3Mbps	12Mbps
ADSL2+	1.4Mbps	24Mbps
SDSL	1.5Mbps	1.5Mbps
IDSL (ISDN DSL)	144Kbps	144Kbps
RADSL (Rate-adaptive DSL)	1Mbps	7Mbps

DSL Variation	Upload Speed	Download Speed
VHDSL	1.6Mbps	13Mbps
HDSL (High bit rate DSL)	768Kbps	768Kbps

PPP

Point-to-Point Protocol (PPP) is a common Layer 2 protocol used on dedicated leased lines. It can carry multiple Layer 3 protocols, such as IPv4 and IPv6. IP uses PPP's IP control protocol (IPCP). When a link is configured with IP and PPP, IPCP initiates the Link Control Protocol (LCP), which can provide any or all of the following features:

- **Multilink interface**—PPP multilink allows multiple interfaces to be combined into one logical interface.

- **Looped link detection**—A Layer 2 loop (of PPP links) can be detected and prevented.

- **Error detection**—Frames containing errors can be detected and discarded by PPP.

- **Authentication**—PPP provides three methods of authentication methods:

  - **Password Authentication Protocol (PAP)**—PAP performs one-way authentication. Passwords are sent in clear text.

  - **Challenge Handshake Authentication Protocol (CHAP)**—CHAP performs one-way authentication using a three-way handshake (challenge, response, and acceptance). Passwords are not sent across the link.

  - **Microsoft Challenge Handshake Authentication Protocol (MS-CHAP)**—MS-CHAP is a Microsoft-enhanced version of CHAP, offering a collection of additional features, including two-way authentication.

Broadband Cable

Broadband cable is an always-on Internet access method available in areas that have digital cable television. Connectivity is achieved by using a device called a cable modem. It has a coaxial connection for connecting to the provider's outlet and an unshielded twisted-pair (UTP) connection for connecting directly to a system or to a hub, switch, or router.

The provider's infrastructure probably has a mix of coaxial and fiber cabling called hybrid fiber-coax (HFC). A broadband cable network is shown in Figure 29-5.

Figure 29-5   Broadband Cable Topology

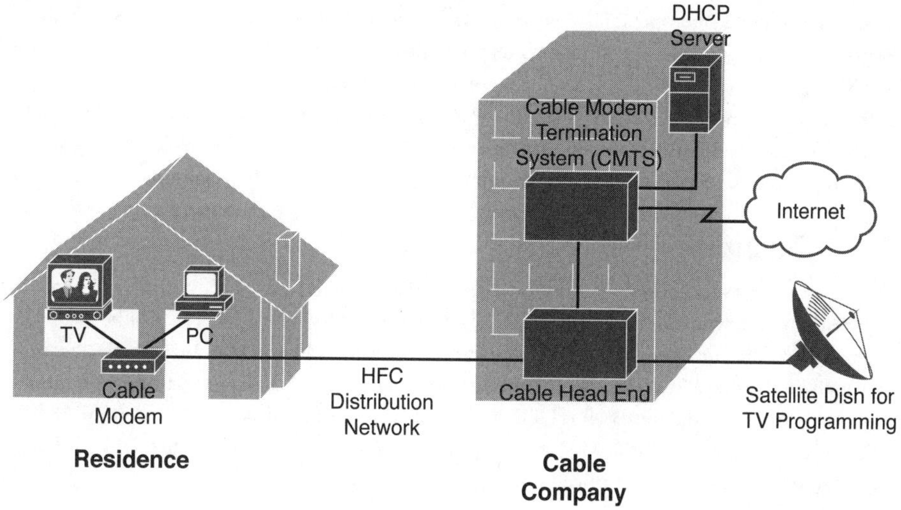

Wireless

Wireless WAN connection options include satellite, Worldwide Interoperability for Microwave Access (WiMAX), and several varieties of cellular technologies.

Satellite

Some locations do not have the WAN connectivity options, such as DSL connections or cable modems, commonly available in urban areas. However, these locations might be able to connect to the Internet or to a remote office using satellite communications, where a transmission is bounced off of a satellite, received by a satellite ground station, and then sent to its destination using either another satellite hop or a wired WAN connection.

Two different types of broadband Internet satellite services are deployed:

- **One-way satellite system**—A one-way satellite system requires a satellite card and a satellite dish installed at the end user's site. Outgoing requests are sent using a phone line. Inbound traffic returns on the satellite link.

- **Two-way satellite system**—A two-way satellite system, in contrast, provides data paths for both upstream and downstream data. Bidirectional communication occurs directly between the end user's site and the satellite.

WiMAX

WiMAX (Worldwide Interoperability for Microwave Access) provides wireless Internet broadband access to fixed locations (as an alternative to technologies such as DSL or cable). Depending on the WiMAX service provider, WiMAX coverage areas could encompass entire cities or small countries. Based on the IEEE 802.16 standard, WiMAX can provide data rates up to 1Gbps. Although WiMAX can send data up to 31 miles (50 km), it is most effective within one mile. WiMAX is a popular choice for connecting cell towers in cellular networks.

Cellular Technologies

Some cellular phone technologies (for example, Long-Term Evolution [LTE], which supports a 100Mbps data rate to mobile devices and a 1Gbps data rate for stationary devices) can be used to connect a mobile device (such as a smartphone) to the Internet. Other technologies for cellular phones include the older 2G edge, which provides slow data rates. 2G edge was improved upon with 3G, in addition to the newer 4G, LTE, and Evolved High-Speed Packet Access (HSPA+). Code division multiple access (CDMA) and Global System for Mobile Communications (GSM) are the two major radio systems used in cell phones.

SONET

Synchronous Optical Network (SONET) is a fiber-optic WAN technology that delivers voice, data, and video at speeds starting at 51.84Mbps. SONET uses dense wavelength-division multiplexing (DWDM), which uses erbium-doped fiber amplifiers (EDFA) to amplify the signal and allow it to travel greater distances. An alternative to DWDM is CWDM (coarse wavelength-division multiplexing), which is commonly used with television cable networks. SONET is classified into various Optical Carrier (OCx) levels, as shown in Table 29-5.

Table 29-5   Optical Carrier Data Rates

OCx Level	Data Rate
OC-1	51.84Mbps
OC-3	155.52Mbps
OC-12	622.08Mbps
OC-24	1.244Gbps
OC-48	2.488Gbps
OC-96	4.976Gbps
OC-192	9.953Gbps
OC-768	39.813Gbps

SONET can connect as many as 16 other devices in a linear fashion (similar to a bus topology) or in a ring topology. A metropolitan area network (MAN), as depicted in Figure 29-6, often uses SONET in a ring topology.

Figure 29-6 SONET Ring Topology

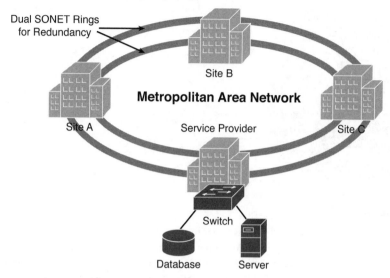

Dedicated Leased Lines

A dedicated leased line is typically a point-to-point digital circuit interconnecting two sites. All the bandwidth on that circuit is available to those sites. These circuits can use multiplexing technology to simultaneously carry multiple conversations in different 64Kbps channels. A single 64Kbps channel is called a Digital Signal 0 (DS0). WAN technologies commonly used with dedicated leased lines include the following:

- **T1**—T1 circuits were originally used in telephony networks, with the intent of one voice conversation being carried in a single channel. A T1 circuit is composed of 24 DS0s, which is called a Digital Signal 1 (DS1). The bandwidth of a T1 circuit is 1.544Mbps.

- **T3**—T3 circuits combine 672 DS0s into a single physical connection, which is called a Digital Signal 3 (DS3). A T3 circuit has a bandwidth capacity of 44.7Mbps.

- **E1**—E1 circuits are popular outside of North America and Japan. They contain 32 channels, in contrast to the 24 channels on a T1 circuit, for a bandwidth capacity of 2.048Mbps.

- **E3**—E3 circuits have a bandwidth capacity of 34.4Mbps, which is less than a T3 circuit.

Dedicated leased lines are terminated at the customer's premises with a channel service unit/data service unit (CSU/DSU), as shown in Figure 29-7.

Figure 29-7   Terminating a Leased Line

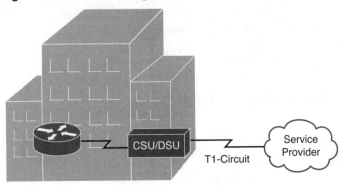

Enterprise WANs

Initially, dedicated leased lines were used by enterprises to connect various sites. However, as network traffic and the number of required WAN connections grew, leased lines became cost prohibitive. Several technologies emerged to answer the need, including Frame Relay, Asynchronous Transfer Mode (ATM), Multiprotocol Label Switching (MPLS), and Metro Ethernet.

Frame Relay

Frame Relay sites are interconnected using virtual circuits (VCs). Frame Relay is a Layer 2 technology that uses locally significant identifiers called data-link connection identifiers (DLCI). DLCIs identify the VC. A single router interface can have multiple VCs, as shown in Figure 29-8.

Figure 29-8   Frame Relay Topology

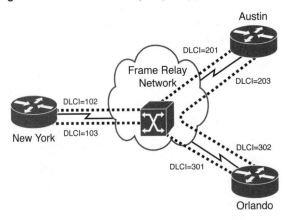

Unlike a dedicated leased line, Frame Relay shares a service provider's bandwidth with other customers of its service provider. Therefore, subscribers might purchase a service level agreement (SLA) to guarantee a minimum level of service. Part of the Frame Relay SLA would be a minimum bandwidth guarantee called a committed information rate (CIR).

During times of congestion, the service provider manages transmission rates using the backward explicit congestion notification (BECN) and forward explicit congestion notification (FECN) bits in the frame relay header. The BECN and FECN bits inform the customers to slow down the transmission rates.

If the service is not congested, a customer might have an SLA that allows transmission rates higher than the CIR. In such cases, the discard eligibility (DE) bit is set in each frame. If the service becomes congested, these frames can be discarded by the Frame Relay service provider.

ATM

ATM is a Layer 2 technology that uses VCs. However, ATM uses a fixed-length frame, called a cell, which includes 48 bytes of data and a 5-byte header, as shown in Figure 29-9.

Figure 29-9   ATM Cell Format

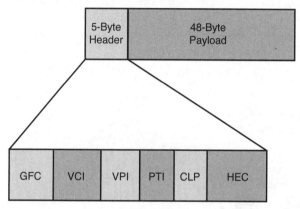

Table 29-6 details the fields of the ATM cell header.

Table 29-6   ATM Header Fields

Field	Description
GFC (4 bits)	The Generic Flow Control (GFC) field is used to indicate congestion.
VCI (16 bits)	The Virtual Circuit Identifier (VCI) field indicates a VC.
VPI (8 bits)	The Virtual Path Identifier (VPI) indicates the virtual path, which could contain multiple VCs.
PTI (3 bits)	The Payload Type Indicator (PTI) indicates the type of payload (for example, user data versus ATM management data).
HEC (8 bits)	The Header Error Control (HEC) field is used to detect and correct errors in the header.

ATM VCs are identified with a VPI/VCI pair, as shown in Figure 29-10.

Figure 29-10   Identifying ATM VCs

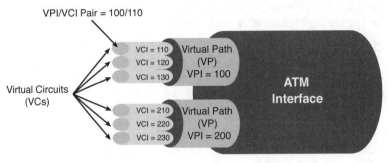

MPLS

Multiprotocol Label Switching (MPLS) can accommodate both Frame Relay and ATM on the same backbone. It does this by inserting a 32-bit header between the Layer 2 and Layer 3 headers. The 32-bit header contains a 20-bit label. This label is used to make forwarding decisions within an MPLS cloud. Therefore, the process of routing MPLS frames through an MPLS cloud is commonly referred to as label switching. Figure 29-11 shows an MPLS topology.

Figure 29-11   MPLS Topology

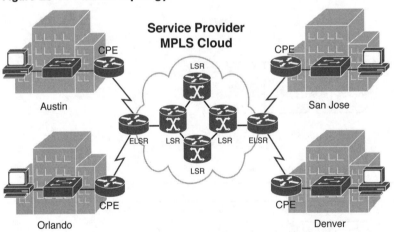

Table 29-7 lists the definitions for the components of the MPLS topology shown in Figure 29-11.

Table 29-7   MPLS Components

Component	Description
CPE	A customer premises equipment (CPE) device resides at a customer site.
ELSR	An edge label switch router (ELSR) resides at the edge of an MPLS service provider's cloud and interconnects a service provider to one or more customers.
LSR	A label switch router (LSR) resides as part of a service provider's MPLS cloud and makes frame-forwarding decisions based on labels applied to frames.

Metro Ethernet

Metro Ethernet is simply Ethernet technology extended into the metropolitan area network (MAN). The customer connects to the service provider through an Ethernet connection (using an RJ-45 connector). This effectively extends the LAN into the MAN. The service provider is responsible for configuring the logical connections between the customer sites. The technologies used with the service provider network are hidden from the customer.

 Video: WAN Links (Circuit Switched)

Refer to the Digital Study Guide to view this video.

 Video: WAN Links (Packet Switched)

Refer to the Digital Study Guide to view this video.

 Activity: Identify the WAN Technology

Refer to the Digital Study Guide to complete this activity.

Study Resources

For today's exam topics, refer to the following resources for more study.

Resource	Location	Topic
Primary Resources		
Certification Guide	7	All
Video Course	5	All
Exam Cram	6	WAN Technologies
		Internet Access Technologies
Supplemental Resources		
Lab Simulator	7	Configuring a VPN Client
Flash Cards	3	WAN Technologies
Quick Reference	3	WAN Technologies

 Check Your Understanding

Refer to the Digital Study Guide to take a 10-question quiz covering the content of this day.

Cable Installation

CompTIA Network+ N10-006 Exam Topics

- 1.5 Install and properly terminate various cable types and connectors using appropriate tools

Key Topics

Today, we review the two main cable types: copper and fiber. We also review the connectors for these cable types and the tools we use to terminate and test the cables.

Copper

Copper media and connectors are used through many different types of networks. They are especially popular in local area network (LAN) installations.

Copper Cables

Copper cabling for networking is either twisted-pair or coaxial. Both have evolved over the years and both are in prevalent use today.

Twisted-Pair Characteristics

The wires in twisted-pair cabling are twisted into pairs to counteract the effects of electromagnetic interference (EMI). This prevents the cable from acting as an antenna, receiving and transmitting EMI.

Two main types of twisted-pair cabling are in use today: unshielded twisted-pair (UTP) and shielded twisted-pair (STP). UTP is significantly more common than STP and is used for most networks. Figure 28-1 compares UTP and STP cabling.

Figure 28-1   UTP and STP Cabling

UTP Cable   Shielding   STP Cable

Although STP prevents interference better than UTP, it is more expensive and difficult to install. In addition, if it is improperly grounded, the shield acts like an antenna and picks up unwanted signals. Because of its cost and difficulty with termination, STP is rarely used in Ethernet networks.

UTP cabling characteristics are shown in Table 28-1.

Table 28-1   UTP Cable Characteristics

Type	Usage	Characteristics
Category 3 (Cat 3)	10BASE-T	Ethernet, 10Mbps; Token Ring, 16Mbps
Category 5 (Cat 5)	100BASE-TX	Ethernet, 100Mbps; ATM, 155Mbps; usually 24 gauge wire
Category 5e (Cat 5e)	1000BASE-T	Gigabit Ethernet, 1Gbps; reduced crosstalk compared to Cat 5
Category 6 (Cat 6)	1000BASE-T	Gigabit Ethernet, 1Gbps; thicker cabling and reduced crosstalk compared to Cat 5e
Category 6a (Cat 6a)	10GBASE-T	10 Gigabit Ethernet (10GigE), 10Gbps; supports twice as many frequencies as Cat 6

Twisted-Pair Cables

Twisted-pair cables can be constructed as straight-through, crossover, or rollover cables. In a straight-through cable, the eight pins in the cable are lined up on both ends, as shown in Figure 28-2.

Figure 28-2   Straight-Through Cable Pinout

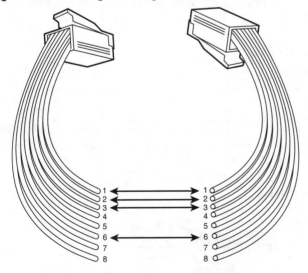

In a crossover cable, the transmit and receive pairs are swapped. Pins 1 and 2 on one end of the cable are matched with (crossed over to) pins 3 and 6 on the other end of the cable, as shown in Figure 28-3.

Figure 28-3   Crossover Cable Pinout

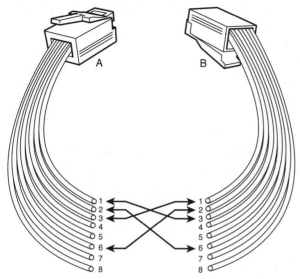

A rollover cable is used for logging in to a Cisco device through the console port. The pins roll over on the other end of the cable. Therefore, the pin mapping for a rollover cable is 1 to 8, 2 to 7, 3 to 6, and 4 to 5.

Plenum and PVC Cables

If cabling catches fire, it can be a source of toxic fumes. These fumes can easily travel through the heating, ventilation, and air conditioning (HVAC) system, especially if cabling is installed in the plenum area. The plenum is the area between a drop ceiling and the true ceiling where HVAC ducts and wiring are often installed. Non-plenum-rated cabling is made of polyvinyl chloride (PVC). Plenum cables are coated with a nonflammable material, often Teflon or Kynar, and they do not give off toxic fumes if they catch fire. Plenum cabling can cost up to three times more than non-plenum cabling.

Coaxial Cables

Although you might still find coaxial (or coax) cable networks in industrial settings, it has all but disappeared in most LAN settings. However, it continues to be a popular cabling choice for cable companies to use in the home market. Coax is constructed to add resistance to attenuation, cross-talk, and EMI. As shown in Figure 28-4, coax is constructed with a copper core at the center (the main wire) that carries the signal, insulation (made of plastic), ground (braided metal shielding), and insulation on the outside (an outer plastic covering).

Figure 28-4   Coaxial Cable

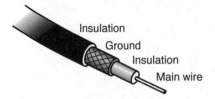

Three of the most common types of coaxial cables include the following:

- **RG-59**—Used for short-distance applications, such as carrying composite video between two nearby devices. It has an impedance of 75 Ohms.

- **RG-6**—Used to connect homes to the cable company's distribution network. It has an impedance of 75 Ohms.

- **RG-58**—Popular with early 10BASE2 Ethernet networks, RG-58 has loss characteristics and distance limitations similar to those of RG-59. It has an impendence of 50 ohms.

Copper Connectors

The type of copper connector used depends on the type of cabling as well as what the cable needs to attach to.

Registered Jack Connectors

A type 11 registered jack (RJ-11) is found in most home telephone networks. However, most home phones only use two of the six pins.

A type 45 registered jack (RJ-45) is an eight-pin connector found in most Ethernet networks. However, most Ethernet implementations only use four of the eight pins.

A type 48C registered jack (RJ-48C) looks like an RJ-45. However, the RJ-48C is used with T1 lines. Pins 1, 2, 4, and 5 are used for data, and pins 7 and 8 are used for cable shield integrity. Pins 3 and 6 are grounded.

Illustrations of the RJ-45 and RJ-11 connectors are shown in Figure 28-5.

Figure 28-5   Registered Jack Connectors

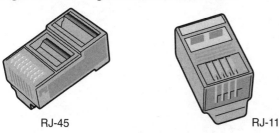

RJ-45   RJ-11

RS-232 Connectors

Recommended Standard 232 (RS-232) is a TIA/EIA standard for serial communications that is commonly used with DB-9 and DB-25 connectors. DB-9 connectors were popular for connecting a serial port on a computer to peripheral devices such as a mouse, keyboard, or external modem. DB-25 connectors were once popular for RS-232 serial connections and parallel printer interfaces. Illustrations of the DB-9 and DB-25 connectors are shown in Figure 28-6.

Figure 28-6   RS-232 Connectors

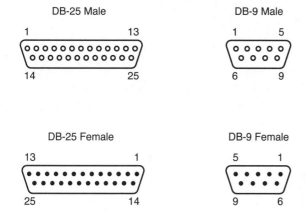

Coaxial Connectors

Coaxial cables are connected to end devices with one of two types of connecters. Bayonet Neill-Concelman (BNC) connectors are used in variety of applications, including 10BASE2 networks. BNC connectors, shown in Figure 28-7, include barrel connectors (not shown), T-connectors, and terminators.

Figure 28-7   BNC Connectors

Terminators

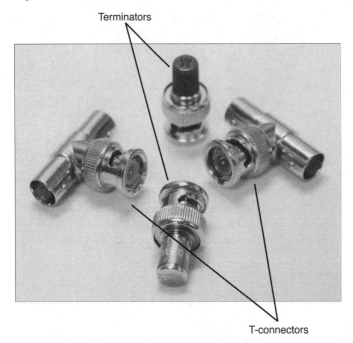

T-connectors

F-type connectors, as shown in Figure 28-8, are screw-on connections used most commonly for connecting modems to cable or satellite Internet service providers' (ISP) equipment.

Figure 28-8   F-Type Connector

Fiber

Fiber media and connectors are primarily used for long–distance wide area network (WAN) connectivity as well as in storage area networks (SANs) and data centers.

Fiber-Optic Cables

An alternative to copper cabling is fiber-optic cabling, which uses light instead of electricity to send bits of data. Fiber-optic cabling doesn't suffer from signal degradation, crosstalk, or EMI. However, fiber-optic cabling is more expensive and more difficult to install than copper cabling.

As shown in Figure 28-9, a fiber-optic cable is composed of two kinds of glass (core and cladding) and a protective outer shield (jacket). Strengthening material surrounds the buffer to prevent the fiber from being stretched when it is pulled. The outer jacket is typically PVC to protect the fiber against abrasion, moisture, and other contaminants.

Figure 28-9   Fiber-Optic Cable

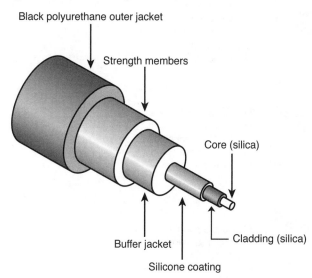

Two types of fiber-optic cable are available:

- **Multimode fiber (MMF)**—MMF uses light-emitting diodes (LED) to send many beams of light through the cable, bouncing off the cable walls. Popular in LANs, MMF provides bandwidth up to 10Gbps over link lengths of up to 550 meters. The wavelengths of light are in the range of 850–1300 nanometers (nm).

- **Single-mode fiber (SMF)**—SMF uses a single direct beam generated from very expensive laser technology, thus allowing for greater distances and increased transfer speeds. SMF is popular in long-distance situations spanning hundreds of kilometers, such as those required in long-haul telephony and cable TV applications. The wavelengths of light are in the range of 1310–1550 nm.

Fiber Connectors

Figure 28-10 shows the fiber connectors you should know for the exam.

Figure 28-10   Fiber Connectors

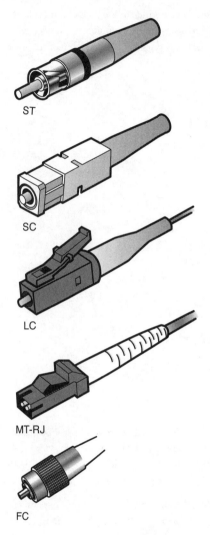

The ST connector uses a half-twist bayonet type of lock.

ST

The SC uses a push-pull connector similar to common audio and video plugs and sockets.

SC

LC connectors have a flange on top, similar to an RJ-45 connector, that aids secure connection.

LC

MT-RJ is a popular connector for two fibers in a very small form factor.

MT-RJ

FC connectors have a threaded body and are used in environments where vibration is a problem.

FC

Connector types can be purchased as Physical Contact (PC), Ultra Physical Contact (UPC), and Angled Physical Contact (APC). These different polishes result in different performance of the connector. The less back reflection, the better the transmission. The PC back reflection is −40 dB, the UPC back reflection is around −55 dB, and the APC back reflection is about −70 dB.

 Video: Media Types Overview

Refer to the Digital Study Guide to view this video.

Activity: Compare Media Types

Refer to the Digital Study Guide to complete this activity.

Media Converters

A media converter is used to convert one type of media to another type of media. Depending on the conversion being done, the converter can be a small device barely larger than the connectors themselves, or a large device within a sizable chassis. Figure 28-11 shows a generic fiber to twisted-pair media converter.

Figure 28-11   Generic Media Converter

Common media converters include the following:

- Single-mode fiber to Ethernet
- Multimode fiber to Ethernet
- Fiber to coaxial
- Single-mode to multimode fiber

NOTE: In contrast to converters, couplers connect the same media type together with the intention of extending the length of a cable that is too short. However, couplers do not regenerate the signal. Therefore, care must be taken not to extend a cable beyond its distance limitations.

Tools

Tools are specially built for terminating twisted-pair, coaxial, and fiber-optic cables. In general, these tools include the following:

- **Wire strippers**—Before a cable can be terminated, a portion of the outer jacket needs to be removed with a wire stripper.

- **Snips**—Wire snips are tools designed to cleanly cut the twisted pair cable. Sometimes network administrators buy cable in bulk and use wire snips to cut the cable into desired lengths.

- **Cable crimpers**—A tool used to crimp a connector to the end of a cable. Many crimpers have a built-in wire stripper and wire snip function as well, as shown in Figure 28-12.

Figure 28-12   Cable Crimper

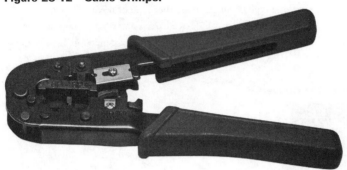

- **Punch down tool**—Specific to twisted-pair cabling, a punch down tool is used to terminate the individual wires in a telecommunications outlet or a patch panel found in an intermediate distribution facility (IDF).

The two types of cross-connect blocks you should be familiar with for the exam are the 66 block and the 110 block. The electrical characteristics of the 66 block, shown in Figure 28-13, connects sets of wires in a telephone system and cannot support 100Mbps Ethernet.

Figure 28-13   A 66 Block

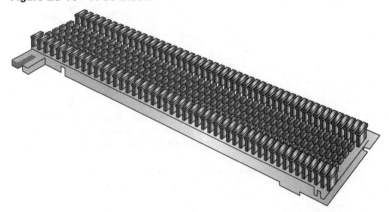

Therefore, LANs today use the 110 block because many are certified for Cat 5, Cat 6, and Cat 6a wiring systems. A 110 block is shown in Figure 28-14.

Figure 28-14   A 110 Block

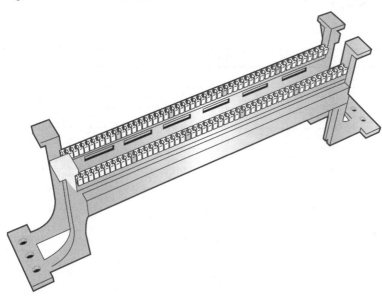

Use a cable tester to verify a newly terminated cable or the signal from one end of the cable to the other. If you need to verify the data throughput of a cable, use a cable certifier.

To test optical cable, you can use an optical time domain reflectometer (OTDR) to send a light signal down the cable. When the light signal encounters a cable fault or the end of the cable run, a portion of the light signal is reflected back. Based on the speed of the light, the OTDR can determine the distance to the cable fault or the other end of the cable run. An OTDR is shown in Figure 28-15.

Figure 28-15   Optical Time Domain Reflectometer (Photo Courtesy of Coral-i Solutions, http://www.coral-i.com)

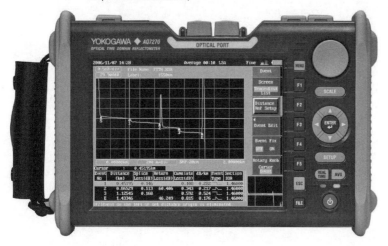

Study Resources

For today's exam topics, refer to the following resources for more study.

Resource	Location	Topic
Primary Resources		
Certification Guide	3	Media
	11	Maintenance Tools
Exam Cram	7	General Media Considerations
Video Course	6	All
Supplemental Resources		
Lab Simulator	3	Create a Straight Cable and Test It
		Create a Crossover Cable
		Create a Console Cable
Flash Cards	4	Install Cables and Connectors
Quick Reference	4	Install Cables and Connectors

 Check Your Understanding

Refer to the Digital Study Guide to take a 10-question quiz covering the content of this day.

Network Topologies and Infrastructure

CompTIA Network+ N10-006 Exam Topics

- 1.6 Differentiate between common network topologies
- 1.7 Differentiate between network infrastructure implementations

Key Topics

Is your local area network (LAN) a star or extended star? Is your wide area network (WAN) a full mesh or a partial mesh? How many point-to-point links do you have? Does your organization use a metropolitan area network (MAN)? Today, we review network topologies and infrastructures.

Network Topologies

Networks come in a variety of topological configurations, including bus, ring, star, extended-star, mesh, point-to-point, point-to-multipoint, client-server, and peer-to-peer.

Bus

A bus topology uses a trunk or backbone to connect all the computers on the network, as shown in Figure 27-1.

Figure 27-1   Bus Topology

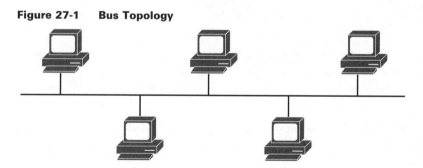

The advantages and disadvantage of a bus topology are listed in Table 27-1.

Table 27-1   Advantages and Disadvantages of the Bus Topology

Advantages	Disadvantages
Cheap and easy to implement	Network disruption when adding or removing devices
Less cable	A break in the cable prevents all systems from accessing the network
No specialized network equipment	Difficult to troubleshoot

Ring

In a ring topology, data travels in a circular fashion from one computer to another on the network, as shown in Figure 27-2.

Figure 27-2   Ring Topology

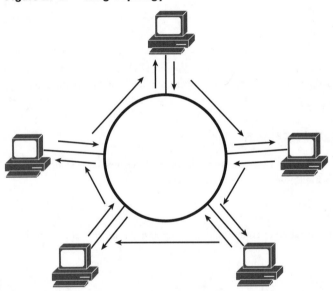

Token Ring, as the name suggests, used a logical ring topology. However, the physical topology was usually set up as a star. Fiber Distributed Data Interface (FDDI) was another variant of a ring-based topology. Most FDDI networks used not just one ring, but two. If one ring broke, the stations on each side of the break interconnected their two rings, resulting in a single ring capable of reaching all stations on the ring.

The advantages and disadvantage of a ring topology are listed in Table 27-2.

Table 27-2   Advantages and Disadvantages of the Ring Topology

Advantages	Disadvantages
Cable faults are easily located	Network disruption when adding or removing devices
Moderately easy to install	Requires more cable than a bus topology

Star, Extended Star, and Hub-and-Spoke

The star topology is the most popular physical LAN topology in use today, with an Ethernet switch at the center of the star and unshielded twisted-pair cable (UTP) used to connect from the switch ports to clients, as shown in Figure 27-3.

Figure 27-3   Star Topology

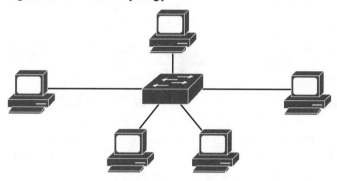

Table 27-3 lists the advantages and disadvantages of star topology.

Table 27-3   Advantages and Disadvantages of a Star Topology

Advantages	Disadvantages
Easy to add new devices without network disruption	Requires more cable than other topologies
Cable failure affects only a single user	Center of star is a single point of failure
Easy to troubleshoot and implement	Requires additional networking equipment

An extended star is simply a star of star topologies, as shown in Figure 27-4.

Figure 27-4   Extended Star Topology

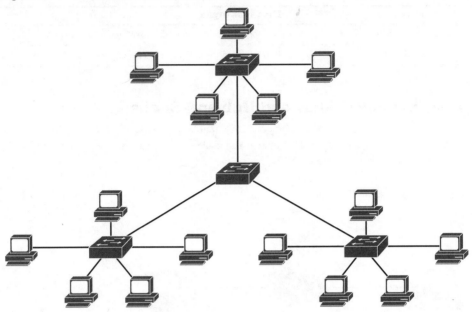

An extended star sometimes is referred to as a star bus or hybrid topology because it is made up of two types of topologies. The links between the three switches in Figure 27-4 form a bus to attach the three star topologies.

The WAN implementation of a star topology is typically called a hub-and-spoke topology. It is used to connect multiple sites to a central site, as shown in Figure 27-5.

Figure 27-5   Hub-and-Spoke Topology

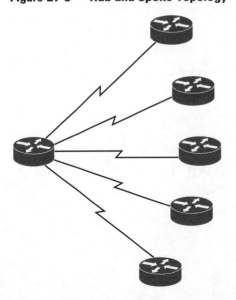

This hub-and-spoke topology might actually be a point-to-multipoint topology, where the hub only has one physical link to a WAN service provider, as shown in Figure 27-6. The hub router is configured with multiple logical interfaces to connect to the remote sites.

Figure 27-6   Hub-and-Spoke as a Point-to-Multipoint Topology

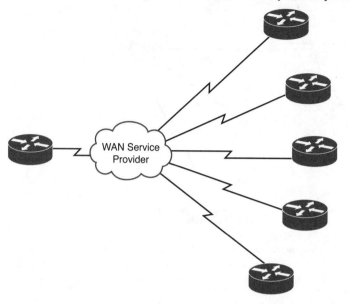

Table 27-4 lists the advantages and disadvantages of hub-and-spoke topology.

Table 27-4   Advantages and Disadvantages of a Hub-and-Spoke Topology

Advantages	Disadvantages
Costs are minimized for WAN links	Suboptimal routing
Easy to add more sites	Hub is single point of failure
Hub can provide security between sites	Lacks redundancy

Full and Partial Mesh

A full-mesh topology, as shown in Figure 27-7, is a collection of point-to-point links that connect every site to every other site.

Figure 27-7   Full Mesh Topology

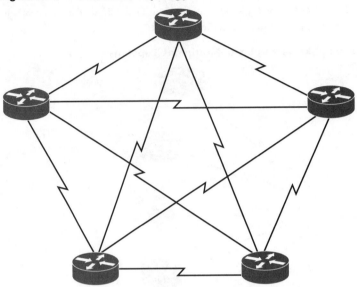

The number of point-to-point links needed in a full mesh topology is calculated with the formula $n*(n-1)/2$, where **n** is the number of devices. Therefore, a five-router topology needs 10 links to be a full mesh ($5*(5-1)/2 = 10$). Add one more router and the number of links increases to 15.

Table 27-5 lists the advantages and disadvantages of a full mesh topology.

Table 27-5   Advantages and Disadvantages of a Full Mesh Topology

Advantage	Disadvantage
Optimal routing	Expensive
Fault tolerant	Difficult to scale
Easy to add new devices without network disruption	Complex implementation

A partial mesh topology lacks some of the point-to-point connections that would make it a full mesh, as shown in Figure 27-8. A partial mesh might also be called a hybrid topology because it can be a combination of topology types.

Figure 27-8   Partial Mesh Topology

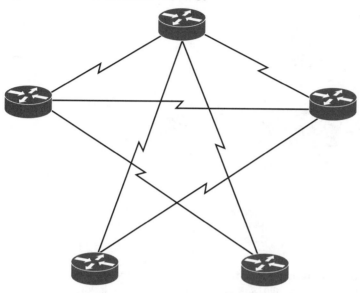

Table 27-6 lists the advantages and disadvantages of a partial mesh topology.

Table 27-6   Advantages and Disadvantages of a Partial Mesh Topology

Advantage	Disadvantage
Optimal routing where needed	Less fault tolerant than full mesh
Less expensive than full mesh	More expensive than hub-and-spoke
More redundant than hub-and-spoke	More complex implementation than hub-and-spoke

Client-Server and Peer-to-Peer

Figure 27-9 shows an example of a client-server network, with a dedicated file server and printer. Both include network operating systems (NOSs) to enable client devices to share these resources.

Table 27-7 lists the advantages and disadvantages of a client-server network.

Table 27-7   Advantages and Disadvantages of a Client-Server Network

Advantage	Disadvantage
Easily scales by adding more clients	Server is a single point of failure
Easier to administer compared to peer-to-peer	More expensive than peer-to-peer

Figure 27-9   Client-Server Network

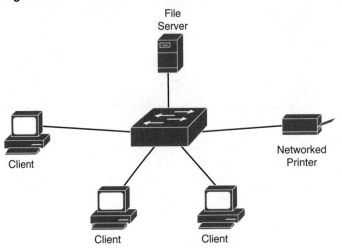

Peer-to-peer networks allow interconnected devices to share their resources with one another. Those resources could be, for example, files or printers. In Figure 27-10, each PC is sharing its hard drive with every other PC. One PC is also sharing a printer.

Figure 27-10   Peer-to-Peer Network

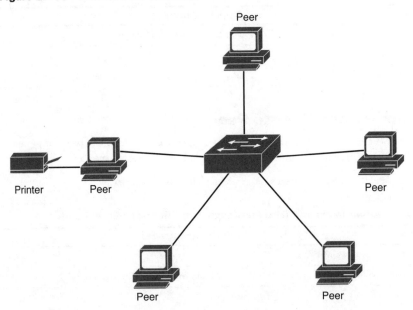

Table 27-8 lists the advantages and disadvantages of a peer-to-peer network.

Table 27-8   Advantages and Disadvantages of a Peer-to-Peer Network

Advantage	Disadvantage
Easy to install because no knowledge of NOSs is required	Not easy to scale
Costs less than client-server	Performance may suffer because peer resources are not dedicated to services

Activity: Identify the Network Topology

Refer to the Digital Study Guide to complete this activity.

Network Infrastructures

Network infrastructures include personal area networks (PANs), local area networks (LAN), wireless LANs (WLAN), campus area networks (CAN), metropolitan area networks (MAN), and wide area networks (WAN).

PANs

A PAN is a network whose scale is limited to just a few meters by the technology used to connect the devices. Table 27-9 lists some examples of PANs and the technology they use.

Table 27-9   PAN Technologies and Examples

Technology	Example
Universal serial bus (USB)	Attaching a digital camera to a PC with a USB cable
FireWire	Attaching an external hard drive to a PC with a FireWire cable
Bluetooth	Used to create a personal hotspot; for example, wirelessly connecting a cell phone to a car's audio system
Infrared (IR)	Security system devices that detect motion when an object crosses the line-of-sight
Near Field Communication (NFC)	An NFC chip in a movie poster will play a YouTube video on a smartphone when the smartphone is within a few centimeters of the chip

LANs and WLANs

A LAN is a data network that typically encompasses a relatively small area, such as a building or school. Some of the network topologies discussed earlier are LANs. The examples of bus, ring, star, extended star, client-server, and peer-to-peer are all LAN infrastructures. The router in Figure 27-11 is attached to two LANs.

Figure 27-11   Two LAN Topology

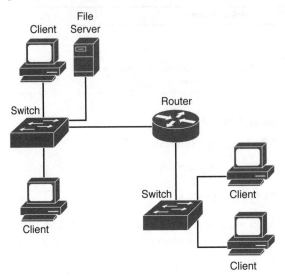

The technology used for data communication in LANs is typically Ethernet (IEEE 802.3), wireless (IEEE 802.11), or a combination of both. For example, a basic home network most likely includes wired and wireless devices, as shown in Figure 27-12.

Figure 27-12   Home Network Topology

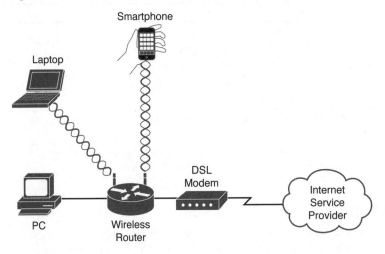

CANs

A CAN is a network of LANs that encompasses a larger area than one LAN, but does not span an entire city. Although a campus is typically associated with universities and colleges, larger organizations also have campuses. For example, Cisco System's campus in San Jose, California spans many buildings spread across a large area within the city.

MANs

No formal guidelines dictate the differences between a MAN and a WAN. Technically, a MAN is a WAN. A MAN interconnects locations scattered throughout a metropolitan area. For example, imagine a Chicago business that has a location near O'Hare Airport, another near the Navy Pier, and another in the Willis Tower. The service provider probably connects the sites using a high-speed service, such as Metro Ethernet, which runs at 10Gbps.

WANs

A WAN interconnects network components that are geographically separated. For example, a corporate headquarters might have multiple WAN connections to remote office sites. Multiprotocol Label Switching (MPLS), Asynchronous Transfer Mode (ATM), and Frame Relay are examples of WAN technologies. Figure 27-13 shows a basic WAN connecting two remote sites.

Figure 27-13   WAN Topology

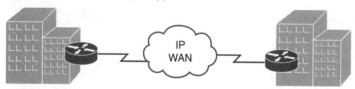

 Video: Network Topology and Infrastructure Overview
Refer to the Digital Study Guide to view this video.

Other Network Infrastructures

Other network infrastructures included in the Network+ exam topics are industrial networks and medianets.

Industrial Networks

Industrial networks are primarily concerned with the remote control of equipment. You should be familiar with the following list of industrial control system concepts:

- **ICS**—An industrial control system (ICS) uses distributed control systems (DCSs) to monitor and control processes and equipment within a facility.

- **SCADA**—A Supervisory Control And Data Acquisition (SCADA) network is generally much larger than an ICS, often spanning multiple sites.

- **RTU**—Remote terminal units (RTUs) are a subsystem of a SCADA that connects to sensors in the system. RTUs are primarily responsible for converting the sensor signals to digital data.

- **PLC**—Programmable logic controllers (PLC) serve the same function as RTUs. PLCs are often used instead of RTUs because they are configurable.

Medianets

Medianet is a term used to describe a network architecture created by Cisco Systems that is optimized for video teleconferencing (VTC) with rich media. Rich media not only includes voice and video, but the mixing together of videos and documents, web pages, text, and other forms of media. The coordination and synchronization of multiple types of rich media into a single experience is a critical aspect of a medianet.

Cisco divides the delivery of the various kinds of functions and benefits of a medianet into the following service categories:

- **Quality of experience (QoE)**—High-quality, real-time interactive video applications have stringent requirements on delay, jitter, loss, reliability, and bandwidth that directly impact the effectiveness of video application.

- **Content virtualization**—Content should be available for consumption by any application in any form of media.

- **Mobility**—The QoE should be seamless as the user moves from location to location and from device to device.

- **Session control**—Session control is responsible for monitoring, authenticating, and managing individual sessions, which includes coordination between different applications across different networks. This is controlled with the Session Initiation Protocol (SIP), which runs over IP.

- **Security**—The identification of users, devices, and applications helps establish a trust boundary for interacting with and accepting information into the network. The security is pervasive and end-to-end.

- **Management**—Management comprises provisioning as well as visibility and monitoring services. With a medianet architecture, device configuration is simplified. Management tools collect information to facilitate troubleshooting as well as provide data for upgrading the network.

NOTE: An Integrated Services Digital Network (ISDN) is often used for medianets when connecting to external customers. ISDN provides a guaranteed level of bandwidth.

To learn more about Cisco's medianet architecture, access the *Medianet Reference Guide* at http://www.cisco.com/c/en/us/td/docs/solutions/Enterprise/Video/Medianet_Ref_Gd/medianet_ref_gd.html.

Study Resources

For today's exam topics, refer to the following resources for more study.

Resource	Location	Topic
Primary Resources		
Certification Guide	1	Networks Defined by Geography
		Networks Defined by Topology
		Networks Define by Resource Location
	8	WLAN Concepts and Components
Exam Cram	1	Network Topologies
Video Course	3	Network Topologies
Supplemental Resources		
Lab Simulator	1	Network Topologies
Flash Cards	5	Network Topologies and Infrastructure
Quick Reference	5	Network Topologies and Infrastructure

 Check Your Understanding

Refer to the Digital Study Guide to take a 10-question quiz covering the content of this day.

Implement IPv4 Addressing

CompTIA Network+ N10-006 Exam Topics

- 1.8 Given a scenario, implement and configure the appropriate addressing schema

Key Topics

Today's exam topic is so broad that we will review it over two days. Today's review focuses on MAC addressing, collision domains, broadcast domains, and IP version 4 (IPv4) addressing. Tomorrow, we will focus on IP version 6 (IPv6) addressing.

Local Addressing

Local addressing refers to the addressing required for devices to communicate on the same local link. That local link could be a LAN or a WAN. For today's review, we will focus on the method and operation of local addressing on LANs.

MAC Addresses

For Ethernet, a MAC address is used to uniquely identify a device on the network. A MAC address is a 6-byte (48-bit) hexadecimal address. The first 3 bytes are known as the organizational unique identifier (OUI) because these bytes define the manufacturer.

For example, consider the MAC address F0-4D-A2-DD-A7-B2. The first 3 bytes (F0-4D-A2) identify the manufacturer of the card. The last 3 bytes (DD-A7-B2) are assigned by the manufacturer and uniquely identify the card.

Collision and Broadcast Domains

Ethernet uses a broadcast topology in which all devices on the local link see the data sent by all other devices. Every frame sent out on the local link must be opened by every other device in order to determine whether the MAC address belongs to that device. This feature of Ethernet makes the local link a broadcast domain.

In older Ethernet implementations, the local link was also a collision domain. If two devices transmitted at the same time, their frames could collide. Collision domains have largely been eliminated with the introduction of switches. Each port on a switch is its own collision domain. If the port and the device attached to the port are both set to full duplex (both devices can send and receive simultaneously), then it is a collision-free connection.

However, a Layer 2 switch cannot divide a broadcast domain. It must forward all broadcast frames out all other ports, except for the port on which the frame was initially received. Because routers are Layer 3 devices, forwarding traffic based on Layer 3 addressing, they can segment broadcast domains. Figure 26-1 shows a topology with eight collision domains and two broadcast domains.

Figure 26-1   Collision and Broadcast Domains

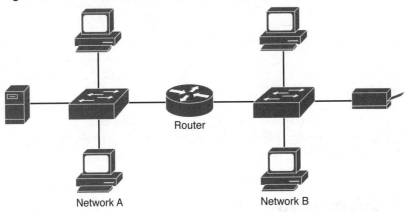

Router

Network A   Network B

Eight Collision Domains
Two Broadcast Domains

NOTE: Ethernet has a method for resolving collisions, which we will review on Day 12, "Network Theory."

IPv4 Addressing

Network addressing or Layer 3 addressing is usually either IPv4 or IPv6. Although IPv6 is increasingly being adopted in corporate networks, IPv4 is still, by far, the most popular Layer 3 addressing scheme.

IPv4 Address Structure

An IPv4 address is 32 bits, represented in dotted decimal notation, such as 10.1.2.3. Each number represents 8 bits, as shown in Figure 26-2. Also, notice there are four separate 8-bit octets.

Figure 26-2   An IP Address in Dotted Decimal and Binary Representations

Dotted Decimal Notation	10	1	2	3
Binary Bits	00001010	00000001	00000010	00000011
	Octet 1	Octet 2	Octet 3	Octet 4

An IP address is divided into two parts at a bit boundary. The bit boundary can be just about any-where. On the left side of the bit boundary is the network portion, and on the right side of the bit boundary is the host portion. For example, assume that the bit boundary for 10.1.2.3 occurs between the first and second octet. Then 10 is the network portion, and 1.2.3 is the host portion.

A subnet mask is used to determine the bit boundary between the network and host. Like the IPv4 address, a subnet mask is 32 bits. The subnet mask consists of a series of contiguous 1s followed by a set of contiguous 0s. For example, Figure 26-3 shows the subnet mask 255.0.0.0 in dotted deci-mal and binary.

Figure 26-3   A Subnet Mask in Dotted Decimal and Binary Representations

Dotted Decimal Notation	255	0	0	0
Binary Bits	11111111	00000000	00000000	00000000
	Octet 1	Octet 2	Octet 3	Octet 4

Using the logical ANDing process, computers can determine the network address for any IPv4 address if given the subnet mask. The binary values for the AND operations are as follows:

- 1 AND 1 = 1

- 1 AND 0 = 0

- 0 AND 1 = 0

- 0 AND 0 = 0

Matching an IPv4 address to its subnet mask, bit for bit, and then performing the ANDing opera-tion will yield the network address, as shown in Figure 26-4.

Figure 26-4   Calculating the Network Address

IPv4 Address	10	1	2	3
IPv4 Address (in Binary)	00001010	00000001	00000010	00000011
Subnet Mask	11111111	00000000	00000000	00000000
Network Address	00001010	00000000	00000000	00000000
Network Address (in Dotted Decimal)	10	0	0	0
	Network Portion	Host Portion		

Video: Calculating the Network Address

Refer to the Digital Study Guide to view this video.

You should be familiar with the default subnet masks specified for Class A, B, and C network addresses, as shown in Table 26-1.

Table 26-1   IPv4 Classful Addresses

Address Class	Value in First Octet	Classful Mask (Dotted Decimal)	Classful Mask (Prefix Notation)
Class A	1–126	255.0.0.0	/8
Class B	128–191	255.255.0.0	/16
Class C	192–223	255.255.255.0	/24
Class D	224–239	—	—
Class E	240–255	—	—

NOTE: The 127.0.0.0 network is reserved for loopback testing.

Private and Public IP Addressing

RFC 1918, "Address Allocation for Private Internets," eased the demand for IP addresses by reserving the following addresses for use in private internetworks.

- **Class A**—10.0.0.0/8 (10.0.0.0 to 10.255.255.255)

- **Class B**—172.16.0.0/12 (172.16.0.0 to 172.31.255.255)

- **Class C**—192.168.0.0/16 (192.168.0.0 to 192.168.255.255)

If you are addressing a nonpublic intranet, these private addresses are normally used instead of globally unique public addresses. This provides flexibility in your addressing design. Any organization can take full advantage of an entire Class A address (10.0.0.0/8). Forwarding traffic to the public Internet requires translation to a public address using Network Address Translation (NAT). However, by overloading an Internet routable address with many private addresses, a company needs only a handful of public addresses. We reviewed NAT on Day 30, "Network Services and Applications."

IPv4 Address Types

Communication between devices connected to an IPv4 network occurs in one of three ways:

- **Unicast**—The process of sending a packet from one host to an individual host, as shown in Figure 26-5

Figure 26-5   Unicast Transmission

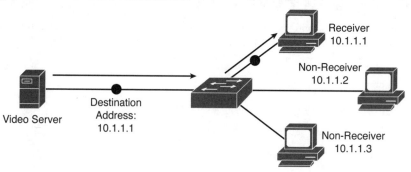

- **Broadcast**—The process of sending a packet from one host to all hosts in the network, as shown in Figure 26-6

Figure 26-6   Broadcast Transmission

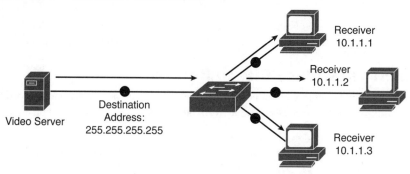

- **Multicast**—The process of sending a packet from one host to a selected group of hosts, as shown in Figure 26-7

Figure 26-7   Multicast Transmission

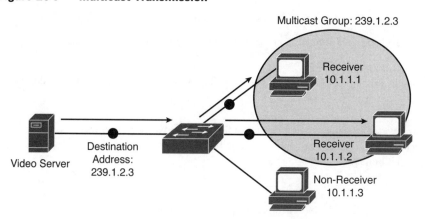

Subnetting in Four Steps

Everyone has a preferred method of subnetting. Each teacher will use a slightly different strategy to help students master this crucial skill. Each of the suggested "Study Resources" has a slightly different way of approaching this subject.

The method I prefer can be broken down into four steps:

Step 1.   Determine how many bits to borrow based on the host requirements.

Step 2.   Determine the new subnet mask.

Step 3.   Determine the subnet multiplier.

Step 4.   List the subnets, including subnetwork address, host range, and broadcast address.

The best way to demonstrate this method is to use an example. Let's assume you are given the network address 192.168.1.0, with the default subnet mask 255.255.255.0. The network address and subnet mask can be written as 192.168.1.0/24. The "slash 24" represents the subnet mask in a shorter notation and means the first 24 bits are network bits.

Let's further assume you need 30 hosts per network and want to create as many subnets for the given address space as possible. With these network requirements, let's subnet the address space.

Determine How Many Bits to Borrow

To determine the number of bits you can borrow, you first must know how many host bits you have to start with. Because the first 24 bits are network bits in our example, the remaining 8 bits are host bits.

Because our requirement specifies 30 host addresses per subnet, we need to first determine the minimum number of host bits to leave. The remaining bits can be borrowed:

Host Bits = Bits Borrowed + Bits Left

To provide enough address space for 30 hosts, we need to leave 5 bits. Use the formula

$2^{BL} - 2$ = number of host addresses

where the exponent BL is the bits left in the host portion.

Remember, the "minus 2" is to account for the network and broadcast addresses that cannot be assigned to hosts.

In this example, leaving 5 bits in the host portion will provide the right amount of host addresses:

$2^5 - 2 = 30$.

Because we have 3 bits remaining in the original host portion, we borrow all these bits to satisfy the requirement to "create as many subnets as possible." To determine how many subnets we can create, use the formula

2^{BB} = number of subnets

where the exponent BB is the bits borrowed from the host portion.

In this example, borrowing 3 bits from the host portion will create 8 subnets: $2^3 = 8$.

As shown in Table 26-2, the 3 bits are borrowed from the leftmost bits in the host portion. The highlighted bits in the table show all possible combinations of manipulating the 8 bits borrowed to create the subnets.

Table 26-2   Binary and Decimal Value of the Subnetted Octet

Subnet Number	Last Octet Binary Value	Last Octet Decimal Value
0	00000000	.0
1	00100000	.32
2	01000000	.64
3	01100000	.96
4	10000000	.128
5	10100000	.160
6	11000000	.192
7	11100000	.224

Determine the New Subnet Mask

Notice in Table 26-2 that the network bits now include the 3 borrowed host bits in the last octet. Add these 3 bits to the 24 bits in the original subnet mask, and you have a new subnet mask, /27. In decimal format, you turn on the 128, 64, and 32 bits in the last octet for a value of 224. So the new subnet mask is 255.255.255.224.

Determine the Subnet Multiplier

Notice in Table 26-2 that the last octet decimal value increments by 32 with each subnet number. The number 32 is the subnet multiplier. You can quickly find the subnet multiplier using one of two methods:

- **Method 1**—Subtract the last nonzero octet of the subnet mask from 256. In this example, the last nonzero octet is 224, so the subnet multiplier is $256 - 224 = 32$.

- **Method 2**—The decimal value of the last bit borrowed is the subnet multiplier. In this example, we borrowed the 128 bit, the 64 bit, and the 32 bit. The 32 bit is the last bit we borrowed and is, therefore, the subnet multiplier.

By using the subnet multiplier, you no longer have to convert binary subnet bits to decimal. Because this method makes subnetting easier, the subnet multiplier is often called the magic number.

List the Subnets, Host Ranges, and Broadcast Addresses

Listing the subnets, host ranges, and broadcast addresses helps you see the flow of addresses within one address space. Table 26-3 documents our subnet addressing scheme for the 192.168.1.0/24 address space.

Table 26-3   Subnet Addressing Scheme for 192.168.1.0/24: 30 Hosts Per Subnet

Subnet Number	Subnet Address	Host Range	Broadcast Address
0	192.168.1.0	192.168.1.1–192.168.1.30	192.168.1.31
1	192.168.1.32	192.168.1.33–192.168.1.62	192.168.1.63
2	192.168.1.64	192.168.1.65–192.168.1.94	192.168.1.95
3	192.168.1.96	192.168.1.97–192.168.1.126	192.168.1.127
4	192.168.1.128	192.168.1.129–192.168.1.158	192.168.1.159
5	192.168.1.160	192.168.1.161–192.168.1.190	192.168.1.191
6	192.168.1.192	192.168.1.193–192.168.1.222	192.168.1.223
7	192.168.1.224	192.168.1.225–192.168.1.254	192.168.1.255

The following are three examples using the four subnetting steps. For brevity, only the first three subnets are listed in step 4.

Subnetting Example 1

Subnet the address space 172.16.0.0/16 to provide at least 80 host addresses per subnet while creating as many subnets as possible:

1. There are 16 host bits. Leave 7 bits for host addresses ($2^7 - 2 = 126$ host addresses per subnet). Borrow the first 9 host bits to create as many subnets as possible ($2^9 = 512$ subnets).

2. The original subnet mask is /16, or 255.255.0.0. Turn on the next 9 bits starting in the second octet for a new subnet mask of /25, or 255.255.255.128.

3. The subnet multiplier is 128, which can be found as $256 - 128 = 128$, or because the 128 bit is the last bit borrowed.

Table 26-4 lists the first three subnets, host ranges, and broadcast addresses.

Table 26-4   Subnet Addressing Scheme for Example 1

Subnet Number	Subnet Address	Host Range	Broadcast Address
0	172.16.0.0	172.16.0.1–172.16.0.126	172.16.0.127
1	172.16.0.128	172.16.0.129–172.16.0.254	172.16.0.255
2	172.16.1.0	172.16.1.1–172.16.1.126	172.16.1.127

Subnetting Example 2

Subnet the address space 172.16.0.0/16 to provide at least 80 subnet addresses:

1. There are 16 host bits. Borrow the first 7 host bits to create at least 80 subnets ($2^7 = 126$ subnets). That leaves 9 bits for host addresses or $2^9 - 2 = 510$ host addresses per subnet.

2. The original subnet mask is /16, or 255.255.0.0. Turn on the next 7 bits starting in the second octet for a new subnet mask of /23, or 255.255.254.0.

3. The subnet multiplier is 2, which can be found as 256 − 254 = 2, or because the 2 bit is the last bit borrowed.

Table 26-5 lists the first three subnets, host ranges, and broadcast addresses.

Table 26-5   Subnet Addressing Scheme for Example 2

Subnet Number	Subnet Address	Host Range	Broadcast Address
0	172.16.0.0	172.16.0.1–172.16.1.254	172.16.1.255
1	172.16.2.0	172.16.2.1–172.16.3.254	172.16.3.255
2	172.16.4.0	172.16.4.1–172.16.5.254	172.16.5.255

Subnetting Example 3

Subnet the address space 172.16.10.0/23 to provide at least 60 host addresses per subnet while creating as many subnets as possible:

1. There are 9 host bits. Leave 6 bits for host addresses ($2^6 − 2 = 62$ host addresses per subnet). Borrow the first 3 host bits to create as many subnets as possible ($2^3 = 8$ subnets).

2. The original subnet mask is /23, or 255.255.254.0. Turn on the next 3 bits starting with the last bit in the second octet for a new subnet mask of /26, or 255.255.255.192.

3. The subnet multiplier is 64, which can be found as 256 − 192 = 64, or because the 64 bit is the last bit borrowed.

Table 26-6 lists the first three subnets, host ranges, and broadcast addresses.

Table 26-6   Subnet Addressing Scheme for Example 3

Subnet Number	Subnet Address	Host Range	Broadcast Address
0	172.16.10.0	172.16.10.1–172.16.10.62	172.16.10.63
1	172.16.10.64	172.16.10.65–172.16.10.126	172.16.10.127
2	172.16.10.128	172.16.10.129–172.16.10.190	172.16.10.191

Video: Basic Subnetting Overview

Refer to the Digital Study Guide to view this video.

VLSM and Classless Addressing

You probably noticed that the starting address space in Subnetting Example 3 is not an entire classful address. In fact, it is subnet 5 from Subnetting Example 2. Thus, in Subnetting Example 3, we "subnetted a subnet." That is what VLSM is in a nutshell—subnetting a subnet.

With VLSM, you can customize your subnets to fit your network. Subnetting works the same way. You just have to do it more than once to complete your addressing scheme. To avoid overlapping address spaces, start with your largest host requirement, create a subnet for it, and then continue with the next largest host requirement.

Let's use a small example. Given the address space 172.30.4.0/22 and the network requirements shown in Figure 26-8, apply an addressing scheme that conserves the most amount of addresses for future growth.

Figure 26-8   VLSM Example Topology

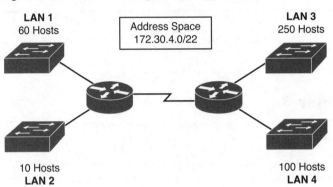

| LAN 1 | Address Space | LAN 3 |
| 60 Hosts | 172.30.4.0/22 | 250 Hosts |

10 Hosts   100 Hosts
LAN 2   **LAN 4**

We need five subnets: four LAN subnets and one WAN subnet. Starting with the largest host requirement on LAN 3, begin subnetting the address space.

To satisfy the 250 hosts requirement, we leave 8 hosts bits ($2^8 - 2 = 254$ hosts per subnet). Because we have 10 host bits total, we borrow 2 bits to create the first round of subnets ($2^2 = 4$ subnets). The starting subnet mask is /22, or 255.255.252.0. We turn on the next two bits in the subnet mask to get /24, or 255.255.255.0. The multiplier is 1. The four subnets are as follows:

- **Subnet 0**—172.30.4.0/24

- **Subnet 1**—172.30.5.0/24

- **Subnet 2**—172.30.6.0/24

- **Subnet 3**—172.30.7.0/24

Assigning Subnet 0 to LAN 3, we are left with three /24 subnets. Continuing on to the next largest host requirement on LAN 4, we take Subnet 1, 172.30.5.0/24, and subnet it further.

To satisfy the 100 hosts requirement, we leave 7 bits ($2^7 - 2 = 128$ hosts per subnet). Because we have 8 host bits total, we can borrow only 1 bit to create the subnets ($2^1 = 2$ subnets). The starting subnet mask is /24, or 255.255.255.0. We turn on the next bit in the subnet mask to get /25, or 255.255.255.128. The multiplier is 128. The two subnets are as follows:

- **Subnet 0**—172.30.5.0/25

- **Subnet 1**—172.30.5.128/25

Assigning Subnet 0 to LAN 4, we are left with one /25 subnet and two /24 subnets. Continuing on to the next largest host requirement on LAN 1, we take Subnet 1, 172.30.5.128/25, and subnet it further.

To satisfy the 60 hosts requirement, we leave 6 bits ($2^6 - 2 = 62$ hosts per subnet). Because we have 7 host bits total, we borrow 1 bit to create the subnets ($2^1 = 2$ subnets). The starting subnet mask is /25, or 255.255.255.128. We turn on the next bit in the subnet mask to get /26, or 255.255.255.192. The multiplier is 64. The two subnets are as follows:

- **Subnet 0**—172.30.5.128/26

- **Subnet 1**—172.30.5.192/26

Assigning Subnet 0 to LAN 1, we are left with one /26 subnet and two /24 subnets. Finishing our LAN subnetting with LAN 2, we take Subnet 1, 172.30.5.192/26, and subnet it further.

To satisfy the 10 hosts requirement, we leave 4 bits ($2^4 - 2 = 14$ hosts per subnet). Because we have 6 host bits total, we borrow 2 bits to create the subnets ($2^2 = 4$ subnets). The starting subnet mask is /26, or 255.255.255.192. We turn on the next two bits in the subnet mask to get /28, or 255.255.255.240. The multiplier is 16. The four subnets are as follows:

- **Subnet 0**—172.30.5.192/28
- **Subnet 1**—172.30.5.208/28
- **Subnet 2**—172.30.5.224/28
- **Subnet 3**—172.30.5.240/28

Assigning Subnet 0 to LAN 2, we are left with three /28 subnets and two /24 subnets. To finalize our addressing scheme, we need to create a subnet for the WAN link, which needs only two host addresses. We take Subnet 1, 172.30.5.208/28, and subnet it further.

To satisfy the two host requirement, we leave 2 bits ($2^2 - 2 = 2$ hosts per subnet). Because we have 4 host bits total, we borrow 2 bits to create the subnets ($2^2 = 4$ subnets). The starting subnet mask is /28, or 255.255.255.240. We turn on the next two bits in the subnet mask to get /30, or 255.255.255.252. The multiplier is 4. The four subnets are as follows:

- **Subnet 0**—172.30.5.208/30
- **Subnet 1**—172.30.5.212/30
- **Subnet 2**—172.30.5.216/30
- **Subnet 3**—172.30.5.220/30

We assign Subnet 0 to the WAN link. We are left with three /30 subnets, two /28 subnets, and two /24 subnets.

Video: Design a VLSM Addressing Scheme

Refer to the Digital Study Guide to view this video.

Activity: Design a VLSM Addressing Scheme

Refer to the Digital Study Guide to complete this activity.

Study Resources

For today's exam topics, refer to the following resources for more study.

Resource	Location	Topic
Primary Resources		
Certification Guide	5	IPv4 Addressing
		Assigning IPv4 Addresses
		Subnetting
Exam Cram	3	IPv4
		IP Address Classes
		Subnet Mask Assignment
		Subnetting
		Identifying the Difference Between IPv4 Public and Private Networks
		Classless Interdomain Routing
		Default Gateways
		IPv4 Address Types
		Assigning IP Addresses
		Identifying MAC Addresses
Video Course	10	MAC Addresses
		IPv4 Addressing
Supplemental Resources		
Lab Simulator	5	IPv4 Address Types and Classes
		Intermediate IPv4 Addressing Practice 1
		Configuring a Client Network Adapter with an IPv4 Address
		Configuring an Ethernet Interface on a Router
		Configure an IP Address on a Switch with a Default Gateway
		Connecting Two Routers to Each Other
Flash Cards		
Quick Reference		

Check Your Understanding

Refer to the Digital Study Guide to take a 10-question quiz covering the content of this day.

Implement IPv6 Addressing

CompTIA Network+ N10-006 Exam Topics

- 1.8 Given a scenario, implement and configure the appropriate addressing schema

Key Topics

Today, we continue our review of IP addressing, focusing solely on IPv6. Topics include an overview of IPv6, the IPv6 address structure and types, configuring IPv6, and IPv6 migration techniques.

IPv6 Addressing Overview

The capability to scale networks for future demands requires a limitless supply of IP addresses and improved mobility that private addressing and NAT alone cannot meet. IPv6 satisfies the increasingly complex requirements of hierarchical addressing that IPv4 does not provide. Here are several of the main benefits and features of IPv6:

- **Extended address space**—A 128-bit address space represents about 340 trillion trillion trillion addresses. That's enough to assign an address to every atom on the earth and still have enough addresses for another 100 earths.

- **Stateless autoconfiguration**—IPv6 provides host devices with a method for generating their own routable IPv6 address, called EUI-64 (Extended Unique Identifier that is 64 bits). IPv6 also supports stateful configuration using DHCPv6.

- **Eliminates the need for NAT/PAT**—NAT/PAT was conceived as a part of the solution to IPv4 address depletion. With IPv6, address depletion is no longer an issue. NAT64, however, does play an important role in providing backward compatibility with IPv4.

- **Simpler header**—A simpler header offers several advantages over IPv4:

    - Better routing efficiency for performance and forwarding-rate scalability

    - No broadcasts and thus no potential threat of broadcast storms

    - No requirement for processing checksums

    - Simpler and more efficient extension header mechanisms

- **Mobility and security**—Mobility and security help ensure compliance with mobile IP and IPsec standards functionality. Mobility enables people with mobile network devices—many with wireless connectivity—to move around in networks:

  - IPv4 does not automatically enable mobile devices to move without breaks in established network connections.

  - In IPv6, mobility is built in, which means that any IPv6 node can use mobility when necessary.

  - IPsec is enabled on every IPv6 node and is available for use, making the IPv6 Internet more secure.

- **Transition strategies**—You can incorporate existing IPv4 capabilities with the added features of IPv6 in several ways:

  - You can implement a dual-stack method, with both IPv4 and IPv6 configured on the interface of a network device.

  - You can use tunneling, which will become more prominent as the adoption of IPv6 grows.

Representing the IPv6 Address

The IPv6 address can look rather intimidating to someone who is used to IPv4 addressing. However, the IPv6 address can be easier to read and is much simpler to subnet than IPv4.

Conventions for Writing IPv6 Addresses

IPv6 conventions use 32 hexadecimal numbers, organized into eight hextets of four hex digits separated by a colon, to represent a 128-bit IPv6 address. Here's an example:

        2340:1111:AAAA:0001:1234:5678:9ABC

To make things a little easier, two rules allow you to shorten what must be typed for an IPv6 address:

- **Rule 1**—Omit the leading 0s in any given hextet.

- **Rule 2**—Omit the all-0s hextets. Represent one or more consecutive hextets of all hex 0s with a double colon (::), but only for one such occurrence in a given address.

NOTE: The term *hextet* refers to four consecutive hexadecimal digits. Eight hextets are in each IPv6 address.

For example, consider the following address. The highlighted hex digits represent the portion of the address that could be abbreviated.

        FE00:**0000:0000:0001:0000:0000:0000:00**56

This address has two locations in which one or more hextets have four hex 0s, so two main options exist for abbreviating this address, using the :: abbreviation in one or the other location. The following two options show the two briefest valid abbreviations:

- FE00::1:0:0:0:56

- FE00:0:0:1::56

In the first example, the second and third hextets preceding 0001 were replaced with ::. In the second example, the fifth, sixth, and seventh hextets were replaced with ::. In particular, note that the :: abbreviation, meaning "one or more hextets of all 0s," cannot be used twice, because that would be ambiguous. Therefore, the abbreviation FE00::1::56 would not be valid.

Conventions for Writing IPv6 Prefixes

IPv6 prefixes represent a range or block of consecutive IPv6 addresses. The number that represents the range of addresses, called a *prefix*, is usually seen in IP routing tables, just like you see IP subnet numbers in IPv4 routing tables.

As with IPv4, when you are writing or typing a prefix in IPv6, the bits past the end of the prefix length are all binary 0s. The following IPv6 address is an example of an address assigned to a host:

2000:1234:5678:9ABC:1234:5678:9ABC:1111/64

The prefix in which this address resides would be as follows:

2000:1234:5678:9ABC:**0000:0000:0000:0000**/64

When abbreviated, this would be

2000:1234:5678:9ABC::/64

If the prefix length does not fall on a hextet boundary (is not a multiple of 16), the prefix value should list all the values in the last hextet. For example, assume the prefix length in the previous example is /56. Therefore, by convention, the rest of the fourth hextet should be written, after being set to binary 0s, as follows:

2000:1234:5678:9A**00**::/56

The following list summarizes some key points about how to write IPv6 prefixes:

- The prefix has the same value as the IP addresses in the group for the first number of bits, as defined by the prefix length.

- Any bits after the prefix length number of bits are binary 0s.

- The prefix can be abbreviated with the same rules as IPv6 addresses.

- If the prefix length is not on a hextet boundary, write down the value for the entire hextet.

Table 25-1 shows several sample prefixes, their format, and a brief explanation.

Table 25-1   Example IPv6 Prefixes and Their Meanings

Prefix	Explanation	Incorrect Alternative
2000::/3	All addresses whose first 3 bits are equal to the first 3 bits of hex number 2000 (bits are 001)	2000/3 (omits ::) 2::/3 (omits the rest of the first hextet)
2340:1140::/26	All addresses whose first 26 bits match the listed hex number	2340:114::/26 (omits the last digit in the second hextet)
2340:1111::/32	All addresses whose first 32 bits match the listed hex number	2340:1111/32 (omits ::)

 Video: IPv6 Address Representation

Refer to the Digital Study Guide to view this video.

 Activity: Compress IPv6 Address Representations

Refer to the Digital Study Guide to complete this activity.

IPv6 Address Types

IPv4 has three address types: unicast, multicast, and broadcast. IPv6 does not use broadcasts. Instead, IPv6 uses unicast, multicast, and anycast. Figure 25-1 illustrates these three types of IPv6 addresses.

Figure 25-1   IPv6 Address Types

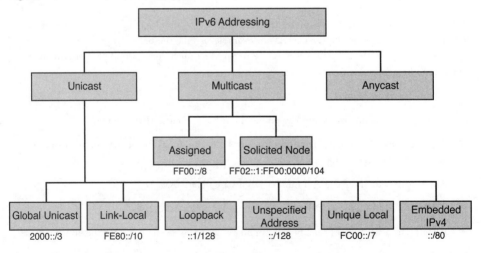

You should be familiar with the global unicast address and the link-local address. The other IPv6 address types are beyond the scope of the Network+ Exam.

NOTE: To learn more about IPv6, I recommend purchasing Rick Graziani's book *IPv6 Fundamentals: A Straightforward Approach to Understanding IPv6.*

Global Unicast Addresses

An IPv6 global unicast address is globally unique. Similar to a public IPv4 address, it can be routed in the Internet without any modification. An IPv6 global unicast address consists of a 48-bit global routing prefix, a 16-bit subnet ID, and a 64-bit interface ID. Use Rick Graziani's method of breaking down the IPv6 address with the 3-1-4 Rule (also known as the *pi rule* for 3.14), as shown in Figure 25-2.

Figure 25-2   Graziani's 3-1-4 Rule for Remembering the Global Unicast Address Structure

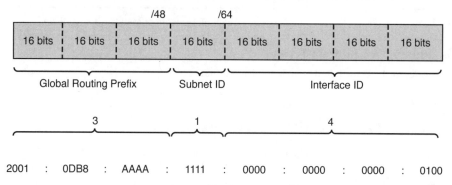

Each number refers to the number of hextets, or 16-bit segments, of that portion of the address.

- **3**—Three hextets for the global routing prefix
- **1**—One hextet for the subnet ID
- **4**—Four hextets for the interface ID

Link-Local Addresses

As shown earlier in Figure 25-1, link-local addresses are a type of unicast address. Link-local addresses are confined to a single link. They only need to be unique to that link because packets with a link-local source or destination address are not routable off the link.

Link-local addresses provide a unique benefit in IPv6. A device can create its own link-local address completely on its own. Link-local unicast addresses are in the range from FE80::/10 to FEBF::/10, as shown in Table 25-2.

Table 25-2   Range of Link-local Unicast Addresses

Link-local Unicast Address	Range of First Hextet	Range of First Hextet in Binary
FE80::/10	FE80	1111 1110 10 00 0000
	FEBF	1111 1110 10 11 1111

Figure 25-3 shows the format of a link-local unicast address.

Figure 25-3   Link-local Unicast Address

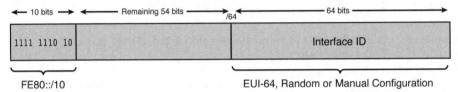

FE80::/10

EUI-64, Random or Manual Configuration

 Video: IPv6 Address Types

Refer to the Digital Study Guide to view this video.

Configuring IPv6 Addressing

Global unicast addresses can be configured using any one of the options shown in Table 25-3.

Table 25-3   Summary of Global Unicast Configuration Options

Global Unicast Configuration Option		Description
Manual	Static	Similar to IPv4, the IPv6 address and prefix are statically configured on the interface.
	EUI-64	The prefix is configured manually and the EUI-64 process uses the MAC address to generate the 64-bit interface ID.
	IPv6 Unnumbered	Similar to IPv4, an interface can be configured to use the IPv6 address of another interface on the same device.
Dynamic	Stateless Address Autoconfiguration	SLAAC determines the prefix and prefix length from Neighbor Discovery Router Advertisement messages and then creates the interface ID using the EUI-64 method.
	DHCPv6	Similar to IPv4, a device can receive some or all of its addressing from a DHCPv6 server.

Link-local addresses are configured in one of three ways:

- Dynamically, using EUI-64

- Randomly generated interface ID

- Statically, with the link-local address entered manually

EUI-64 Concept

Recall from Figures 25-2 and 25-3 that the second half of the IPv6 address is called the interface ID. The value of the interface ID portion can be set to any value, as long as no other host in the same subnet attempts to use the same value. However, the size of the interface ID was chosen to allow easy autoconfiguration of IP addresses by plugging the MAC address of a network card into the interface ID field in an IPv6 address.

MAC addresses are 6 bytes (48 bits) in length. Therefore, to complete the 64-bit interface ID, IPv6 fills in 2 bytes more by separating the MAC address into two 3-byte halves. It then inserts hex **FFFE** in between the halves and sets the seventh bit in the first byte to binary 1 to form the interface ID field. Figure 25-4 shows this format, called the EUI-64 format.

Figure 25-4   IPv6 Address Format with Interface ID and EUI-64

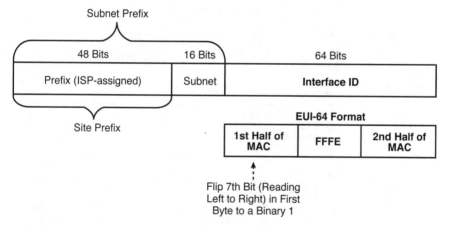

For example, the following two lines list a host's MAC address and corresponding EUI-64 format interface ID, assuming the use of an address configuration option that uses the EUI-64 format:

- **MAC address**—0034:5678:9ABC

- **EUI-64 interface ID**—0234:56**FF:FE**78:9ABC

NOTE: To change the seventh bit (reading left to right) in the example, convert hex 00 to binary 00000000, change the seventh bit to 1 (00000010), and then convert back to hex, for hex 02 as the first two digits.

Stateless Address Autoconfiguration

As previously mentioned in Table 25-3, IPv6 supports two methods of dynamic configuration of IPv6 addresses:

- **Stateless Address Autoconfiguration (SLAAC)**—A host dynamically learns the /64 prefix through the IPv6 Neighbor Discovery Protocol (NDP) and then calculates the rest of its address by using an EUI-64 method.

- **DHCPv6**—Works the same conceptually as DHCP in IPv4, which we reviewed on Day 30, "Network Services and Applications."

By using the EUI-64 process and the Neighbor Discovery Protocol (NDP), SLAAC allows a device to determine its entire global unicast address without any manual configuration or a DHCPv6 server. Figure 25-5 illustrates the SLAAC process between a host and a router configured with the **ipv6 unicast-routing** command, which means it will send and receive NDP messages.

Figure 25-5   Neighbor Discovery and the SLAAC Process

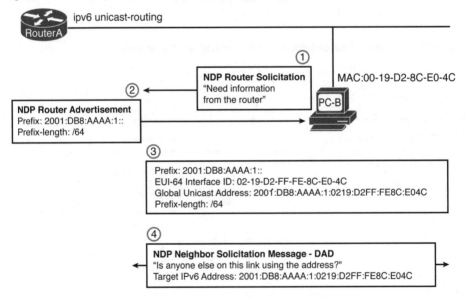

Migration to IPv6

Two major transition strategies are currently used to migrate to IPv6: dual-stack and tunneling.

Dual-Stack

A dual-stack device has complete support for both IPv4 and IPv6. It can be a host, printer, server, router, or any device that can be configured to support both protocols. When communicating with another IPv4 device, it behaves like an IPv4-only device. When communicating with another IPv6 device, it acts like an IPv6-only device.

Although an application can support both IPv4 and IPv6, the device doesn't just randomly select which protocol to use. Figure 25-6 shows an example of a dual-stack host.

Figure 25-6   Dual-Stack Example

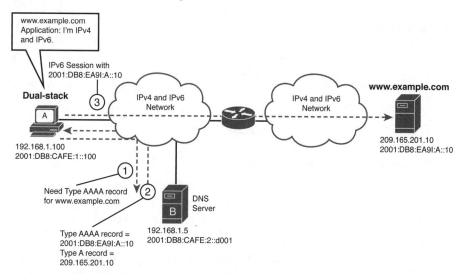

In step 1, dual-stack host A sends a DNS query for the quad-A (AAAA) record for www.example. com. In step 2, the DNS server returns a DNS query response containing both the quad-A and A records for www.example.com. Host A uses the quad-A record to begin communications with the www.example.com server.

Tunneling

A tunnel is nothing more than encapsulating one IP packet inside another. In IPv6, this is known as an overlay tunnel. Overlay tunnels encapsulate IPv6 packets in IPv4 packets for delivery across an IPv4 infrastructure, as shown in the examples in Figure 25-7.

Figure 25-7   Tunneling Examples

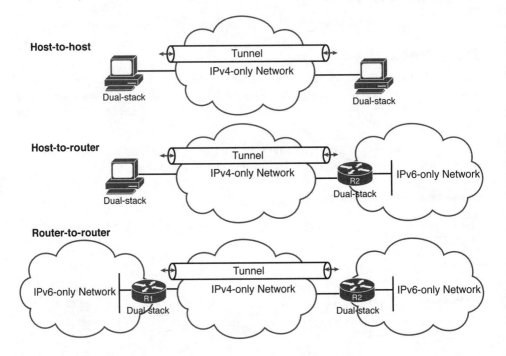

Tunneling types include the following:

- **Manual**—Manually configured, bidirectional, point-to point tunnels are the easiest to configure. However, they don't scale well. If the environment requires multiple tunnels between several routers, a separate tunnel is required between every two endpoints or routers.

- **6to4**—Defined in RFC 3056, a 6to4 tunnel is a point-to-multipoint connection, which mitigates the scalability issue with manually configured tunnels. A single 6to4 tunnel can be used to connect to any number of IPv6 networks, as shown in Figure 25-8. Viewed from the perspective of an IPv4-only network tunneling to an IPv6-only network, the tunnel is called 4to6.

Figure 25-8   6to4 Tunnel Example

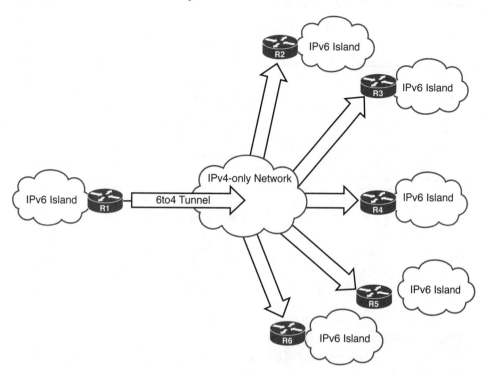

- **ISATAP**—ISATAP is defined in RFC 5214, "Intra-Site Automatic Tunnel Addressing Protocol (ISATAP)." ISATAP is designed for transporting IPv6 packets within a site, but not between sites.

- **GRE**—Generic Routing Encapsulation is similar to a manual tunnel. A GRE tunnel is a point-to-point tunnel for secure communication between two endpoints but can carry protocols other than IP, such as IS-IS (Intermediate System–to–Intermediate System). IS-IS is beyond the scope of the Network+ Exam.

- **Teredo (RFC 4380)**—Teredo, also known as shipworm, allows two dual-stack devices to send IPv6 packets when one is located behind an IPv4 NAT. Although Teredo was proposed by Microsoft, there exists a version for Linux known as Miredo, which is designed to allow full IPv6 connectivity to systems that are strictly IPv4 based.

Study Resources

For today's exam topics, refer to the following resources for more study.

Resource	Location	Topic
Primary Resources		
Certification Guide	5	IP Version 6
Exam Cram	3	IPv6 Addressing
		Comparing IPv4 and IPv6 Addressing
Video Course	10	IPv6 Addressing
Supplemental Resources		
Lab Simulator	5	IPv6 Addressing Terminology
		Truncating IPv6 Addresses
		Configuring a Network Adapter with an IPv6 Address
Flash Cards	6	Addressing Schemes
Quick Reference	6	Addressing Schemes

Check Your Understanding

Refer to the Digital Study Guide to take a 10-question quiz covering the content of this day.

Day 24

Routing Concepts

CompTIA Network+ N10-006 Exam Topics

- 1.9 Explain the basics of routing concepts and protocols

Key Topics

Today's review focuses on the various ways routers learn and advertise in a network to ensure that end devices have connectivity to network resources. Routing methods include static and dynamic configurations. Dynamic routing can be achieved with a variety of routing protocols.

Static and Default Routing Overview

A device such as a router can learn about other networks either through static configuration or dynamically through the processes of a routing protocol. Table 24-1 compares dynamic and static routing.

Table 24-1   Dynamic Versus Static Routing

Feature	Dynamic Routing	Static Routing
Configuration complexity	Generally independent of the network size	Increases with network size
Required administrator knowledge	Advanced knowledge required	No extra knowledge required
Topology changes	Automatically adapts to topology changes	Administrator intervention required
Scaling	Suitable for simple and complex topologies	Suitable for simple topologies
Security	Less secure	More secure
Resource usage	Uses CPU, memory, and link bandwidth	No extra resources needed
Predictability	Route depends on the current topology	Route to destination is always the same

When a router is configured with a dynamic routing protocol, it can learn routes without any additional input from the network administrator, so why would you use static routing? Situations vary, and there may be other reasons unique to a particular implementation. However, in general, you would use static routes in the following situations:

- In a small network that requires only simple routing
- In a hub-and-spoke network topology

- When you want to create a quick ad hoc route

- As a backup when there is failure on the primary route

Conversely, you would probably not use static routes in these situations:

- In a large network

- When the network is expected to scale

Static routes are commonly used when you are routing from a larger network to a stub network (a network that is accessed by a single link). Static routes can also be useful for specifying a default route. For example, in Figure 24-1, R2 is attached to a stub network.

Figure 24-1   Example of a Stub Network

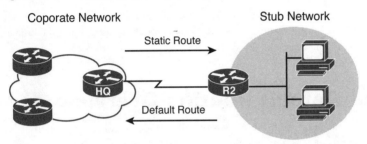

In Figure 24-1, there is no other route out of the stub network except to send packets to HQ. Therefore, it makes sense to configure R2 with a default route pointing out the interface attached to HQ. Similarly, there is only one way for HQ to route packets destined for the stub network attached to R2. Therefore, it makes sense to configure HQ with a static route pointing out the interface attached to R2. Yes, you could configure both routers with a dynamic routing protocol, but this can introduce a level of complexity that may not be necessary in a stub network situation.

 Video: Static and Default Routing

Refer to the Digital Study Guide to view this video.

 Activity: Compare Dynamic and Static Routing

Refer to the Digital Study Guide to complete this activity.

Dynamic Routing Protocols

Figure 24-2 shows a timeline of IP routing protocols along with a chart that will help you memorize the various ways to classify routing protocols.

Figure 24-2   Routing Protocols' Evolution and Classification

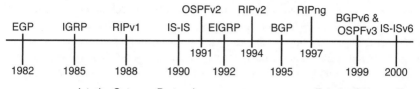

	Distance Vector Routing Protocols		Link State Routing Protocols		Path Vector
Classful	RIP	IGRP			EGP
Classless	RIPv2	EIGRP	OSPFv2	IS-IS	BGPv4
IPv6	RIPng	EIGRP for IPv6	OSPFv3	IS-IS for IPv6	MP BGP-4 (IPv6)

Table 24-2 expands the routing protocol acronyms and briefly lists some characteristics of each.

Table 24-2   Routing Protocols

Acronym	Expansion	Characteristics
RIP	Routing Information Protocol	Distance vector routing protocol with a maximum of 15 hops and updates sent every 30 seconds
RIPv2	Routing Information Protocol version 2	Same as RIP but sends subnet mask information in updates
RIPng	Routing Information Protocol next generation	Supports IPv6
IGRP	Interior Gateway Routing Protocol	Cisco proprietary routing protocol that has been replaced by EIGRP
EIGRP	Enhanced Interior Gateway Routing Protocol	Fast convergence; uses bandwidth and delay as its metric; includes IPv4 and IPv6 versions
OSPF	Open Shortest Path First	Link-state protocol offering fast convergence; uses cost as its metric; open standard; includes versions for IPv4 (version 2) and IPv6 (version 3)
IS-IS	Intermediate System-to-Intermediate System	Link-state protocol offering fast convergence; uses same algorithm as OSPF; not as widely deployed as OSPF; includes version for IPv4 and IPv6
EGP	Exterior Gateway Protocol	First exterior protocol now replaced by BGP
BGP	Border Gateway Protocol	Path-vector routing protocol; uses number of autonomous system hops as the metric; includes other parameters that can be configured

Route Redistribution

A network can simultaneously support more than one routing protocol through the process of route redistribution. For example, a router could have one of its interfaces participating in an OSPF area of the network and have another interface participating in an EIGRP area of the network. This router could then take routes learned via OSPF and inject those routes into the EIGRP routing process. Similarly, EIGRP-learned routes could be redistributed into the OSPF routing process.

IGP and EGP Routing Protocols

An autonomous system (AS) is a collection of routers under one administration that presents a common, clearly defined routing policy to the Internet. Typical examples are a large company's internal network and an ISP's network. Most company networks are not autonomous systems, only a network within their own ISP's autonomous system. Autonomous systems numbers are used in some routing protocols, such as BGP and EIGRP, to identify the autonomous system. Because the Internet is based on the autonomous system concept, two types of routing protocols are required:

- **Interior Gateway Protocols (IGP)**—Used for intra-AS routing (that is, routing inside an AS)

- **Exterior Gateway Protocols (EGP)**—Used for inter-AS routing (that is, routing between autonomous systems)

Distance Vector Routing Protocols

Distance vector means that routes are advertised as vectors of distance and direction. Distance is defined in terms of a metric, such the hop count in RIP, and direction is the next-hop router or exit interface. Distance vector protocols typically use the Bellman-Ford algorithm for the best-path route determination.

Some distance vector protocols periodically send complete routing tables to all connected neighbors. In large networks, these routing updates can become enormous, causing significant traffic on the links.

Although the Bellman-Ford algorithm eventually accumulates enough knowledge to maintain a database of reachable networks, the algorithm does not allow a router to know the exact topology of an internetwork. The router knows only the routing information received from its neighbors.

Distance vector protocols use routers as signposts along the path to the final destination. The only information a router knows about a remote network is the distance or metric to reach that network and which path or interface to use to get there. Distance vector routing protocols do not have an actual map of the network topology.

Distance vector protocols work best in the following situations:

- The network is simple and flat and does not require a hierarchical design.

- The administrators do not have enough knowledge to configure and troubleshoot link-state protocols.

- Specific types of networks, such as hub-and-spoke networks, are being implemented.

- Worst-case convergence times in a network are not a concern.

Link-State Routing Protocols

In contrast to distance vector routing protocol operation, a router configured with a link-state routing protocol can create a "complete view," or topology, of the network by gathering information from all the other routers. Think of a link-state routing protocol as having a complete map of the network topology. The signposts along the way from source to destination are not necessary, because all link-state routers are using an identical "map" of the network. A link-state router uses the link-state information to create a topology map and to select the best path to all destination networks in the topology. Link-state routing protocols include OSPF and IS-IS.

With some distance vector routing protocols, routers send periodic updates of their routing information to their neighbors. Link-state routing protocols do not use periodic updates. After the network has converged, a link-state update is sent only when there is a change in the topology.

Link-state protocols work best in the following situations:

- The network design is hierarchical, usually occurring in large networks.

- The administrators have a good knowledge of the implemented link-state routing protocol.

- Fast convergence of the network is crucial.

Classful Routing Protocols

Classful routing protocols do not send subnet mask information in routing updates. The first routing protocols, such as RIP and IGRP, were classful. This was at a time when network addresses were allocated based on classes: Class A, B, or C. A routing protocol did not need to include the subnet mask in the routing update because the network mask could be determined based on the first octet of the network address.

Classful routing protocols can still be used in some of today's networks, but because they do not include the subnet mask, they cannot be used in all situations. Classful routing protocols cannot be used when a network is subnetted using more than one subnet mask. In other words, classful routing protocols do not support variable-length subnet masking (VLSM).

Other limitations exist for classful routing protocols, including their inability to support noncontiguous networks and supernets. Classful routing protocols include Routing Information Protocol version 1 (RIPv1) and Interior Gateway Routing Protocol (IGRP).

Classless Routing Protocols

Classless routing protocols include the subnet mask with the network address in routing updates. Today's networks are no longer allocated based on classes, and the subnet mask cannot be determined by the value of the first octet. Classless routing protocols are required in most networks today because of their support for VLSM, noncontiguous networks, and supernets. Classless routing protocols are RIPv2, EIGRP, OSPF, IS-IS, and BGP.

Dynamic Routing Metrics

There are cases when a routing protocol learns of more than one route to the same destination from the same routing source. To select the best path, the routing protocol must be able to evaluate and differentiate among the available paths. A metric is used for this purpose. Two different routing protocols might choose different paths to the same destination because of using different metrics. Metrics used in IP routing protocols include the following:

- **RIP—Hop count**—Best path is chosen by the route with the lowest hop count.

- **IGRP and EIGRP—Bandwidth, delay, reliability, and load**—Best path is chosen by the route with the smallest composite metric value calculated from these multiple parameters. By default, only bandwidth and delay are used. For the Network+ exam objectives, the term latency is the same as delay. When an EIGRP router has two or more paths of equal cost, it will use the one with the larger maximum transmission unit (MTU).

- **IS-IS and OSPF—Cost**—Best path is chosen by the route with the lowest cost. The Cisco implementation of OSPF uses bandwidth to determine the cost.

NOTE: Although you will see SPB listed in the exam topics under routing metrics, SPB is not a routing metric. SPB stands for Shortest Path Bridging, which is an IEEE 802.1aq standard meant to replace the Spanning Tree Protocol (STP) in situations where a Layer 2 network has hundreds or thousands of switches, such as a data center. SPB relies on IS-IS at Layer 3.

The metric associated with a certain route can be best viewed by looking at the routing table. On Cisco routers, you use the command **show ip route** to view the routing table. The metric value is the second value in the brackets for a routing table entry. In Example 24-1, R2 has a route to the 192.168.8.0/24 network that is two hops away.

Example 24-1 Routing Table for R2

```
R2# show ip route

<output omitted>

Gateway of last resort is not set

R 192.168.1.0/24 [120/1] via 192.168.2.1, 00:00:24, Serial0/0/0
C 192.168.2.0/24 is directly connected, Serial0/0/0
C 192.168.3.0/24 is directly connected, FastEthernet0/0
C 192.168.4.0/24 is directly connected, Serial0/0/1
R 192.168.5.0/24 [120/1] via 192.168.4.1, 00:00:26, Serial0/0/1
R 192.168.6.0/24 [120/1] via 192.168.2.1, 00:00:24, Serial0/0/0
                 [120/1] via 192.168.4.1, 00:00:26, Serial0/0/1
R 192.168.7.0/24 [120/1] via 192.168.4.1, 00:00:26, Serial0/0/1
R 192.168.8.0/24 [120/2] via 192.168.4.1, 00:00:26, Serial0/0/1
```

Administrative Distance

There can be times when a router learns a route to a remote network from more than one routing source. For example, a static route might have been configured for the same network/subnet mask that was learned dynamically by a dynamic routing protocol such as RIP. The router must choose which route to install.

Although less common, more than one dynamic routing protocol can be deployed in the same network. In some situations, it might be necessary to route the same network address using multiple routing protocols such as RIP and OSPF. Because different routing protocols use different metrics—RIP uses hop count and OSPF uses bandwidth—it is not possible to compare metrics to determine the best path.

Administrative distance (AD) defines the preference of a routing source. Each routing source—including specific routing protocols, static routes, and even directly connected networks—is prioritized in order of most to least preferable using an AD value. Cisco routers use the AD feature to select the best path when they learn about the same destination network from two or more different routing sources.

The AD value is an integer value from 0 to 255. The lower the value, the more preferred the route source. An administrative distance of 0 is the most preferred. Only a directly connected network has an AD of 0, which cannot be changed. An AD of 255 means the router will not believe the source of that route, and it will not be installed in the routing table.

In the routing table shown in Example 24-1, the AD value is the first value listed in the brackets. You can see that the AD value for RIP routes is 120. Table 24-3 shows a chart of the different administrative distance values for various routing protocols.

Table 24-3   Default Administrative Distances

Route Source	AD
Connected	0
Static	1
EIGRP summary route	5
External BGP	20
Internal EIGRP	90
IGRP	100
OSPF	110
IS-IS	115
RIP	120
External EIGRP	170
Internal BGP	200

Routing Loop Prevention

Without preventive measures, distance vector routing protocols could cause severe routing loops in the network. A routing loop is a condition in which a packet is continuously transmitted within a series of routers without ever reaching its intended destination network. A routing loop can occur when two or more routers have inaccurate routing information to a destination network.

A number of mechanisms are available to eliminate routing loops, primarily with distance vector routing protocols. These mechanisms include the following:

- **Defining a maximum metric to prevent count to infinity**—To eventually stop the incrementing of a metric during a routing loop, "infinity" is defined by setting a maximum metric value. For example, RIP defines infinity as 16 hops—an "unreachable" metric. When the routers "count to infinity," they mark the route as unreachable.

- **Hold-down timers**—Used to instruct routers to hold any changes that might affect routes for a specified period of time. If a route is identified as down or possibly down, any other information for that route containing the same status, or worse, is ignored for a predetermined amount of time (the hold-down period) so that the network has time to converge.

- **Split horizon**—Used to prevent a routing loop by not allowing advertisements to be sent back through the interface they originated from. The split horizon rule stops a router from incrementing a metric and then sending the route back to its source.

- **Route poisoning or poison reverse**—Used to mark the route as unreachable in a routing update that is sent to other routers. Unreachable is interpreted as a metric that is set to the maximum.

- **Triggered updates**—A routing table update that is sent immediately in response to a routing change. Triggered updates do not wait for update timers to expire. The detecting router immediately sends an update message to adjacent routers.

- **TTL field in the IP header**—The purpose of the Time to Live (TTL) field is to avoid a situation in which an undeliverable packet keeps circulating on the network endlessly. With TTL, the 8-bit field is set with a value by the source device of the packet. The TTL is decreased by 1 by every router on the route to its destination. If the TTL field reaches 0 before the packet arrives at its destination, the packet is discarded and the router sends an ICMP error message back to the source of the IP packet.

Link-State Routing Protocol Features

Like distance vector protocols that send routing updates to their neighbors, link-state protocols send link-state updates to neighboring routers, which in turn forward that information to their neighbors, and so on. At the end of the process, like with distance vector protocols, routers that use link-state protocols add the best routes to their routing tables, based on metrics. However, beyond this level of explanation, these two types of routing protocol algorithms have little in common.

Building the LSDB

Link-state routers flood detailed information about the internetwork to all the other routers so that every router has the same information about the internetwork. Routers use this link-state database (LSDB) to calculate the currently best routes to each subnet.

OSPF, the most popular link-state IP routing protocol, advertises information in routing update messages of various types, with the updates containing information called link-state advertisements (LSA).

Figure 24-3 shows the rather basic flooding process, with R8 sending the original LSA for itself, and the other routers flooding the LSA by forwarding it until every router has a copy.

Figure 24-3   Flooding LSAs Using a Link-State Routing Protocol

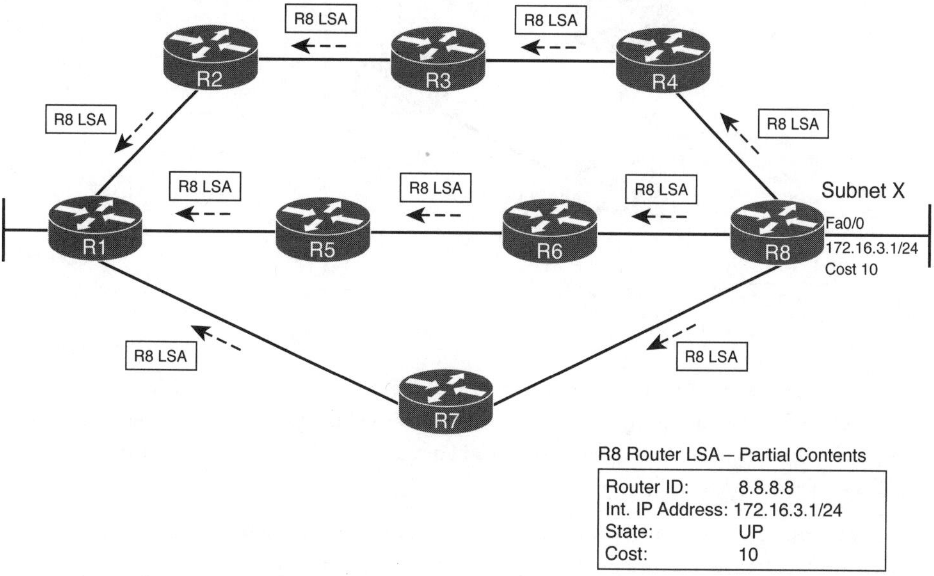

R8 Router LSA – Partial Contents

Router ID:	8.8.8.8
Int. IP Address:	172.16.3.1/24
State:	UP
Cost:	10

Calculating the Dijkstra Algorithm

The flooding process alone does not cause a router to learn what routes to add to the IP routing table. Link-state protocols must then find and add routes to the IP routing table using the Dijkstra Shortest Path First (SPF) algorithm.

The SPF algorithm is run on the LSDB to create the SPF tree. The LSDB holds all the information about all the possible routers and links. Each router must view itself as the starting point and each subnet as the destination, and use the SPF algorithm to build its own SPF tree to pick the best route to each subnet.

Figure 24-4 shows a graphical view of the results of the SPF algorithm run by router R1 when trying to find the best route to reach subnet 172.16.3.0/24 (based on Figure 24-3).

Figure 24-4   SPF Tree to Find R1's Route to 172.16.3.0/24

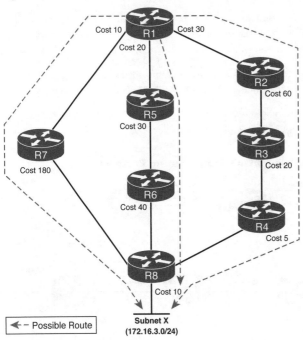

To pick the best route, a router's SPF algorithm adds the cost associated with each link between itself and the destination subnet, over each possible route. Figure 24-4 shows the costs associated with each route beside the links, with the dashed lines showing the three routes R1 finds between itself and subnet X (172.16.3.0/24).

Table 24-4 lists the three routes shown in Figure 24-4 with their cumulative costs, showing that R1's best route to 172.16.3.0/24 starts by going through R5.

Table 24-4   Comparing R1's Three Alternatives for the Route to 172.16.3.0/24

Route	Location in Figure 24-4	Cumulative Cost
R1–R7–R8	Left	10 + 180 + 10 = 200
R1–R5–R6–R8	Middle	20 + 30 + 40 + 10 = 100
R1–R2–R3–R4–R8	Right	30 + 60 + 20 + 5 + 10 = 125

As a result of the SPF algorithm's analysis of the LSDB, R1 adds a route to subnet 172.16.3.0/24 to its routing table, with the next-hop router of R5.

Convergence with Link-State Protocols

Remember, when an LSA changes, link-state protocols react swiftly, converging the network and using the currently best routes as quickly as possible. For example, imagine that the link between

R5 and R6 fails in the internetwork of Figures 24-3 and 24-4. The following list explains the process R1 uses to switch to a different route:

1. R5 and R6 flood LSAs that state that their interfaces are now in a "down" state.

2. All routers run the SPF algorithm again to see if any routes have changed.

3. All routers replace routes, as needed, based on the results of SPF. For example, R1 changes its route for subnet X (172.16.3.0/24) to use R2 as the next-hop router.

These steps allow the link-state routing protocol to converge quickly—much more quickly than distance vector routing protocols.

Route Aggregation

Route aggregation is the process of summarizing multiple routes into one router advertisement. This is also called classless interdomain routing (CIDR). CIDR allows contiguous classful networks to be aggregated. Instead of sending a collection of networks in routing updates, a border router can send one summary route to the next router.

A typical use of CIDR is as a service provider summarizing multiple Class C networks, assigned to their various customers. For example, imagine that a service provider is responsible for advertising the Class C networks shown in Figure 24-5.

Figure 24-5   Route Aggregation Example

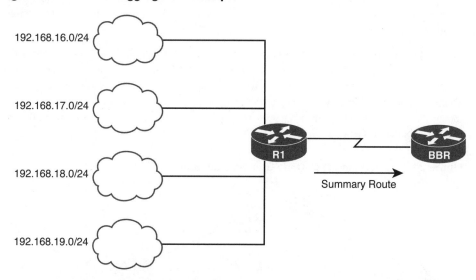

Use the following steps to calculate a summary route:

Step 1.   Write out the networks that you want to summarize in binary, as shown following step 4.

Step 2.   To find the subnet mask for summarization, start with the leftmost bit.

Step 3.   Work your way to the right, finding all the bits that match consecutively.

Step 4.   When you find a column of bits that do not match, stop. You are at the summary
boundary.

```
11000000.10101000.00010000.00000000
11000000.10101000.00010001.00000000
11000000.10101000.00010010.00000000
11000000.10101000.00010011.00000000
```

Step 5.   Count the number of leftmost matching bits, which in this example is 22. This number
becomes your subnet mask for the summarized route (/22, or 255.255.252.0).

Step 6.   To find the network address for summarization, copy the matching 22 bits and add all
0 bits to the end to make 32 bits. In this example, the network address with prefix is
192.168.16.0/22.

Video: Route Summary Calculation

Refer to the Digital Study Guide to view this video.

High Availability

The availability of a network is measured by its uptime during a year. For example, if a network
has five nines of availability, it is up 99.999 percent of the time, which translates to a maximum of
5 minutes of downtime per year. One way to ensure high availability is to provide default gateway
redundancy.

Most end devices do not store routes to reach remote networks. Instead, they are configured with
a default gateway that will handle routing for them. To ensure that a device will still have access to
remote networks, you should implement some type of default gateway redundancy in the network.
That is the role of first-hop redundancy protocols (FHRP). FHRPs allow you to install multiple
routers in a subnet to collectively act as a single default router. These routers share a virtual IP
address, as shown in Figure 24-6.

Figure 24-6   Redundant Default Gateway Example

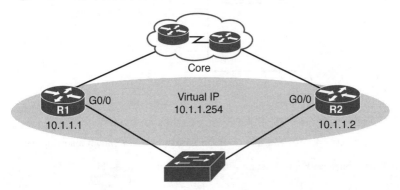

In the figure, the G0/0 interfaces on R1 and R2 are configured with the IP addresses shown. However, both routers are also configured with the virtual IP. This virtual IP address is the default gateway address configured on end devices. A redundancy protocol provides the mechanism for determining which router should take the active role in forwarding traffic. It also determines when the forwarding role must be taken over by a standby router. The transition from one forwarding router to another is transparent to the end devices. It is this ability of a network to dynamically recover from the failure of a device acting as a default gateway that is known as first-hop redundancy.

Regardless of which FHRP is implemented, the steps that take place when the active router fails are as follows:

Step 1.   The standby router stops seeing hello messages from the forwarding router.

Step 2.   The standby router assumes the role of the forwarding router.

Step 3.   Because the new forwarding router assumes both the IP and MAC addresses of the virtual router, the end stations do not recognize a disruption in service.

The following list defines the three options available for first-hop redundancy protocols (FHRPs).

- **Hot Standby Router Protocol (HSRP)**—A Cisco-proprietary FHRP designed to allow for transparent failover of a first-hop IPv4 device. The function of the HSRP standby router is to monitor the operational status of the HSRP group and to quickly assume packet-forwarding responsibility if the active router fails. HSRP for IPv6 provides support for IPv6 networks.

- **Virtual Router Redundancy Protocol (VRRP)**—An IETF standard that dynamically assigns responsibility for one or more virtual routers to the VRRP routers on an IPv4 LAN. Operation is very similar to HSRP. VRRPv3 supports IPv4 and IPv6.

- **Gateway Load Balancing Protocol (GLBP)**—Cisco-proprietary FHRP that protects data traffic from a failed router or circuit, like HSRP and VRRP, while also allowing load balancing (also called load sharing) between a group of redundant routers. GLBP for IPv6 provides support for IPv6 networks.

Study Resources

For today's exam topics, refer to the following resources for more study.

Resource	Location	Topic
Primary Resources		
Certification Guide	5	Classless Interdomain Routing
	6	All
	9	Layer 3 Redundancy
Exam Cram	3	Managing TCP/IP Routing
		Configuring Routers and Switches
Video Course	11	All

Resource	Location	Topic
Supplemental Resources		
Lab Simulator	6	Reading a Routing Table
		Using the `route print` Command
Flash Cards	7	Routing Concepts
Quick Reference	7	Routing Concepts

 Check Your Understanding

Refer to the Digital Study Guide to take a 10-question quiz covering the content of this day.

Unified Communications, Virtualization, and Cloud

CompTIA Network+ N10-006 Exam Topics

- 1.10 Identify the basics elements of unified communication technologies

- 1.11 Compare and contrast technologies that support cloud and virtualization

Key Topics

Today's review focuses on several important trends in networking technologies. Unified communications is concerned with merging the data and telephone networks onto one platform along with all the tools users expect to use to keep in touch with each other: email, voice mail, instant messaging, video conferencing, and presence. Quality of Service (QoS) ensures that network traffic is appropriately classified. Virtualization decouples the software from the hardware and has played a primary role in the rise of cloud computing. Cloud computing depends on the evolution of storage area networks, particularly Fibre Channel over Ethernet (FCoE) and iSCSI SAN implementations.

Unified Communications

Unified communications is the integration of real-time services such as presence, instant messaging, VoIP, and audio/videoconferencing with non-real-time communication services such as email and voicemail. Unified communication devices include using specialized servers, devices, and gateways.

At its most fundamental level, unified communications merges the data and telephone networks. Figure 23-1 shows a small Voice over IP (VoIP) network with only a call agent to manage the VoIP connections.

Figure 23-1   Sample VoIP Network Topology

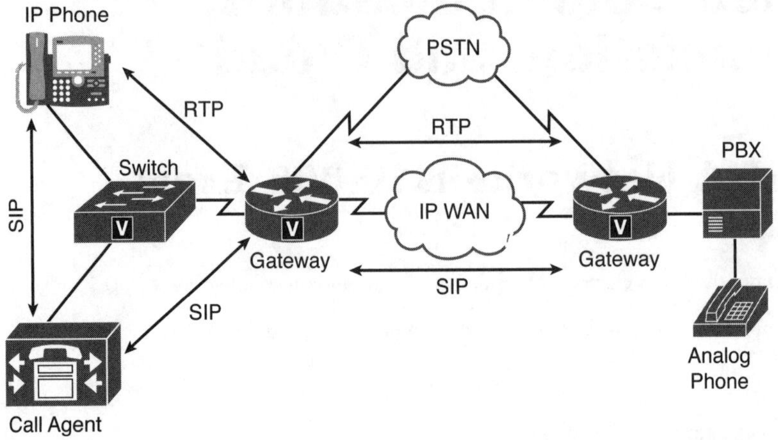

Table 23-1 provides a definition for each of the devices and protocols shown in Figure 23-1.

Table 23-1   VoIP Network Elements

Protocol/Device	Description
IP phone	An IP phone digitizes the spoken voice, packetizes it, and sends it out over a data network (via the IP phone's Ethernet port).
Call agent	The call agent analyzes the dialed digits and determines how to route the call toward the destination.
Gateway	A gateway in a VoIP network acts as a translator between two different telephony signaling environments.
PBX	A Private Branch Exchange (PBX) can connect into a VoIP network through a gateway.
Analog phone	An analog phone can connect into a VoIP network via a PBX, which is connected to a VoIP network.
SIP	Session Initiation Protocol (SIP) is a VoIP signaling protocol used to set up, maintain, and tear down VoIP phone calls.
RTP	Real-time Transport Protocol (RTP) is a protocol that carries voice (and interactive video).

Dozens of vendors provide unified communications equipment, applications, and services, including Microsoft, NEC, IBM, Dell, and HP. To focus today's review, I will discuss the unified communications solutions from Cisco Systems. Core products for Cisco's Unified Communications include the following:

- Cisco Unified Communications Manager Express (CME)
- Cisco Unified Communications Manager (CUCM)
- Cisco Unity Connection (Unity)
- Cisco Unified Communications Manager IM and Presence

The CME solution acts as the call agent in small organizations. Integrated into the default gateway router, CME controls virtually every action performed on an IP phone. Figure 23-2 shows a CME router controlling a call to an analog phone that is connected to the public switched telephone network (PSTN).

Figure 23-2   CME Controlling Calls to the PSTN

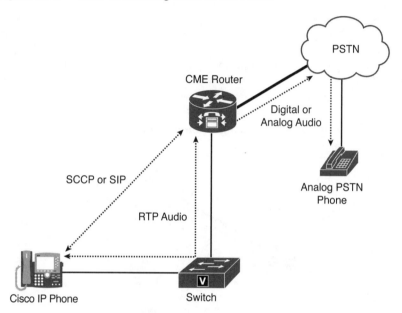

If a user picks up the handset, an off-hook state is sent from the IP phone to the CME router using either Skinny Client Control Protocol (SCCP) or SIP. After the user finishes dialing the phone number of the PSTN phone, the CME router forwards the call out a PSTN-connected interface. CME now assumes the role of voice gateway and signals to the PSTN to establish the call on behalf of the Cisco IP Phone. The CME router has now established two different "legs" of the call: one to the PSTN and the other to the Cisco IP Phone. It stands in the middle, independently handling signaling from both sides in two different formats.

CUCM serves the same function as a CME, but is scaled for midsize to global enterprise-class corporations. CUCM features include the following:

- Full support for audio and video telephony

- Appliance-based operation that runs on top of a hardened and secure operating system

- VMware installation for deployment in virtual machines

- Redundant server cluster that scales to 40,000 phones

- Built-in Disaster Recovery System (DRS) that allows database backup to a secure FTP server

- Directory service support that can incorporate user accounts or integrate with an existing directory structure

The goal of Cisco Unity Connection is to make any message retrievable from any voice-enabled device or application. Regardless of how a message was left, you could retrieve it using a variety of clients. Here's a list of some of the Cisco Unity Connection features:

- Up to 20,000 mailboxes per server

- Access voicemails from anywhere

- Directory server integration

- Microsoft Exchange support

Cisco Unity Connection operates independently from CUCM and is not tied exclusively to the CUCM product. Therefore, Cisco Unity Connection must be set up as an outside system that the CUCM can communicate with using SIP or SCCP, as shown in Figure 23-3.

Figure 23-3   CUCM and Cisco Unity Connection Integration

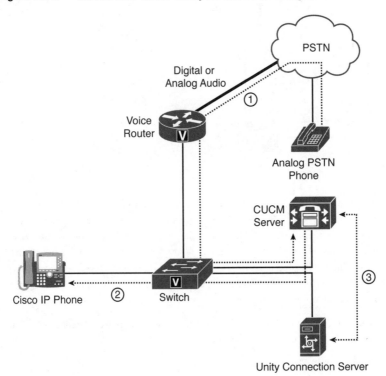

The steps in Figure 23-3 are as follows:

1. An incoming call from the PSTN arrives at the voice gateway. The voice gateway routes the incoming call to the CUCM server.

2. CUCM receives the call and directs it to the appropriate IP phone (signaling using SCCP or SIP). If someone does not answer the IP phone or diverts the call to voicemail, CUCM forwards the call to the preconfigured voicemail pilot number that rings the Unity Connection server.

3. CUCM transfers the call (once again using SCCP or SIP) to the Unity Connection server. The extension of the originally called phone is contained in the signaling messages, which allows Unity Connection to send the call to the correct voicemail box.

After the caller leaves a message on the voicemail server, Cisco Unity Connection signals the CUCM to light the voicemail indicator on the Cisco IP Phone, alerting the user that he or she has a voice message waiting.

Cisco Unified Communications Manager Instant Messaging and Presence (IMP) is server software, in conjunction with a variety of IM clients, that gives people secure IM with full presence status indication. This allows them to see the status of their friends and co-workers before they pick up the phone to dial their number or IM chat with them. Status indicators include on the phone, off the phone, not available, and in a meeting.

IMP can operate in Unified Communications mode, which is integrated with CUCM and supports up to 45,000 users, or in IM-Only mode, which sets up IMP as a standalone app without an integrated CUCM and supports up to 75,000 users. A third mode, Microsoft Lync interoperability mode, provides integration with users of Microsoft Office Communicator and CUCM for up to 40,000 users.

Quality of Service

Unified communications intrinsically relies upon strong QoS policies. Real-time voice and video data streams are particularly sensitive to the quality issues shown in Table 23-2.

Table 23-2   Quality Issues

Issue	Description
Delay	Delay is the time required for a packet to travel from its source to its destination.
Jitter	Jitter is the uneven arrival, or variable delay, of packets.
Drops	Packet drops occur when a link is congested and a router's interface queue overflows.

Routers and switches can be configured with QoS features to mitigate these issues by classifying and prioritizing traffic. For example, voice and video traffic should probably have no more than 150 ms of one-way delay, no more than 30 ms of jitter, and no more than 1 percent packet loss. Data traffic can be further classified with specific delay and loss characteristics. For example, normal web traffic should probably be classified differently than traffic to and from the point-of-sale databases.

QoS can be implemented in three different ways, as shown in Table 23-3.

Table 23-3   QoS Implementation

Issue	Description
Best-effort	Same as no QoS, best-effort uses a first-in, first-out (FIFO) queuing strategy, where packets are emptied from a queue in the same order that they entered the queue.
Integrated services (IntServ)	IntServ is often referred to as hard QoS because it can make strict bandwidth reservations. Because IntServ must be configured on every router along a packet's path, the main drawback of IntServ is its lack of scalability.
Differentiated services (DiffServ)	Packets are marked, and routers and switches can drop or forward based on those markings. Because DiffServ does not make an explicit reservation, it is often called soft QoS. Most modern QoS configurations are based on the DiffServ approach.

The following is a collection of commonly used QoS mechanisms for the treatment of packets using the DiffServ QoS approach:

- **Classification**—Traffic is placed into different categories. No bits are altered.

- **Marking**—Bits are altered within a frame, cell, or packet to indicate how the network should treat that traffic. For example, the bits type of service (ToS) octet in the IPv4 packet header can be altered to indicate priority, as shown in Figure 23-4. The first three bits are the IP Precedence markings, which can range from 0 to 7. For more granularity, QoS could use the differentiated service code point (DSCP) bits, which are the first 6 bits. This allows the QoS mechanism to mark packets from 0 to 63. At Layer 2, a 3-bit class of service (CoS) field is used to mark tagged frames as they traverse a switch trunk.

Figure 23-4   The ToS Octet in the IPv4 Header

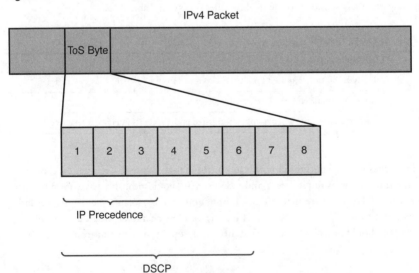

- **Congestion management**—A queuing algorithm is used to divide an interface's buffer into multiple logical queues, as shown in Figure 23-5.

Figure 23-5   Queuing Algorithm Example

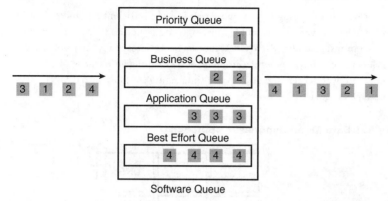

- **Congestion avoidance**—To avoid packet drops when a queue fills to capacity, you can configure a minimum threshold for random early detection (RED). Once it is triggered, packets of low priority can be randomly discarded. This discard rate can then increase to a maximum, at which point all low-priority packets are discarded.

- **Policing and shaping**—Instead of making a minimum amount of bandwidth available for specific traffic types, you might want to limit available bandwidth. Both policing and traffic-shaping tools can accomplish this objective. Collectively, these tools are called traffic conditioners.

- **Link efficiency**—To make the most of the limited bandwidth available on slower-speed links, you might choose to implement compression or link fragmentation and interleaving (LFI). RTP header compression (cRTP) can take the Layer 3 and Layer 4 headers and compress them to only 2 or 4 bytes, as shown in Figure 23-6. LFI can fragment large data packets and interleave smaller time-sensitive packets among the fragments.

Figure 23-6   RTP Header Compression (cRTP)

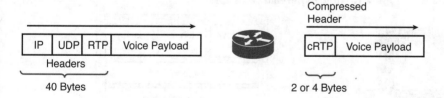

Virtualization

Unified communications platforms are often virtualized, especially in large implementations. For example, the CUCM clusters discussed earlier are installed as virtual machines. Device, network, and data virtualization are trends that will continue to impact the design and implementation of computer networks.

Server Virtualization

The computing power available in a single high-end server is often sufficient to handle the tasks of multiple independent servers. For example, the single high-end server shown in Figure 23-7 might be running an instance of a Microsoft Windows Server providing Microsoft Active Directory (AD) services to an enterprise, while simultaneously running an instance of a Linux server acting as a corporate web server, and at the same time acting as a Sun Solaris UNIX server providing corporate DNS services.

Figure 23-7   Type 1 Bare Metal Hypervisor Approach

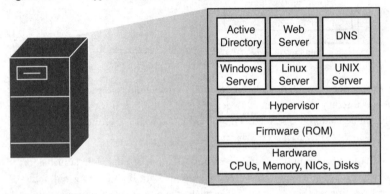

There are two approaches to implementing a hypervisor: the Type 1 bare-metal approach (shown in Figure 23-7) and the Type 2 hosted approach. Type 1 hypervisors are installed directly on the hardware. They use a management console to install operating systems and manage the allocation of hardware resources. VMware ESXi and Oracle VM Server are examples of Type 1 hypervisors.

Type 2 hypervisors are installed on top of an existing operating system, which then hosts additional operating system installations, as shown in Figure 23-8. VMware Player and Oracle VirtualBox are examples of Type 2 hypervisors.

Figure 23-8   Type 2 Hosted Hypervisor Example

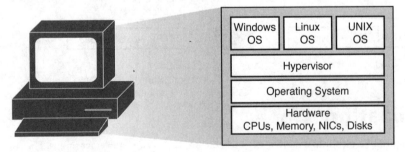

Activity: Identify the Type of Hypervisor

Refer to the Digital Study Guide to complete this activity.

In data centers, server hardware is specialized to provide an efficient and flexible platform for meeting customer needs. For example, the four Cisco UCS B460 M4 blade servers shown in Figure 23-9 provide full redundancy.

Figure 23-9   Cisco UCS B460 M4 Blade Servers; Courtesy of Cisco Systems, Inc. Unauthorized use not permitted.

These servers are incredibly powerful. For example, one possible configuration might be the following:

- Two CPUs providing up to 15 3.5GHz cores

- Ninety-six DIMM slots for a maximum total memory of 6TB

- Three virtual NICs supporting 16 10GigE interfaces and up to 768 virtualized connections

- Two 1.2TB HDDs or two 800GB SSDs

Networking Device Virtualization

The benefits of virtualization are also extended into the networking realm where just about any device can be virtualized, including switches, routers, and firewalls. The connection between the virtual world and the physical world is achieved through a physical interface that connects to the virtual interfaces. More than one virtual interface can be configured to use the same physical interface.

Using virtual interfaces allows a network administrator to apply the same QoS and security policies that she would normally use on physical networking devices. For example, the virtual servers you saw earlier in Figure 23-7 can be separated on individual VLANs by using a virtual switch, as shown in Figure 23-10.

Figure 23-10   Virtual Servers Segmented with a Virtual Switch

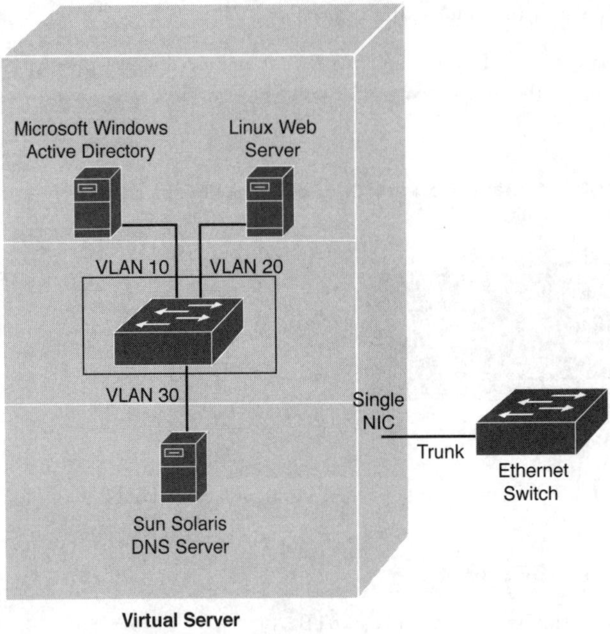

Microsoft Windows
Active Directory

Linux Web
Server

VLAN 10   VLAN 20

VLAN 30

Single
NIC

Trunk

Ethernet
Switch

Sun Solaris
DNS Server

Virtual Server

Similar to the virtual switch shown in Figure 23-10, routers and firewalls can also be virtualized.

Software-Defined Networking

Large implementations of many virtualized servers and networking devices would be difficult to manage without some type of orchestration software. The role of software-defined networking (SDN) is to manage this complexity. SDN solutions allow the administrator to implement features, functions, and configurations without the need to do the individual command-line configuration on the network devices. This is done by separating the physical network control plane from the data plane. The control plane can then manage several devices. For example, in Figure 23-11, the data planes on five physical devices are managed by one centralized controller.

SDN is the future of networking. If you are interested in exploring SDN further, I recommend the excellent "live lessons" by Terry Slattery titled, An Introduction to Software Defined Networking (SDN) LiveLessons—Networking Talks.

Figure 23-11   Separating the Control Plane from the Data Plane

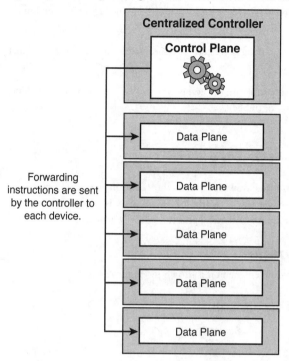

 Video: Virtualization Overview

Refer to the Digital Study Guide to view this video.

Cloud Concepts

Virtualization is the foundation upon which cloud computing stands. The NIST (National Institute of Standards and Technology) defines three service models for cloud computing in its Special Publication 800-145. These are as follows:

- **Software as a Service (SaaS)**—The cloud service provider is responsible for access to services such as email, communication, and virtual desktops that are delivered over the Internet.

- **Platform as a Service (PaaS)**—The cloud service provider is responsible for access to the development tools and services used to deliver the applications.

- **Infrastructure as a Service (IaaS)**—The cloud service provider is responsible for access to the network equipment, virtualized network services, and supporting network infrastructure.

NIST also defines four possible delivery models, which are described as follows:

- **Private cloud**—A private cloud is created exclusively for a single organization. It may be owned by the organization or by a third party, such as a cloud service provider.

- **Public cloud**—A public cloud is created for use by the general public. The infrastructure is physically located on the cloud service provider's site, but may be owned by one or multiple organizations.

- **Community cloud**—A community cloud is created for a specific group of organizations that have shared concerns.

- **Hybrid cloud**—A hybrid cloud infrastructure is a composition of two or more distinct cloud infrastructures (private, community, or public).

Storage Area Networks

The physical location of the data that is made available through virtualization and cloud services is usually stored in a data center within storage area networks (SANs). A SAN is a network containing storage devices that can make those storage devices appear to be locally attached.

Directly Attached Storage

A directly attached storage (DAS) SAN implementation is shown in Figure 23-12.

Figure 23-12   Directly Attached Storage SAN

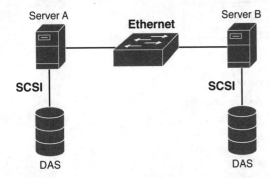

Each server in Figure 23-12 has a direct connection to its own hard drives, which could be internal or external. That connection is typically achieved through a Small Computer System Interface (SCSI), which is a collection of standards used to exchange data between computers and storage devices. Users connect to the servers over Ethernet.

Network-Attached Storage

A network-attached storage (NAS) SAN implementation is shown in Figure 23-13.

Figure 23-13   Network Attached Storage SAN

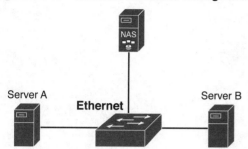

NAS allows the two servers in Figure 23-13 to share storage resources. A NAS is a network appliance that acts like a file server and can be accessed over an Ethernet connection.

Fibre Channel

A fibre channel SAN implementation is shown in Figure 23-14.

Figure 23-14   Fibre Channel SAN

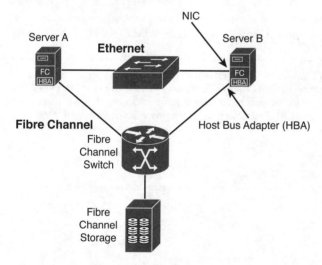

Fibre channel is a technology that allows high-speed access to storage devices over a fibre channel (FC) network. These implementations are common in enterprise-level SANs. Servers that connect to an FC network require two different network adapters: a standard Ethernet NIC for the LAN and a host bus adapter (HBA) for the SAN. The HBA card allows the server to connect the FC network.

Fibre Channel over Ethernet

A fibre channel over Ethernet (FCoE) SAN implementation is shown in Figure 23-15.

Figure 23-15   Fibre Channel over Ethernet SAN

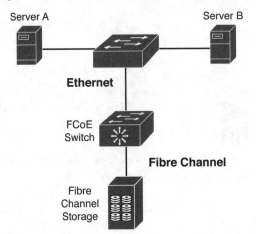

FC networks have now evolved to FCoE where the servers only need one adapter to connect to the network. FCoE is a technology that allows FC frames to be encapsulated inside Ethernet frames and sent over the Ethernet LAN, running at speeds up to 10Gbps. The data transport is Ethernet until the traffic reaches the FCoE switch. Then the data transport is FC to the FC SAN.

NOTE: Encapsulating an FC frame inside an Ethernet frame increases the FC payload to 2,112 bytes, which is larger than the maximum size for an Ethernet frame (1518 bytes). To prevent fragmentation of FCoE traffic, you must enable jumbo frames. This will increase the maximum transmission unit (MTU) size so that FC frames will not be fragmented.

---

iSCSI

An Internet Small Computer System Interface (iSCSI) SAN implementation is shown in Figure 23-16.

Figure 23-16   iSCSI SAN

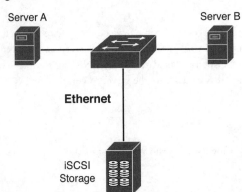

FC SANs and the newer FCoE SANs might be too expensive a solution for small to medium implementations. The iSCSI technology allows SCSI commands to be sent inside IP packets, allowing access to a remote SAN over an IP network. Although the performance is not as good as FCoE, the lower cost makes iSCSI a popular choice for some SAN implementations.

Study Resources

For today's exam topics, refer to the following resources for more study.

Resource	Location	Topic
Primary Resources		
Certification Guide	3	Virtual Network Devices
		Voice over IP Protocols and Components
	9	High Availability
		QoS Technologies
		Real-World Case Study
Exam Cram	5	All
	10	Unified Communication Technologies
Video Course	12	Unified Communication Fundamentals
	13	Virtualization Fundamentals
Supplemental Resources		
CCNA Collaboration Cert Guide	2	All
SDN LiveLessons	2	What Is SND?
Lab Simulator	3	Contrast Virtualization Technologies and Services
		Workstation Virtualization
Flash Cards	8	Unified Communications Technologies
Quick Reference	8	Unified Communications Technologies

 Check Your Understanding

Refer to the Digital Study Guide to take a 10-question quiz covering the content of this day.

Network Design and Documentation

CompTIA Network+ N10-006 Exam Topics

- .1.12 Given a set of requirements, implement a basic network
- 2.3 Given a scenario, use appropriate resources to support configuration management

Key Topics

Today's review focuses on network design and network monitoring. Designing networks is somewhat of an art. However, there are certain steps you should always consider when designing a network. Documentation is an important ingredient in network design and operation.

Network Design

A well-designed network is important to ensuring that the network not only serves the needs of the business, but can also scale as the business grows. Additionally, a network design considers the requirements for security and its impact on the environment.

Sample Design Approach

There is no one, right approach to designing a network. However, most approaches will incorporate the following steps:

Step 1 **Determine customer requirements.**

Budget is a major factor that impacts the requirements. For example, redundant equipment and network paths increase the expense. The type of business will impact the level of redundancy.

Step 2 **Examine the current network.**

Take an inventory of the current network, including equipment and cabling to help determine what needs to be changed to meet customer requirements.

Step 3 **Select the topology and network services.**

Design a topology with the necessary services to meet customer services. Does the network only need to support email and web traffic, or will the network also need to support IP telephony and video?

Step 4   **Mock up the design in a lab.**

Every network is different and has unique characteristics. For larger deployments, it is not possible to foresee the impact of complex interactions. Therefore, you should test the design prior to deployment.

Step 5   **Create an installation schedule.**

More often than not, a network design is meant to replace or augment an existing network. Therefore, the designers must coordinate with management to determine when to implement the design.

Step 6   **Create comprehensive documentation.**

A design document will include information such as the location and type of devices, how devices are connected, port assignments, and configuration details.

Step 7   **Install and verify the design.**

The network is installed according to the plan. A verification plan is also designed that will effectively test the network once it is implemented. What routes should be in the routing table? What path is data taking from A to B?

Step 8   **Perform ongoing monitoring and updates.**

After the network is installed and verified, continue to monitor the network to determine when to update or patch aspects of the network.

 Activity: Order the Steps in Network Design

Refer to the Digital Study Guide to complete this activity.

Design Considerations for Layers 1, 2, and 3

At Layer 1, the following design considerations will impact what media you decide to use:

- Speed that needs to be supported now and in the future
- Maximum distance between devices
- Impact of electromagnetic interference (EMI) and crosstalk

At Layer 2, the following design considerations will impact what switches you decide to use:

- Location of switches
- Required port density of switches
- Required switch features
- Supported media types

At Layer 3, the following design considerations will impact what routers or multilayer switches you decide to use:

- Number of interfaces
- Interface types
- Supported routing protocols
- Other required router features

Wireless Design Considerations

Most network designs today require a wireless component. Wireless design considerations include the following:

- Wireless speeds and 802.11 standards are required.
- Complete a site survey to determine the number of wireless access points (APs) required.
- Location of APs.
- Wireless channels to be used.
- Heat map to show AP coverage and overlap.

 Video: Wireless Heat Maps
Refer to the Digital Study Guide to view this video.

Documentation

Step 7 in the preceding network design process explicitly calls out creating comprehensive documentation. In fact, each step of the process requires some type of documentation.

IP Addressing Scheme

The IP addressing documentation should include a listing of all the unused subnets. These subnets should be organized in a logical manner so that when they are assigned, route summaries are not adversely impacted.

Most IPv4 addressing will be private addresses assigned from the following address spaces:

- 10.0.0.0/8
- 172.16.0.0/12
- 192.168.0.0/16

The network administrator has complete control over how private addresses are assigned to devices within the organization. The 10.0.0.0/8 address space is a popular choice because of its size and ease of use. It has over 16 million possible addresses and can be easily divided into logical subnets for assignment. For example, the 10.1.0.0/16 subnet could be used for all the devices at headquarters. Within the headquarters building, the 10.1.0.0/16 could be further divided into /24 subnetworks for each floor, as shown in Figure 22-1. The network administrator could then add more subnets within the 10.1.0.0/16 address space without affecting the route summary sent to the branch locations.

Figure 22-1   Sample IP Addressing Scheme

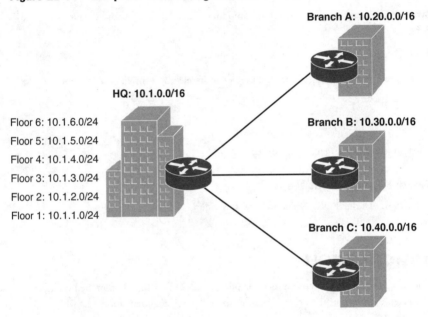

Network Diagrams

Network topology documentation typically consists of a diagram or diagrams labeling all critical components used to create the network. These diagrams include such components as routers, switches, hubs, gateways, and firewalls. Network diagrams come in two basic types:

- **Physical topology diagrams**—Identify the physical location of intermediary devices and cable installation, as shown in Figure 22-2.

  Wiring scheme documentation complements a network's physical topology map. It answers questions such as what conduit systems exist? How many copper pairs are in the riser cable interconnecting the first and second floors? How are pairs of fiber-optic cables numbered?

- **Logical topology diagrams**—Identify devices, ports, and addressing scheme, as shown in Figure 22-3.

Figure 22-2   Physical Topology

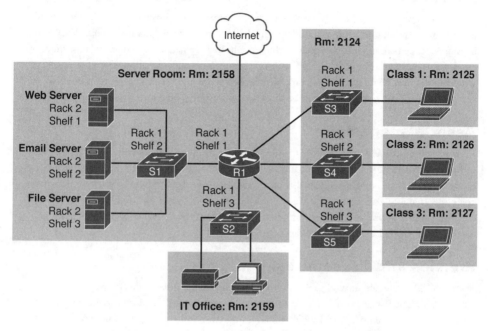

Figure 22-3   Logical Topology

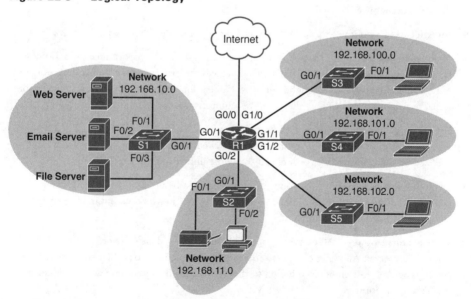

Baselines

Baseline documentation is an important resource for network administrators. The collection of meaningful network operation data under normal conditions is known as baselining. With comprehensive baseline data in your possession (which might include data collected at different times of the day and different days of the week), you can better notice any deviations from the norm when analyzing the data you collect when a problem exists on a network. A baseline is an integral part of network monitoring tasks, which will be discussed in Day 21, "Network Monitoring and Metrics."

Asset Management

Even a small office network will have a wide variety of equipment that connects to the network, including computers, servers, printers, mobile devices, access points, routers, and cable or DSL modems. Asset management, as related to networks, is a formalized system of tracking network components and managing the lifecycle of those components. Network administrators often work closely with accounting and financial business managers to track the value of network assets and determine when replacement is necessary.

Policies and Procedures

Policies are the rules about who can do what, when, and why. Policies dictate who can and cannot access what particular network resources, server rooms, backup tapes, and more. Policies specify how often tasks should occur and why tasks are important. Some examples of network policies include the following:

- **Network usage policy**—Defines who can use network resources and what can be done with those resources once accessed.

- **Internet usage policy**—Typically, Internet usage is limited to business-related tasks.

- **Mobile device policy**—This policy specifies the rules for employees connecting and using personal devices on the network. The policy specifies the procedures for onboarding and offboarding employee-owned mobile devices. Onboarding may scan for viruses and add additional security software. Offboarding removes company-owned resources.

- **Email usage policy**—Email must follow the same code of conduct as expected in any other form of written or face-to-face communication. All emails are company property and can be accessed by the company. Personal emails should be immediately deleted.

- **Personal software policy**—No outside software should be installed on network computer systems. All software installations must be approved by the network administrator. No software can be copied or removed from a site.

- **User account policy**—All users are responsible for keeping their password and account information secret. All staff are required to log off and sometimes lock their systems after they finish using them. Attempting to log on to the network with another user account is considered a serious violation.

- **Ownership policy**—The company owns all data, including users' email, voice mail, and Internet usage logs.

Network procedures differ from policies in that they describe how tasks are to be performed.

- **Backup procedures**—Backup procedures specify when they are to be performed, how often a backup occurs, who does the backup, what data is to be backed up, and where and how it will be stored.

- **Procedures for adding new users**—Users should only have access to the resources they need. This is called the principle of least privilege.

- **Security procedures**—Specifies incident response steps when a security breach occurs. Also includes security monitoring, security reporting, and updating the OS and applications for potential security holes.

- **Network monitoring procedures**—This includes procedures for tracking such things as bandwidth usage, remote access, user logons, and more.

- **Software procedures**—Documented procedures dictate when, how often, why, and for whom software updates are done.

- **Procedures for reporting violations**—Documented procedures should exist to properly handle the violations or network policies. The Human Resources (HR) department is typically in charge of disciplinary action.

- **Network admission procedures**—Network Access Control (NAC) is a feature offered by some authentication servers. Beyond just checking credentials, NAC can check the characteristics of the device seeking admission to the network. The client's operating system and version of antivirus software are examples of these characteristics.

Study Resources

For today's exam topics, refer to the following resources for more study.

Resource	Location	Topic
Primary Resources		
Certification Guide	9	Case Study: SOHO Network Design
	11	Configuration Management
Exam Cram	9	Documentation Management
Video Course	7	All
Supplemental Resources		
Flash Cards	10	Implement a Basic Network
Quick Reference	10	Implement a Basic Network

 Check Your Understanding

Refer to the Digital Study Guide to take a 10-question quiz covering the content of this day.

Network Monitoring and Metrics

CompTIA Network+ N10-006 Exam Topics

- 2.1 Given a scenario, use appropriate monitoring tools

- 2.2 Given a scenario, analyze metrics and reports from monitoring and tracking performance tools

Key Topics

Network monitoring can help you determine whether your network is operating as intended as well as warn you of events that might impact network performance. A variety of metrics can be used to gather statistics on network performance.

Types of Metrics

Network monitoring is the process of observing, measuring, and comparing the performance of the network. The purpose of network monitoring is to detect problems early in order to minimize the disruptions to network operations. A variety of tools is available for monitoring the network. Some of these tools run autonomously and can be configured to send alerts, such as an email or SMS text message, when a deviation from the norm occurs. Measurements of network performance are called metrics. Monitoring tools can gather a variety of metrics from various sources, including the following metrics:

- **Bandwidth**—Which devices are sending the most traffic (top talkers) and which devices are receiving the most traffic (top listeners)?

- **Storage space**—What percent of total storage is available? Do any quotas need to be adjusted? For example, storage space can be limited per user with disk quotas.

- **CPU and memory usage**—What are the CPU utilization rates? Do any devices need extra memory in the near future?

- **Wireless monitoring**—What steps need to be taken to keep channel utilization below 50%? Has the heat map of all the access points changed recently? Are there any rogue access points?

- **Fault detection**—What alerts are in place to ensure that notifications are sent when there is a device or link failure?

- **Security monitoring**—Who is currently using the network, what do they have access to, and what are they doing? Has the SIEM database information been analyzed recently for trends or security violations.

NOTE: Security Information and Event Management (SIEM) is a broad term that describes a collection of hardware and software services that can monitor various types of network activity and report specific events back to a single server.

- **Interface monitoring**—What is the current status of all interfaces and ports in the network? Are any interfaces "down" that should be "up"? Conversely, are any "up" that should be "down"? Network devices typically have a quick method for viewing interface statistics. On Cisco routers and switches, the **show interface** command displays a wealth of information about the operational status of an interface. Example 21-1 shows the output for GigabitEthernet 0/0 on a Cisco router. The highlighted portions of the output show examples of link status (up or down), utilization (transmit and receive loads), duplex and speed setting, errors, interface resets, and packet drops.

Example 21-1 Output for the show interface gigabitethernet 0/0 **Command**

```
Router# show interface gigabitethernet 0/0
GigabitEthernet0/0 is up, line protocol is up
  Hardware is CN Gigabit Ethernet, address is 30f7.0da3.0da0 (bia 30f7.0da3.0da0)
  Description: R1 LAN
  Internet address is 192.168.1.1/24
  MTU 1500 bytes, BW 100000 Kbit/sec, DLY 100 usec,
     reliability 255/255, txload 1/255, rxload 1/255
  Encapsulation ARPA, loopback not set
  Keepalive set (10 sec)
  Full Duplex, 100Mbps, media type is RJ45
  output flow-control is unsupported, input flow-control is unsupported
  ARP type: ARPA, ARP Timeout 04:00:00
  Last input 00:00:00, output 00:00:01, output hang never
  Last clearing of "show interface" counters never
  Input queue: 0/75/0/0 (size/max/drops/flushes); Total output drops: 0
  Queueing strategy: fifo
  Output queue: 0/40 (size/max)
  5 minute input rate 0 bits/sec, 0 packets/sec
  5 minute output rate 0 bits/sec, 0 packets/sec
     387 packets input, 59897 bytes, 0 no buffer
     Received 252 broadcasts (0 IP multicasts)
     0 runts, 0 giants, 0 throttles
     0 input errors, 0 CRC, 0 frame, 0 overrun, 0 ignored
     0 watchdog, 86 multicast, 0 pause input
     281 packets output, 35537 bytes, 0 underruns
     0 output errors, 0 collisions, 1 interface resets
     56 unknown protocol drops
     0 babbles, 0 late collision, 0 deferred
     0 lost carrier, 0 no carrier, 0 pause output
     0 output buffer failures, 0 output buffers swapped out
Router#
```

- **Environmental monitoring**—What is the current temperature and humidity in the server room and wiring closets? For example, is humidity about 50 percent to guard against electro-static discharge? Is the temperature between 50 and 80 degrees Fahrenheit (10 to 28 degrees Celsius)?

- **Power monitoring**—What are the current power utilization statistics? Are the universal power supply (UPS) batteries in good condition? Have the backup generators been recently tested?

Several network monitoring tools are important for gathering metrics about network performance, including SNMP, Syslog, port scanners, packet sniffers, and packet flow monitors (such as Cisco's NetFlow).

SNMP

SNMP began with a series of three RFCs back in 1988 (1065, 1066, and 1067). The SNMP name is derived from RFC 1067, "A Simple Network Management Protocol." Since then, SNMP has undergone several revisions.

SNMP Message Types

SNMP is an application layer protocol that provides a standardized way of communicating informa-tion between SNMP agents and SNMP managers using UDP port 162. The SNMP manager is part of a network management system (NMS). The SNMP manager can collect information from agents using "get" messages. Each agent stores data about the device in the Management Information Base (MIB) locally so that it is ready to respond to these messages from the NMS. Agents can also be configured to forward directly to the NMS using "trap" messages. Figure 21-1 shows a server configured as an SNMP manager. The switch and router can both be configured as SNMP agents, replying to "get" requests and sending "trap" messages.

Figure 21-1   SNMP Example

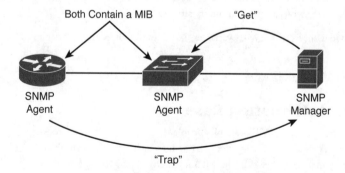

SNMP
Agent

SNMP
Agent

SNMP
Manager

Both Contain a MIB   "Get"

"Trap"

Table 21-1 lists and describes the SNMP message types.

Table 21-1   SNMP Message Type

Operation	Description
get-request	Retrieves a value from a specific variable.
get-next-request	Retrieves a value from a variable within a table; the SNMP manager does not need to know the exact variable name—a sequential search is performed to find the needed variable from within a table. This sequential search is called an SNMP walk.
get-bulk-request	Retrieves large blocks of data, such as multiple rows in a table; only works with SNMPv2 or later.
get-response	Replies to messages sent by an NMS.
set-request	Stores a value in a specific variable.
trap	An unsolicited message sent by an SNMP agent to an SNMP manager when some event has occurred.

 Activity: Identify the SNMP Message Type

Refer to the Digital Study Guide to complete this activity.

SNMP Versions

There are several versions of SNMP, including the following:

- **SNMPv1**—The Simple Network Management Protocol defined in RFC 1157

- **SNMPv2c**—Defined in RFCs 1901 to 1908; utilizes the community-string-based Administrative Framework

- **SNMPv3**—Interoperable standards-based protocol originally defined in RFCs 2273 to 2275; provides secure access to devices by authenticating and encrypting packets over the network

SNMPv1 and SNMPv2c use community strings that control access to the MIB. Community strings are plain-text passwords. There are two types of community strings:

- **Read-only (ro)**—Provides access to the MIB variables, but does not allow these variables to be changed, only read

- **Read-write (rw)**—Provides read and write access to all objects in the MIB

The Management Information Base

The MIB organizes variables hierarchically. MIB variables enable the management software to monitor and control the network device. Formally, the MIB defines each variable as an object ID (OID). OIDs uniquely identify managed objects in the MIB hierarchy. The MIB organizes the OIDs based on RFC standards into a hierarchy of OIDs, usually shown as a tree.

RFCs define some common public variables. Figure 21-2 shows portions of the MIB structure defined by Cisco Systems, Inc.

Figure 21-2   Management Information Base Object IDs

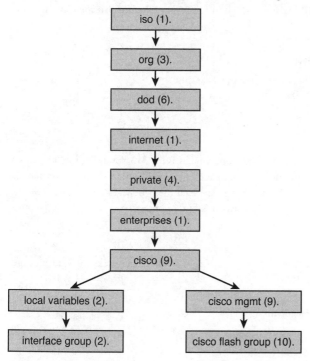

Note how the OID can be described in words or numbers to help locate a particular variable in the tree. For example, OIDs belonging to Cisco are numbered as follows: iso(1). org(3). dod(6). internet(1). private(4). enterprises(1). cisco(9). This is displayed or configured as 1.3.6.1.4.1.9.

One way to demonstrate using these OIDs is to look at how they could be implemented in the freeware SNMPGET utility. Example 21-2 shows how you might configure SNMPGET to obtain a 5-minute exponential moving average of the CPU busy percentage from a router.

Example 21-2 Obtaining a MIB Value with SNMPGET

```
[13:22][cisco@NMS~ ]$ snmpget -v2c -c community 10.250.250.14
  1.3.6.1.4.1.9.2.1.58.0
SNMPv2-SMI::enterprises.9.2.1.58.0 = INTEGER: 11
```

The bold text shows a rather long command with several parameters highlighted, as follows:

- **-v2c**—The version of SNMP in use

- **-c community**—The SNMP password, called a community string

- **10.250.250.14**—The IP address of the monitored device

- **1.3.6.1.4.1.9.2.1.58.0**—The numeric OID of the MIB variable

The last line shows the response. The output shows a shortened version of the MIB variable. It then lists the actual value in the MIB location, which in this example means that the CPU is at 11 percent utilization.

 Video: SNMP Overview

Refer to the Digital Study Guide to view this video.

Syslog

Syslog is a term used to describe a standard first documented as RFC 3164 by IETF in 2001. It is a popular protocol used by many networking devices, including routers, switches, application servers, firewalls, and other network appliances. These devices can send their messages across the network to be stored on syslog servers for later access by network administrators.

Syslog Operation

Syslog uses UDP port 514 to send event notification messages across IP networks to event message collectors, as illustrated in Figure 21-3.

Figure 21-3   Syslog Server Example

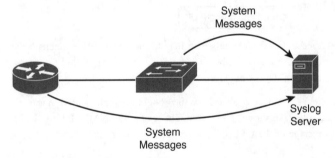

The syslog logging service provides three primary functions:

- The ability to gather logging information for monitoring and troubleshooting
- The ability to select the type of logging information that is captured
- The ability to specify the destinations of captured syslog messages

Severity Levels

Cisco devices produce syslog messages as a result of network events. Every syslog message contains a severity level and a facility. Table 21-2 shows the complete list of syslog severity levels.

Table 21-2   Syslog Severity Level

Severity Name	Severity Level	Explanation
Emergency	Level 0	System unusable
Alert	Level 1	Immediate action needed
Critical	Level 2	Critical condition
Error	Level 3	Error condition
Warning	Level 4	Warning condition
Notification	Level 5	Normal but significant condition
Informational	Level 6	Informational message
Debugging	Level 7	Debugging message

In addition to specifying the severity, syslog messages also contain information on the syslog facility. Syslog facilities are service identifiers that identify and categorize system state data for error and event message reporting. The logging facility options that are available are specific to the networking device. Common syslog message facilities reported on Cisco IOS routers include the following:

- IP

- OSPF protocol

- SYS operating system

- IP security (IPsec)

- Interface IP

Syslog Message Format

The default format for syslog messages is as follows:

```
seq no: timestamp: %facility-severity-MNEMONIC: description
```

Table 21-3 summarizes each field of the syslog message.

Table 21-3   Syslog Message Format

Field	Explanation
seq no	Stamps log messages with a sequence number
timestamp	Date and time of the message or event
facility	The facility to which the message refers
severity	Single-digit code from 0 to 7 that is the severity of the message
MNEMONIC	Text string that uniquely describes the message
description	Text string containing detailed information about the event being reported

Using the message format and Table 21-3, you can easily interpret the following message:

```
000031: *Aug  4 15:24:01.543: %LINK-3-UPDOWN: Interface GigabitEthernet0/1, changed
    state to up
```

The sequence number is **000031** and the timestamp is **Aug 4 15:24:01.543**. The facility is **LINK**, the severity is **3**, and the MNEMONIC is **UPDOWN**. The rest of the message provides a description of the event.

Port Scanners

A port scanner is a utility designed to search a network or host for any open TCP or UDP ports. Hackers use open ports to attempt to gain access to a system. When a port scanner is used, several port states may be reported:

- **Open/listening**—The host sent a reply indicating that a service is listening on the port. There was a response from the port.

- **Closed or denied or not listening**—No process is listening on that port. Access to this port will likely be denied.

- **Filtered or blocked**—There was no reply from the host, meaning that the port is not listening or the port is secured and filtered.

Network administrators should regularly monitor what ports are open on hosts and networking devices. The **netstat –a** command will list all of the active connections on a system, as shown in Example 21-3.

Example 21-3 Sample netstat -a **Output**

```
C:\> netstat -a
<output truncated>
Active Connections

  Proto  Local Address           Foreign Address         State
  TCP    0.0.0.0:135             allan-pc:0              LISTENING
  TCP    0.0.0.0:443             allan-pc:0              LISTENING
  TCP    0.0.0.0:445             allan-pc:0              LISTENING
  TCP    0.0.0.0:554             allan-pc:0              LISTENING
  TCP    10.10.10.4:32419        209.165.200.225:https   ESTABLISHED
  TCP    127.0.0.1:1025          allan-pc:1026           ESTABLISHED
  TCP    127.0.0.1:1026          allan-pc:1025           ESTABLISHED
  TCP    127.0.0.1:1027          allan-pc:1028           ESTABLISHED
  TCP    169.254.223.93:139      allan-pc:0              LISTENING
  TCP    169.254.243.238:139     allan-pc:0              LISTENING
  TCP    192.168.56.1:139        allan-pc:0              LISTENING
  TCP    [::]:135                allan-pc:0              LISTENING
  TCP    [::]:443                allan-pc:0              LISTENING
  TCP    [::]:445                allan-pc:0              LISTENING
```

```
TCP     [::]:554               allan-pc:0          LISTENING
TCP     [::]:1043              allan-pc:0          LISTENING
UDP     [::]:500               *:*
UDP     [::]:3702              *:*
UDP     [::]:3702              *:*
UDP     [::]:4500              *:*


C:\>
```

To test for actual vulnerabilities, it is best to use a port scanner. Many free versions are available on the Internet.

Packet Sniffers

Packet sniffers or packet analyzers can either be hardware or software that quietly captures traffic traversing the network and saves it for review later. Wireshark is a popular free version available that can be downloaded and installed on any computer.

There are two primary defenses against packet sniffers:

- **Fully switched networks**—A packet sniffer installed on a LAN that uses a hub would be able to capture all the traffic destined for any device on the LAN. In a switched network, devices only receive traffic destined for that particular device.

- **Encrypt all sensitive traffic**—Use HTTPS for connections to web servers and SSL for connections to email servers. Use IPsec for connections out to public networks.

Packet Flow Monitors (NetFlow)

Packet flow monitors are powerful network monitoring tools that surpass the capabilities of SNMP and syslog. To describe this tool, we will focus on Cisco's NetFlow. NetFlow tracks TCP/IP flows in the network. You can use the information from these flows for a variety of purposes, including the following:

- Identify potential bottlenecks.

- Provide data for network improvements and redesigns.

- Assist in monitoring customer usage of links.

NetFlow became so popular that it is now a standard used by other networking equipment manufacturers. Flexible NetFlow is the latest NetFlow technology. Flexible NetFlow (Version 9) improves on "original NetFlow" by adding the capability to customize the traffic analysis parameters for the specific requirements of a network administrator.

Most organizations use NetFlow for some or all of the following important data-collection purposes:

- Measuring who is using what network resources for what purpose

- Accounting and charging back according to the resource-utilization level

- Using the measured information to do more effective network planning so that resource allocation and deployment are well aligned with customer requirements

- Using the information to better structure and customize the set of available applications and services to meet user needs and customer service requirements

When Cisco sought out to create NetFlow, two key criteria provided guidance in its creation:

- NetFlow should be completely transparent to the applications and devices in the network.

- NetFlow should not have to be supported and running on all devices in the network to function.

The original NetFlow distinguishes flows using a combination of seven fields. Should one of these fields vary in value from another packet, the packets could be safely determined to be from different flows:

- Source IP address

- Destination IP address

- Source port number

- Destination port number

- Layer 3 protocol type

- Type of Service (ToS) marking

- Input logical interface

Much like SNMP managers, NetFlow uses collectors to store data. NetFlow data is written to the collector's drive at specified intervals. The administrator may run multiple collection schemes or threads concurrently. For example, different cuts of data can be stored to support planning versus billing. A NetFlow collector can easily produce the appropriate aggregation schemes. Figure 21-4 illustrates a NetFlow collector passively listening for exported NetFlow datagrams.

Figure 21-4   NetFlow Collector Functions

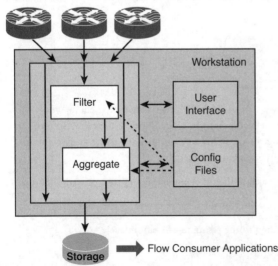

Collecting data provides a network administrator with data on top talkers, top hosts, and top listeners. Because data is preserved over time, after-the-fact network traffic analyses can determine network-use trends.

You can use many different freeware and paid applications to collect NetFlow data. Typical reports that these applications generate include the following:

- Top talkers in the network

- Top listeners in the network

- Most frequently visited websites

- Most frequently downloaded content

- Systems with the least available bandwidth

As shown in Figure 21-5, a NetFlow collector displays the kinds of traffic. Each pie slice in the chart represents a specific type of traffic on the network and the devices that send and receive most of the traffic.

Figure 21-5   NetFlow Collector Top Talkers

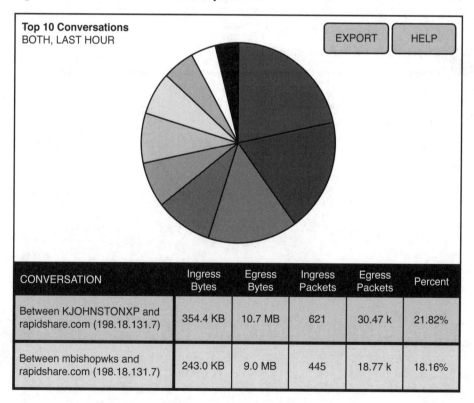

CONVERSATION	Ingress Bytes	Egress Bytes	Ingress Packets	Egress Packets	Percent
Between KJOHNSTONXP and rapidshare.com (198.18.131.7)	354.4 KB	10.7 MB	621	30.47 k	21.82%
Between mbishopwks and rapidshare.com (198.18.131.7)	243.0 KB	9.0 MB	445	18.77 k	18.16%

You can sort and visualize the data in a manner that makes sense to you. You can then export the data to spreadsheets, such as Microsoft Excel, for more detailed analysis, trending, and reporting.

Study Resources

For today's exam topics, refer to the following resources for more study.

Resource	Location	Topic
Primary Resources		
Certification Guide	11	Maintenance Tools
		Monitoring Resources and Reports
		Real-World Case Study
Exam Cram	1	Creating a SOHO Network
	2	Simple Network Management Protocol (SNMP)
	9	Monitoring Network Performance
Video Course	15	All
Supplemental Resources		
Flash Cards	11	Monitoring Tools
Quick Reference	11	Monitoring Tools

Check Your Understanding

Refer to the Digital Study Guide to take a 10-question quiz covering the content of this day.

Network Segmentation, Patches, and Updates

CompTIA Network+ N10-006 Exam Topics

- 2.4 Explain the importance of implementing network segmentation

- 2.5 Given a scenario, install and apply patches and updates

Key Topics

Today's review covers the importance of separating network traffic. The policies of the organization and the nature of the data that travels the network will usually dictate what segmentation strategy you should employ. In addition, government regulations often mandate certain types of data traffic be isolated and secured.

Patches and updates to software and firmware are ongoing concerns for network administrators. Also, upgrading networking equipment and computers is rarely a seamless process. You should always test an upgrade before deploying it on production networks.

Network Segmentation

Network segmentation is the process of implementing a network design that effectively isolates a network so that only authorized devices are allowed access. Depending on organizational policy, segmentation can be logical, such as with VLANs, or physical. For example, in an educational institution it might be the policy to keep student and faculty traffic isolated from each other. This can be done easily with a comprehensive VLAN implementation. Traffic would be travelling through some of the same devices and cables, but it would be logically separated. Access lists on routers and switches would help to keep student traffic off of the faculty VLANs.

However, in a network that connects, say, military assets, these assets should be physically isolated from any other network traffic. It should be impossible for traffic on one network, such as a data network, to be able to access the isolated military network. Routers and switches would not be linked to both types of networks.

The Network+ exam objective "Explain the importance of implementing network segmentation" lists a variety of situations and reasons to implement network segmentation policies, as detailed in Table 20-1.

Table 20-1   Reasons for Network Segmentation

Reason for Segmentation	Description
SCADA systems or industrial control systems	Industrial networks, reviewed on Day 27, "Network Topologies and Infrastructure," are used to control sensitive equipment such as power generators and traffic management systems. These networks should be isolated from data networks to avoid opportunity for malicious or non-malicious interference.
Legacy systems	Many production facilities maintain legacy systems that predate more modern security measures. Although outdated, these critical systems may represent a significant investment.
Separate private/public networks	Organizations frequently provide guest access to the data network for the use of customers or visitors. These public guest nets must be appropriately isolated from the organization's private network to avoid intentional or unintentional access.
Honeypot/honeynet	A honeypot draws attackers to a specific server or network. The honeypot server could have enticing ports open that lure the attacker. The administrator observes the attacker's actions and gathers data in order to better secure "live production" systems and avoid emerging security threats. This honeypot can keep attackers busy with non-critical servers, delaying them from focusing on real network assets. Similarly, a honeynet is a network set up with vulnerabilities.
Testing lab	Testing labs are an important tool for verifying a new network implementation or upgrade. These labs should be kept isolated from production networks.
Load balancing	Load balancing is a technique in which the workload is distributed among several servers. The process of load balancing is generally transparent to the end user. You can isolate the servers on the back end from the users on the front end who are making the requests. This separation enables you to send resource requests to multiple servers in a round-robin fashion.
Performance optimization	Network performance is often a byproduct of network segmentation. For example, using proxy servers to cache web content for quicker access also reduces the load on core routers and switches that connect users to the Internet. VLANs also help to isolate heavy traffic to a separate network so that it does not impact performance on other parts of the network.
Security	Use VLANs for users who have similar needs on the network. Use access control lists to control and filter traffic between the subnets. This type of isolation improves security.
Compliance	Regulations may mandate isolation between various parts of the network to maintain compliance. For example, the U.S. Office of Civil Rights enforces health information privacy and publishes best practices for keeping electronic medical records secure.

Video: Network Segmentation Overview

Refer to the Digital Study Guide to view this video.

Activity: Identify Network Segmentation Terminology

Refer to the Digital Study Guide to complete this activity.

Patches and Updates

Patching and updating software and firmware is an important role of the network administrator. Patches and updates are often released specifically to address potential security weaknesses. Administrators must keep an eye out for these patches and install them when they are released.

Regardless of the size of the organization, patches and updates should always be fully tested before being deployed to production networks. Table 20-2 describes the patches and updates listed in the Network+ exam objective "Given a scenario, install and apply patches and updates."

Table 20-2   Common Patches and Updates

Patch/Update	Description
OS updates	Software vendors release regular updates to their operating systems, which can be minor or major. Often, these updates address security issues.
Firmware updates	Networking devices commonly use firmware to hold the operating system. New releases should be tested and then implemented in a limited portion of the network. If an issue arises, the firmware update can be quickly rolled back.
Driver updates	NICs, video cards, and hard drive systems all rely on driver software to control their processes. Updates often address known performance issues and security weaknesses. Be sure to test all the devices and applications that will be impacted by driver updates.
Feature changes and updates	Normally not critical to your production network, feature updates and changes can often extend the life of the software and/or hardware.
Major and minor updates	Major updates typically increase by one full version number, such as going from version 2.0 to 3.0. A major update will completely change the version number. Minor updates are incremented within the major version number. For example, going from version update 2.0 to 2.1 to 2.2 and so on. In general, the smaller the number, the less significant the update. Hardware and software risks are involved with both major and minor updates. For example, the hardware or software may not work after the updates. Typically, minor updates address "bugs" in previous updates and can be more easily reversed than major updates if problems occur.
Vulnerability patches	Many of the updates previously reviewed might also include vulnerability patches meant to address specific security weaknesses discovered after the release of the software. Vulnerability patches have a high priority for implementation after thorough testing.
Upgrading and downgrading	Before upgrading any system with a new update or patch, make sure it is fully backed up. Configuration files for network devices should be saved offline, ready for easy access in case you need to roll back any changes. Rolling back an upgrade is also called downgrading. A system upgrade should be successful without having to update other drivers or applications. If an upgrade causes problems, you should downgrade the update rather than upgrade a set of additional drivers and software.

Study Resources

For today's exam topics, refer to the following resources for more study.

Resource	Location	Topic
Primary Resources		
Certification Guide	12	Defending Against Attacks
Exam Cram	9	Patches and Update
	10	Network Segmentation
Supplemental Resources		
Flash Cards	12	Network Segmentation
	13	Patches and Updates
Quick Reference	12	Network Segmentation
	13	Patches and Updates

Check Your Understanding

Refer to the Digital Study Guide to take a 10-question quiz covering the content of this day.

Switch Configuration

CompTIA Network+ N10-006 Exam Topics

- 2.6 Given a scenario, configure a switch using proper features

Key Topics

The Network+ exam topic that covers switching requires two days to review. Today, we focus on switching concepts and basic configurations. We will also review AAA, port bonding, and port mirroring configurations.

Evolution to Switching

Today's LANs almost exclusively use switches to interconnect end devices; however, this was not always the case. Initially, devices were connected to a physical bus—a long run of coaxial backbone cabling. With the introduction of 10BASE-T and UTP cabling, the hub gained popularity as a cheaper, easier way to connect devices. But even 10BASE-T with hubs had the following limitations:

- A frame being sent from one device may collide with a frame sent by another device attached to that LAN segment. Devices were in the same collision domain sharing the bandwidth.

- Broadcasts sent by one device were heard by, and processed by, all other devices on the LAN. Devices were in the same broadcast domain. Similar to hubs, switches forward broadcast frames out all ports except for the incoming port. Switch ports can be configured on various VLANs, which will segment them into broadcast domains.

From Bridges to Switches

Ethernet bridges were soon developed to solve some of the inherent problems in a shared LAN. A bridge basically segmented a LAN into two collision domains, which had the following benefits:

- Reduced the number of collisions that occurred in a LAN segment

- Increased the available bandwidth

When switches arrived on the scene, these devices provided the same benefits of bridges, as well as the following:

- A larger number of interfaces to break up the collision domain into more segments

- Hardware-based switching instead of using software to make the decisions

In a LAN where all nodes are connected directly to the switch, the throughput of the network increases dramatically. With each computer connected to a separate port on the switch, each is in a separate collision domain and has its own dedicated segment. Here are the three primary reasons for this increase:

- Dedicated bandwidth to each port

- Collision-free environment

- Full-duplex operation

Switch Types

In today's marketplace, switches can be purchased based on several different factors:

- **Managed and unmanaged**—If the switch can be configured by the network administrator, it is said to be managed. If not, then it is unmanaged. Typically, unmanaged switches are low-cost, plug-and-play devices intended for the home or small office.

- **Fixed and modular**—Fixed switches have a set number of ports, such as 24 ports for connecting hosts and two uplink ports for connecting to another switch or router. Modular switches typically come in different chassis sizes and allow for line cards to be installed based on the need of the network.

- **Powered and unpowered ports**—Switches can provide power to the devices connected to the ports using the IEEE 802.3af standard called Power over Ethernet (PoE). The standard was updated with IEEE 802.at (also known as PoE+), which increased the supplied wattage from 15.4W to 25.5W. PoE is ideal for supplying power to end devices such as IP phones, wireless access points, or another downstream, unpowered switch.

Switching Logic

Ethernet switches selectively forward individual frames from a receiving port to the port where the destination node is connected. During this instant, the switch creates a full bandwidth, logical point-to-point connection between the two nodes.

Switches create this logical connection based on the source and destination Media Access Control (MAC) addresses in the Ethernet header. Specifically, the primary job of a LAN switch is to receive Ethernet frames and then make a decision: either forward the frame or ignore the frame. To accomplish this, the switch performs three actions:

- It decides when to forward a frame or when to filter (not forward) a frame, based on the destination MAC address.

- It learns MAC addresses by examining the source MAC address of each frame received by the switch.

- It creates a (Layer 2) loop-free environment with other switches by using Spanning Tree Protocol (STP).

To make the forward or filter decision, the switch uses a dynamically built MAC address table stored in RAM. By comparing the frame's destination MAC address with the fields in the table, the switch decides how to forward and/or filter the frame.

For example, in Figure 19-1, the switch receives a frame from Host A with the destination MAC address OC. The switch looks in its MAC table and finds an entry for the MAC address and forwards the frame out port 6. The switch also filters the frame by not forwarding it out any other port, including the port on which the frame was received.

Figure 19-1   Switch Forwarding Based on MAC Address

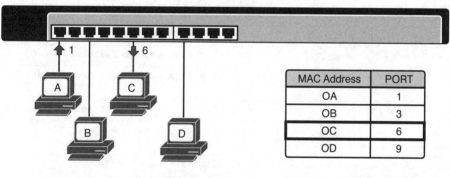

MAC Address	PORT
OA	1
OB	3
OC	6
OD	9

Frame	Preamble	Destination Address	Source Address	Type	Data	Pad	CRC
		OC	OA				

Continuing the example in Figure 19-1, assume another device, Host E, is attached to port 10. Host B then sends a frame to the new Host E. The switch does not yet know where Host E is located, so it forwards the frame out all active ports except for the port on which the frame was received. The new Host E will receive the frame. When it replies to Host B, the switch will learn Host E's MAC address and port for the first time and store it in the MAC address table. Subsequent frames destined for Host E will only be sent out port 10.

Finally, LAN switches must have a method for creating a loop-free path for frames to take within the LAN. The IEEE 802.1D Spanning Tree Protocol (STP) standard provides loop prevention in Ethernet networks where redundant physical links exist.

Basic Switch Configuration

Switch configuration commands may vary, based on the manufacturer of the switch. If you have access to a Cisco Catalyst switch or a simulator, you can practice entering the basic commands listed in Table 19-1.

Table 19-1   Basic Cisco Catalyst Switch Configuration Commands

Command Description	Command Syntax
Enter global configuration mode.	Switch# **configure terminal**
Configure a name for the device.	Switch(config)# **hostname Sw1**
Enter the interface configuration mode for the VLAN 123 interface.	Sw1(config)# **interface vlan 123**
Configure the interface IP address. When possible, using a separate network for management of a managed switch is desired. This is referred to as out-of-band (OOB) management when the management traffic is kept on a separate network than the user traffic.	Sw1(config-if)# **ip address 172.17.99.11 255.255.255.0**
Enable the interface.	Sw1(config-if)# **no shutdown**
Return to global configuration mode.	Sw1(config-if)# **exit**
Enter the interface to assign the VLAN.	Sw1(config)# **interface fastethernet 0/6**
Define the VLAN membership mode for the port.	Sw1(config-if)# **switchport mode access**
Assign the port to a VLAN.	Sw1(config-if)# **switchport access vlan 123**
Configure the interface duplex mode to enable AUTO duplex configuration.	Sw1(config-if)# **duplex auto**
Configure the interface speed and enable AUTO speed configuration.	Sw1(config-if)# **speed auto**
Enable auto-MDIX on the interface.	Sw1(config-if)# **mdix auto**
Return to global configuration mode.	Sw1(config-if)# **exit**
Configure the default gateway on the switch.	Sw1(config)# **ip default-gateway 172.17.50.1**
Switch from global configuration mode to line configuration mode for console 0.	Sw1(config)# **line console 0**
Set **cisco** as the password for the console 0 line on the switch.	Sw1(config-line)# **password cisco**
Set the console line to require the password to be entered before access is granted.	Sw1(config-line)# **login**
Return to global configuration mode.	Sw1(config-if)# **exit**
Switch from global configuration mode to line configuration mode for vty terminals 0 through 15.	Sw1(config)# **line vty 0 15**
Set **cisco** as the password for the vty lines on the switch.	Sw1(config-line)# **password cisco**
Set the vty line to require the password to be entered before access is granted.	Sw1(config-line)# **login**

Command Description	Command Syntax
Return to global configuration mode.	`Sw1(config-line)# exit`
Configure **class** as the enable secret password to enter privileged EXEC mode. This password overrides the **enable password**.	`Sw1(config)# enable secret class`
Encrypt all the system passwords that are stored in clear text.	`Sw1(config)# service password-encryption`
Return to privileged EXEC mode.	`Sw1(config)# end`
Save the running configuration to the switch start-up configuration.	`Sw1# copy running-config startup -config`

 Activity: Match the Command to Its Description

Refer to the Digital Study Guide to complete this activity.

AAA Configuration

In Table 19-1, the configuration for management access allows anyone with the password and IP address to remotely access the switch through the virtual terminal lines (VTY lines). Using authentication, authorization, and accounting (AAA, pronounced "triple A") provides a more secure and scalable method to enable remote access for your network devices.

The authentication part of AAA can be configured locally on the switch, or the switch can direct login requests to a AAA server. The local AAA authentication process is demonstrated in Figure 19-2.

Figure 19-2   Local AAA Authentication

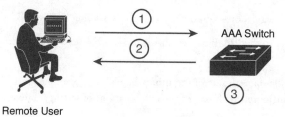

Remote User

1. Remote user attempts to log in to switch
2. Switch prompts the user for a username and password
3. Switch authenticates the username and password using the local database and provides access to user

The process for using a AAA server to authenticate logins is demonstrated in Figure 19-3.

Figure 19-3   Server-Based AAA Authentication

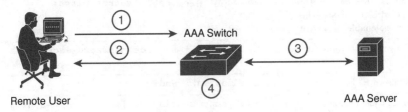

Remote User   AAA Server

1. Remote user attempts to log in to switch
2. Switch prompts the user for a username and password
3. Switch authenticates username and password using a remote AAA server
4. Switch provides access to user based on information in the AAA server

Link Aggregation Configuration

The Network+ exam objectives refer to link aggregation as port bonding. Link aggregation was originally developed by Cisco as EtherChannel, a technology that allows you to bundle multiple physical interfaces into one logical channel to increase the bandwidth on point-to-point links. EtherChannel uses the Cisco proprietary Port Aggregation Protocol (PAgP). Later, IEEE followed with the Link Aggregation Control Protocol (LACP) in its 802.3ad standard.

LACP Modes

LACP allows a switch to negotiate an automatic bundle by sending LACP packets to the peer. LACP uses the following modes:

- **On**—This mode forces the interface to channel without LACP.

- **Active**—The interface initiates negotiations with other interfaces by sending LACP packets.

- **Passive**—The interface responds to the LACP packets that it receives but does not initiate LACP negotiation.

The LACP modes must be compatible on each side of the EtherChannel. For example, Sw1 and Sw2 in Figure 19-4 must be configured with one of the combinations of settings shown in Table 19-2.

Figure 19-4   Two-Switch EtherChannel Topology

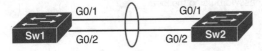

Table 19-2   LACP Mode Settings

Sw1	Sw2	Channel Established?
On	On	Yes
Auto/passive	Active	Yes
On/auto/passive	Not configured	No
On	Active	No
Passive/on	Passive	No

Configuring EtherChannel

To implement EtherChannel on a Cisco Catalyst switch, follow these steps:

Step 1   Specify the interfaces that you want to bundle together in one link using the **interface range** *interfaces* command.

Step 2   Create a port channel using the **channel-group** *identifier* **mode** command. The *identifier* can be any number between 1 and 6, inclusive, and does not have to match the other switch. The mode will be either **on** or one of the LACP modes.

Step 3   Enter interface configuration mode for the new port channel with the **interface port-channel** *identifier* command. The *identifier* is the same number used in the **channel-group** command.

Step 4   Configure the trunking and VLAN settings.

Using the topology in Figure 19-4, assume that Sw1 is already configured for EtherChannel with G0/1 and G0/2 trunking. The allowed VLANs are 1, 10, and 20. EtherChannel is forced on. No PAgP or LACP configuration is needed. Example 19-1 shows the configuration for Sw2. Sw1 would need a similar configuration before the new port channel will become active.

Example 19-1   EtherChannel Configuration

```
Sw2(config)# interface range g0/1-2
Sw2(config-if-range)# channel-group 1 mode on
Creating a port-channel interface Port-channel 1
Sw2(config-if-range)# interface port-channel 1
Sw2(config-if)# switchport mode trunk
Sw2(config-if)# switchport trunk allowed vlan 1,10,20
```

 Video: EtherChannel Configuration

Refer to the Digital Study Guide to view this video.

Port Mirroring Configuration

Port mirroring allows you to configure a switch to make a copy of traffic and send it to another port where a collector is connected. The collector could be a PC with packet capture software, such as Wireshark, installed.

For example, the switch in Figure 19-5 has been configured to copy any inbound traffic on Port 1 and send it out Port 3.

Figure 19-5   Port Mirroring Example

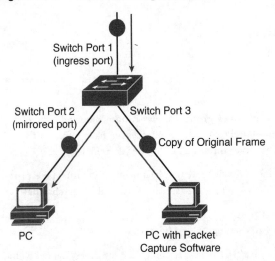

Switch Port 1
(ingress port)

Switch Port 2
(mirrored port)

Switch Port 3

Copy of Original Frame

PC

PC with Packet
Capture Software

On a Cisco Catalyst switch, the configuration would be as shown in Example 19-2.

Example 19-2 Port Mirroring Configuration

```
SW1(config)# monitor session 1 source interface G0/1
SW1(config)# monitor session 1 destination interface G0/3
```

Study Resources

For today's exam topics, refer to the following resources for more study.

Resource	Location	Topic
Primary Resources		
Certification Guide	3	Switches
	4	Ethernet Switch Features
Video Course	8	Switch Configuration
Exam Cram	3	Configuring Routers and Switches

Resource	Location	Topic
Supplemental Resources		
Lab Simulator	4	Connect to Switch Console Port Using PuTTY
		Connect to a Switch and Reconfigure the Hostname and Password
		Switch Management via Telnet
	5	Configure an IP Address on a Switch with a Default Gateway
Flash Cards	14	Implementing Switches
Quick Reference	14	Implementing Switches

Check Your Understanding

Refer to the Digital Study Guide to take a 10-question quiz covering the content of this day.

STP, VLANs, Trunking, and VTP

CompTIA Network+ N10-006 Exam Topics

- 2.6 Given a scenario, configure a switch using proper features

Key Topics

Today, we continue our review of switching technologies. Spanning Tree Protocol (STP) and Rapid STP (RSTP) will be discussed. We will look at the importance of virtual LANs (VLANs) and trunking between switches. We will finish our review of switching technologies by looking at Cisco's VLAN trunking protocol (VTP).

STP and RSTP Concepts and Operation

STP helps to prevent loops in a redundant switched network by providing one switched path. There are many varieties of STP and RSTP, some of which are proprietary to a specific manufacturer's line of switches. However, for the Network+ exam, you should be familiar with the concepts and operation of the IEEE standards for STP (802.1D) and RSTP (802.1w). Figure 18-1 shows an example of a rather complex topology with redundant links.

Figure 18-1   Redundant Switched Topology

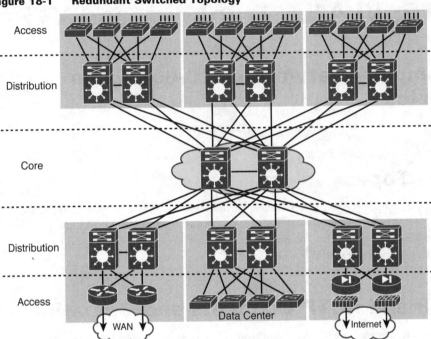

This topology would not be possible without some form of STP. Without STP, redundancy in the switched network could introduce the following issues:

- **Broadcast storms**—Each switch floods broadcasts endlessly, called a broadcast storm.

- **Multiple frame transmission**—Multiple copies of unicast frames may be delivered to the destination, causing unrecoverable errors.

- **MAC database instability**—Instability in the content of the MAC address table results from copies of the same frame being received on different ports of the switch.

STP Algorithm

STP creates a tree that ensures that only one path exists to each network segment at any one time. Then, if any segment experiences a disruption in connectivity, STP rebuilds a new tree by activating the previously inactive, but redundant, path.

The algorithm used by STP chooses the switch ports that should be placed into a forwarding state. For any port not chosen to be in a forwarding state, STP places the port in a blocking state.

Switches exchange STP configuration messages every 2 seconds by default using a multicast frame called the bridge protocol data unit (BPDU). One of the pieces of information included in the BPDU is the bridge ID (BID).

As shown in Figure 18-2, the BID is unique to each switch and is composed of a priority value (2 bytes) and the bridge MAC address (6 bytes).

Figure 18-2   Bridge ID

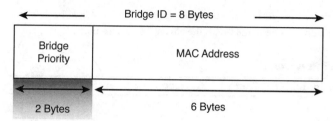

The default priority is 32,768. The root bridge is the bridge with the lowest BID. Therefore, if the default priority value is not changed, the switch with the lowest MAC address becomes root.

STP Convergence

STP convergence is the process by which the switches collectively realize that something has changed in the LAN topology and so the switches might need to change which ports block and which ports forward. The following steps summarize the STP algorithm used to achieve convergence:

Step 1   Elect a root bridge (switch with lowest BID). There can be only one root bridge per network. All ports on the root bridge are forwarding ports.

Step 2   Elect a root port for each nonroot switch, based on lowest root path cost. Each nonroot switch has one root port. The root port is the port through which the nonroot bridge has its best path to the root bridge.

Step 3   Elect a designated port for each segment, based on the lowest root path cost. Each link will have one designated port.

Step 4   The root ports and designated ports transition to the forwarding state, and the other ports stay in the blocking state.

Table 18-1 summarizes the reasons STP places a port in forwarding or blocking state.

Table 18-1   STP: Reasons for Forwarding or Blocking

Characterization of Port	STP State	Description
All the root switch's ports	Forwarding	The root switch is always the designated switch on all connected segments.
Each nonroot switch's root port	Forwarding	The port through which the switch has the least cost to reach the root switch.
Each LAN's designated port	Forwarding	The switch forwarding the lowest-cost BPDU onto the segment is the designated switch for that segment.
All other working ports	Blocking	The port is not used for forwarding frames, nor are any frames received on these interfaces considered for forwarding.

Port Costs

Port bandwidth is used to determine the cost to reach the root bridge. Table 18-2 lists the default port costs defined by IEEE, which had to be revised with the advent of 10Gbps ports.

Table 18-2   Default IEEE Port Costs

Ethernet Speed	Original IEEE Cost	Revised IEEE Cost
10Mbps	100	100
100Mbps	10	19
1Gbps	1	4
10Gbps	1	2

STP uses the four states shown in Figure 18-3 as a port transitions from blocking to forwarding.

Figure 18-3   Spanning Tree Port States

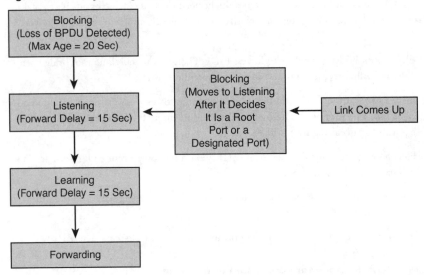

A fifth state, disabled, occurs either when a network administrator manually disables the port or a security violation disables the port.

RSTP Operation

With the RSTP 802.1w standard, IEEE improved the convergence performance of STP from 50 seconds to less than 10 seconds. RSTP is identical to STP in the following ways:

- It elects the root switch using the same parameters and tiebreakers.

- It elects the root port on nonroot switches with the same rules.

- It elects designated ports on each LAN segment with the same rules.

It places each port in either the forwarding or discarding state, although RSTP calls the blocking state the discarding state.

RSTP uses different terminology to describe port states. Table 18-3 lists the port states for RSTP and STP.

Table 18-3   RSTP and STP Port States

Operational State	STP State (802.1D)	RSTP State (802.1w)	Forwards Data Frames in This State?
Enabled	Blocking	Discarding	No
Enabled	Listening	Discarding	No
Enabled	Learning	Learning	No
Enabled	Forwarding	Forwarding	Yes
Disabled	Disabled	Discarding	No

RSTP Port Roles

RSTP also adds three more port roles in addition to the root port and designated port roles defined in STP. Table 18-4 lists and defines the port roles for both RSTP and STP.

Table 18-4   RSTP and STP Port Roles

RSTP Role	STP Role	Definition
Root port	Root port	A single port on each nonroot switch in which the switch hears the best BPDU out of all the received BPDUs
Designated port	Designated port	Of all switch ports on all switches attached to the same segment/collision domain, the port that advertises the "best" BPDU
Alternate port	—	A port on a switch that receives a suboptimal BPDU
Backup port	—	A nondesignated port on a switch that is attached to the same segment/collision domain as another port on the same switch
Disabled	—	A port that is administratively disabled or is not capable of working for other reasons

Figure 18-4 shows an example of these RSTP port roles.

Figure 18-4   RSTP Port Roles

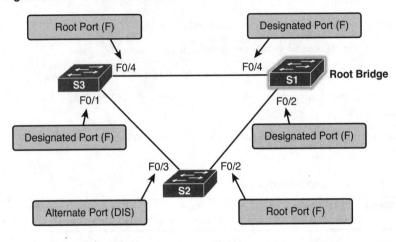

NOTE: Be aware of the IEEE 802.1aq standard, Shortest Path Bridging (SPB), which was meant to replace STP. The primary benefit of SPB over STP is that it is more scalable and enables multiple equal-cost paths within the same switching domain. However, the industry is far from sold on the idea of replacing STP with SPB. A close cousin to SPB is the IETF Transparent Interconnection of Lots of Links (TRILL).

VLAN Concepts

Most large networks today implement virtual local area networks (VLANs). Without VLANs, a switch considers every port to be in the same broadcast domain. With VLANs, switch ports can be grouped into different VLANs, in effect segmenting the broadcast domain.

Although a switch "out of the box" is configured to have only one VLAN, normally a switch will be configured to have two or more VLANs. Doing so creates multiple broadcast domains by putting some interfaces into one VLAN and other interfaces into other VLANs.

Reasons for and Benefit of Using VLANs

Reasons for using VLANs include the following:

- Grouping users by department instead of by physical location

- Segmenting devices into smaller LANs to reduce processing overhead for all devices on the LAN

- Reducing the workload of STP by limiting a VLAN to a single access switch

- Enforcing better security by isolating sensitive data to separate VLANs

- Separating IP voice traffic from data traffic

- Assisting in troubleshooting by reducing the size of the failure domain (the number of devices that can cause or be effected by a failure)

Benefits of using VLANs include the following:

- **Security**—Sensitive data can be isolated to one VLAN, separating it from the rest of the network.

- **Cost reduction**—Cost savings result from less need for expensive network upgrades and more efficient use of existing bandwidth and uplinks.

- **Higher performance**—Dividing flat Layer 2 networks into multiple logical broadcast domains reduces unnecessary traffic on the network and boosts performance.

- **Broadcast storm mitigation**—VLAN segmentation prevents a broadcast storm from propagating throughout the entire network.

- **Ease of management and troubleshooting**—A hierarchical addressing scheme groups network addresses contiguously. Because a hierarchical IP addressing scheme makes problem components easier to locate, network management and troubleshooting are more efficient.

Types of VLANs

Some VLAN types are defined by the type of traffic they support; others are defined by the specific functions they perform. The principal VLAN types and their descriptions follow:

- **Data VLAN**—Configured to carry only user-generated traffic, ensuring that voice and management traffic is separated from data traffic.

- **Default VLAN**—All the ports on a switch are members of the default VLAN when the switch is reset to factory defaults. The default VLAN for Cisco switches is VLAN 1. VLAN 1 has all the features of any VLAN, except that you cannot rename it and you cannot delete it. It is a security best practice to restrict VLAN 1 to serve as a conduit only for Layer 2 control traffic, supporting no other traffic.

- **Black hole VLAN**—A security best practice is to define a black hole VLAN to be a dummy VLAN distinct from all other VLANs defined in the switched LAN. All unused switch ports are assigned to the black hole VLAN so that any unauthorized device connecting to an unused switch port will be prevented from communicating beyond the switch to which it is connected.

- **Native VLAN**—This VLAN type serves as a common identifier on opposing ends of a trunk link. A security best practice is to define a native VLAN to be a dummy VLAN distinct from all other VLANs defined in the switched LAN. The native VLAN is normally not used for any traffic.

- **Management VLAN**—A VLAN defined by the network administrator as a means to access the management capabilities of a switch. By default, VLAN 1 is the management VLAN. It is a security best practice to define the management VLAN to be a VLAN distinct from all other VLANs defined in the switched LAN. You do so by configuring and activating a new VLAN interface.

- **Voice VLANs**—The voice VLAN feature enables switch ports to carry IP voice traffic from an IP phone. The network administrator configures a voice VLAN and assigns it to access ports. Then when an IP phone is connected to the switch port, the switch sends messages that instruct the attached IP phone to send voice traffic tagged with the voice VLAN ID.

Video: VLAN Types

Refer to the Digital Study Guide to view this video.

Activity: Identify the Type of VLAN

Refer to the Digital Study Guide to complete this activity.

Trunking VLANs

A VLAN trunk is an Ethernet point-to-point link between an Ethernet switch interface and an Ethernet interface on another networking device, such as a router or a switch, carrying the traffic of multiple VLANs over the singular link. A VLAN trunk allows you to extend the VLANs across an entire network. A VLAN trunk does not belong to a specific VLAN; rather, it serves as a conduit for VLANs between switches. Figure 18-5 shows a small switched network with a trunk link between S1 and S2 carrying multiple VLAN traffic.

Figure 18-5   Example of a VLAN Trunk

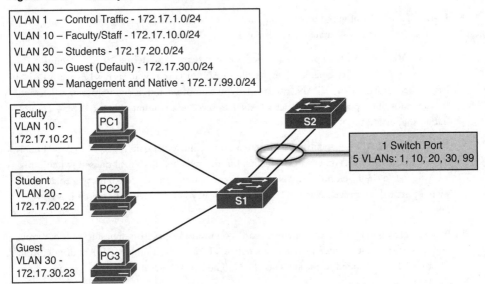

When a frame is placed on a trunk link, information about the VLAN it belongs to must be added to the frame. This is accomplished by using IEEE 802.1Q frame tagging. When a switch receives a frame on a port configured in access mode and destined for a remote device via a trunk link, the switch takes apart the frame and inserts a VLAN tag, recalculates the frame check sequence (FCS), and sends the tagged frame out the trunk port. Figure 18-6 shows the 802.1Q tag inserted in an Ethernet frame.

Figure 18-6   Fields of the 802.1Q Tag Inside an Ethernet Frame

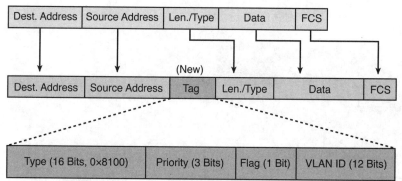

The VLAN tag field consists of a 16-bit Type field called the EtherType field and a Tag control information field. The EtherType field is set to the hexadecimal value of 0x8100. This value is called the tag protocol ID (TPID) value. With the EtherType field set to the TPID value, the switch receiving the frame knows to look for information in the Tag control information field. The Tag control information field contains the following:

- **3 bits of user priority**—Used to provide expedited transmission of Layer 2 frames, such as voice traffic

- **1 bit of Canonical Format Identifier (CFI)**—Enables Token Ring frames to be carried across Ethernet links easily

- **12 bits of VLAN ID (VID)**—VLAN identification numbers

NOTE: Although 802.1Q is the recommended method for tagging frames, you should be aware of Cisco's proprietary legacy trunking protocol called Inter-Switch link (ISL).

VTP Concepts

The name for Cisco's proprietary VLAN Trunking Protocol (VTP) can be confusing. VTP does not provide a method for trunking between devices. Instead, VTP is a Layer 2 messaging protocol that maintains VLAN configuration consistency by managing the additions, deletions, and name changes of VLANs across networks. VTP helps with VLAN management, and although it makes the configuration and troubleshooting of VLANs easier, it is not required.

The benefits of VTP include the following:

- VLAN configuration consistency across the network

- Accurate tracking and monitoring of VLANs

- Dynamic reporting of added VLANs across a network

Figure 18-7 shows an example of how VTP messages can be sent between the VTP server and VTP clients.

Figure 18-7   VTP Server Sends Updates to VTP Clients

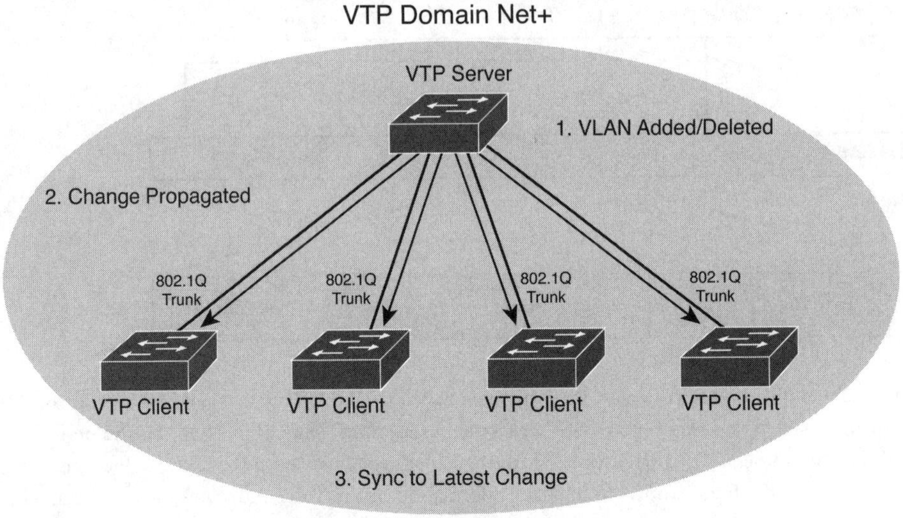

VTP Domain Net+

VTP Server

1. VLAN Added/Deleted

2. Change Propagated

802.1Q Trunk   802.1Q Trunk   802.1Q Trunk   802.1Q Trunk

VTP Client   VTP Client   VTP Client   VTP Client

3. Sync to Latest Change

Notice in the figure that the shaded area is named VTP Domain Net+. A VTP domain is one switch or several interconnected switches that share VTP advertisements. A switch can be in only one VTP domain. A router or Layer 3 switch defines the boundary of each domain.

VTP Modes

VTP operates in one of three modes:

- **Server**—The server is where VLANs can be created, deleted, or renamed for the domain. VTP servers advertise VLAN information to other switches in the same VTP domain and store the VLAN information in NVRAM.

- **Client**—You cannot create, change, or delete VLANs on a VTP client. A switch reset deletes the VLAN information. You must configure a switch to change its VTP mode to client.

- **Transparent**—VTP transparent mode switches forward VTP advertisements to VTP clients and VTP servers, but do not originate or otherwise implement VTP advertisements. VLANs that are created, renamed, or deleted on a VTP transparent mode switch are local to that switch only.

VTP Operation

VTP advertisements are sent by the server every 5 minutes over the default VLAN using a multicast frame. A configuration revision number included in the frame is used by all VTP clients and servers to determine if there has been a change in the VLAN database. Figure 18-8 illustrates VTP operation.

Figure 18-8   VTP Operation

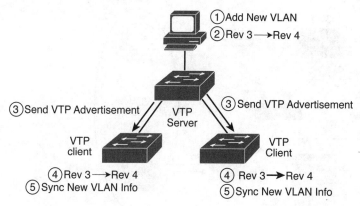

①Add New VLAN
②Rev 3 —→Rev 4

③Send VTP Advertisement   VTP
                             Server

③Send VTP Advertisement

VTP
client

VTP
Client

④Rev 3 —→Rev 4
⑤Sync New VLAN Info

④ Rev 3 —→Rev 4
⑤Sync New VLAN Info

Figure 18-8 begins with all switches having the same VLAN configuration revision number, meaning that they have the same VLAN configuration database; this means that all switches know about the same VLAN numbers and VLAN names. The process begins with each switch knowing that the current configuration revision number is 3. The steps shown in Figure 18-8 are as follows:

1. Someone configures a new VLAN on the VTP server.

2. The VTP server updates its VLAN database revision number from 3 to 4.

3. The server sends VTP update messages out its trunk interfaces, stating revision number 4.

4. The two VTP client switches notice that the updates list a higher revision number (4) than their current revision numbers (3).

5. The two client switches update their VLAN databases based on the server's VTP updates.

VTP defines three types of messages:

- **Summary advertisement**—Sent every 5 minutes by the server; it lists the revision number, domain name, and other information, but no VLAN information.

- **Subset advertisement**—Follows a summary advertisement if something has changed in the VLAN database, indicated by a new, larger revision number.

- **Advertisement request message**—Allows a switch to immediately request VTP messages from a neighboring switch as soon as a trunk comes up.

VTP Pruning

By default, a trunk connection carries traffic for all VLANs in the VTP management domain; however, every switch might not have ports assigned to every VLAN. VTP pruning uses VLAN advertisements to determine when a trunk connection is flooding VLAN traffic needlessly.

Pruning means that the appropriate switch trunk interfaces do not flood frames in that VLAN. Figure 18-9 shows an example, with the dashed-line rectangles denoting the trunks from which VLAN 10 has been automatically pruned.

Figure 18-9   VTP Pruning

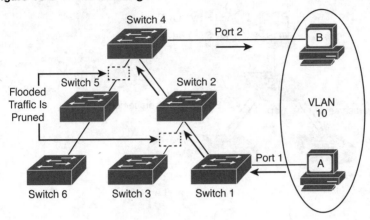

Study Resources

For today's exam topics, refer to the following resources for more study.

Resource	Location	Topic
Primary Resources		
Certification Guide	4	Ethernet Switch Features
Video Course	8	Switch Configuration
Exam Cram	3	Configuring Routers and Switches
Supplemental Resources		
Flash Cards	14	Implementing Switches
Quick Reference	14	Implementing Switches

 Check Your Understanding

Refer to the Digital Study Guide to take a 10-question quiz covering the content of this day.

WLAN Implementation

CompTIA Network+ N10-006 Exam Topics

- 2.7 Install and configure wireless LAN infrastructure and implement the appropriate technologies in support of wireless-capable devices

Key Topics

Wireless networks are becoming increasingly ubiquitous. If you have a router at home, chances are it supports a wireless LAN (WLAN). In the work environment, WLANs provide the ability to connect from any location at any time within the network. WLANs use radio frequencies that present some unique design and implementation considerations. Today, we review the technologies that support WLAN implementations.

WLAN Features

In this section, we will review frequencies, transmission methods, channels, and antenna types.

Frequencies

WLANs use radio waves to send data. Radio waves characteristics include amplitude, frequency, and phase, as shown in Figure 17-1.

Figure 17-1   Example of Amplitude, Frequency, and Phase

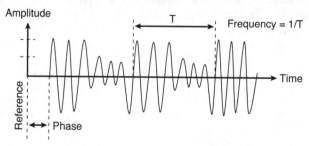

Amplitude is a measure of the amount of power needed to generate a wave of a specific height. *Frequency* is a measure of the number of waves or cycles per second. *Phase* is a measure of how far off a signal is from a given reference point.

These elements are used to modulate digital data onto an analog carrier signal using one of three techniques:

- **Frequency-Shift Keying (FSK)**—Slight changes in the frequency indicate "0" and "1" bits, which overcomes the noise interference common to amplitude-shift keying.

- **Phase-Shift Keying (PSK)**—Frequency remains constant, but the signal is shifted to and from a reference point to indicate "0" and "1" bits.

- **Quadrature Amplitude Modulation (QAM)**—Amplitude and phase of the carrier signal are combined to represent 64 different patterns of data. Each pattern of data can carry 6 bits of data. QAM is used in high-speed WLAN technologies, such as 802.11n and 802.11ac.

Transmission Methods

To avoid the necessity of obtaining a license to use a specific frequency, WLAN transceivers spread the frequency of a modulated signal across a spectrum, as shown in Figure 17-2.

Figure 17-2   Spread Spectrum

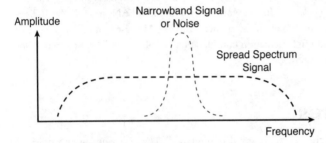

This spread spectrum technology has been used by WLAN components in two different ways:

- **Direct Sequence Spread Spectrum (DSSS)**—This method uses a redundant bit pattern, called a chip, spread across the spectrum to represent bits. For example, the chip for a "1" might be 00010011100 and the chip for a "0" might be the opposite, or 11101100011.

- **Frequency-Hopping Spread Spectrum (FHSS)**—This method uses an algorithm to hop from frequency to frequency, effectively spreading the signal across the spectrum, as shown in Figure 17-3. The boxes labeled A, B, C, D, and E represent the burst of data before the WLAN transceiver hops to the next frequency.

Figure 17-3   FHSS Example

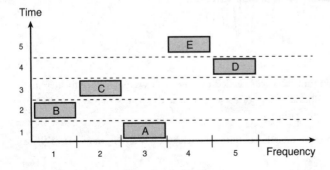

Higher-speed WLAN technologies use Orthogonal Frequency-division Multiplexing (OFDM). OFDM simultaneously encodes data on multiple carrier signals, as shown in Figure 17-4. Each carrier signal is modulated using one of the modulation techniques, such as PSK or QAM.

Figure 17-4   OFDM Example

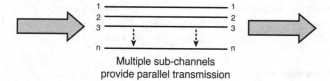

Multiple sub-channels
provide parallel transmission

Channels

WLANs use two frequency bands that are part of the industrial, scientific, and medical bands (ISM bands):

- **2.4GHz band**—Includes a frequency range from 2.4 to 2.5GHz

- **5GHz band**—Includes a frequency range from 5.725 GHz to 5.875GHz

Each of these bands is divided into channels in which wireless devices operate. These channels are what wireless access points (APs) use to prevent interference from each other. For example, the 2.4GHz band has four non-overlapping channels (only three are used in the United States). As shown in Figure 17-5, these channels are 1, 6, 11, and 14.

Figure 17-5   2.4GHz Channels

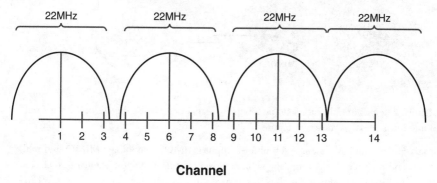

Channel

In a network with multiple APs, you should configure adjacent APs to operate on different channels. This will help provide a better goodput. *Goodput* refers to the number of useful information bits that the network can deliver.

NOTE: The exam topics call out 802.11a-ht and 802.11g-ht. The "ht" stands for high throughput. Although these adjustments to the 802.11a and 802.11g standards do provide better throughput, all WLANs today should, at a minimum, be using 802.11n clients and APs. Preferably, WLANs have migrated to or are migrating to 802.11ac.

Another factor is the density (ratio of users to APs), which if too high could harm performance of the network. Areas expecting high density would include classrooms, hotels, and hospitals. Device or bandwidth saturation could impact performance.

Antennas

WLAN antennas can be omnidirectional or unidirectional. Omnidirectional antennas are typical on wireless routers and APs. They can be internal or external to the devices. These antennas send the signal out in all directions from the location of the AP, as shown in Figure 17-6.

Figure 17-6   Omnidirectional Antenna

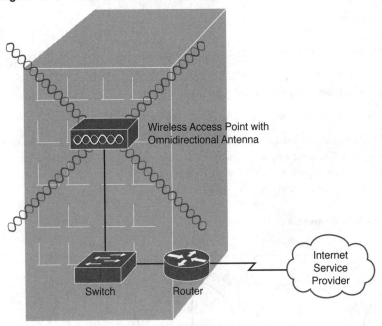

Wireless Access Point with
Omnidirectional Antenna

Internet
Service
Provider

Switch   Router

Unidirectional antennas are ideal for sending a wireless signal in a precise direction, such as from one building to the next, as shown in Figure 17-7.

802.11n incorporates multiple-input and multiple-output (MIMO) technology. MIMO uses multiple antenna and multiple channels to achieve higher data rates than previous standards. 802.11ac improved upon MIMO by allowing multiple users to simultaneously transmit data on the WLAN. Called MU-MIMO or MUMIMO, the MU stands for multiuser.

Figure 17-7   Unidirectional Antenna

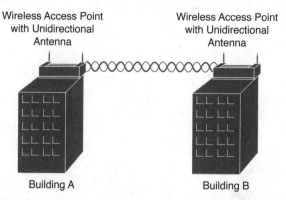

WLAN Topologies
================

WLAN Topologies

The three main 802.11 WLAN topologies are described in the following list:

- **Ad hoc**—This is when two devices connect wirelessly without the aid of an infrastructure device, such as a wireless router or AP. Examples include Bluetooth and Wi-Fi Direct.

- **Infrastructure**—This is when wireless clients interconnect via a wireless router or AP, such as in WLANs. APs connect to the network infrastructure using the wired distribution system (DS), such as Ethernet.

- **Mesh**—This is when there is a mixture of APs all connected to each other wirelessly instead of using an Ethernet connection typical of infrastructure mode. Mesh networks are ideal for residential and city-wide Wi-Fi networks where wiring together many APs is not feasible.

WLAN Devices

For the Network+ exam, you should be familiar with small office or home wireless routers, wireless access points, wireless LAN controllers (WLC), and wireless bridges.

Wireless Routers

Wireless routers include a built-in four-port or five-port switch for wired connections and an Internet or WAN port for connecting to a broadband modem, such as the DSL modem shown in Figure 17-8.

Figure 17-8   Example of a Wireless Router Implementation

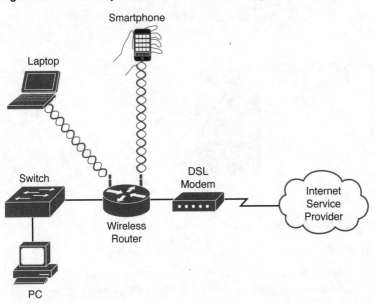

These low-priced wireless routers are ideal for home and small office networks. They provide several essential services, including Dynamic Host Configuration Protocol (DHCP), Network Address Translation (NAT), VPN services, firewall services, port forwarding, and the latest WLAN security.

Wireless Access Points

Wireless access points (APs) are typically used when there is a router already providing Layer 3 services, as shown in Figure 17-9, or in situations where the coverage area of an existing WLAN needs to be extended.

An AP has an Ethernet port that enables it to be connected to a switch port. In a home or small office network, an AP can simply be another wireless router with all the Layer 3 services turned off. You would connect one of the AP's switch ports to the one of the switch ports on the wireless router.

Figure 17-9   Example of an AP Implementation

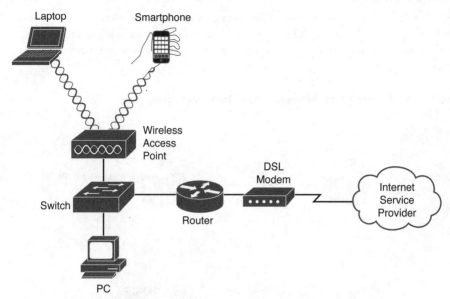

Wireless LAN Controllers

In larger networks, a WLC is typically used to manage multiple APs, as shown in Figure 17-10.

Figure 17-10   Example of a Wireless LAN Controller Implementation

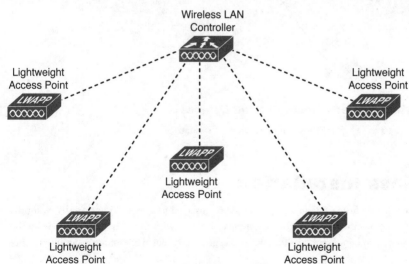

WLCs can use the older Lightweight Access Point Protocol (LWAPP) or the more current Control and Provisioning of Wireless Access Points (CAPWAP). Using a WLC, VLAN pooling can be used to assign IP addresses to wireless clients from a pool of IP subnets and their associated VLANs.

Wireless Bridge

A wireless bridge is primarily responsible for connecting wired and wireless networks. As shown in Figure 17-11, a wireless bridge can connect two networks in two separate buildings using directional antennas, as you saw earlier. A wireless bridge can also be used to connect wired clients to the WLAN.

Figure 17-11   Examples of Wireless Bridge Implementations

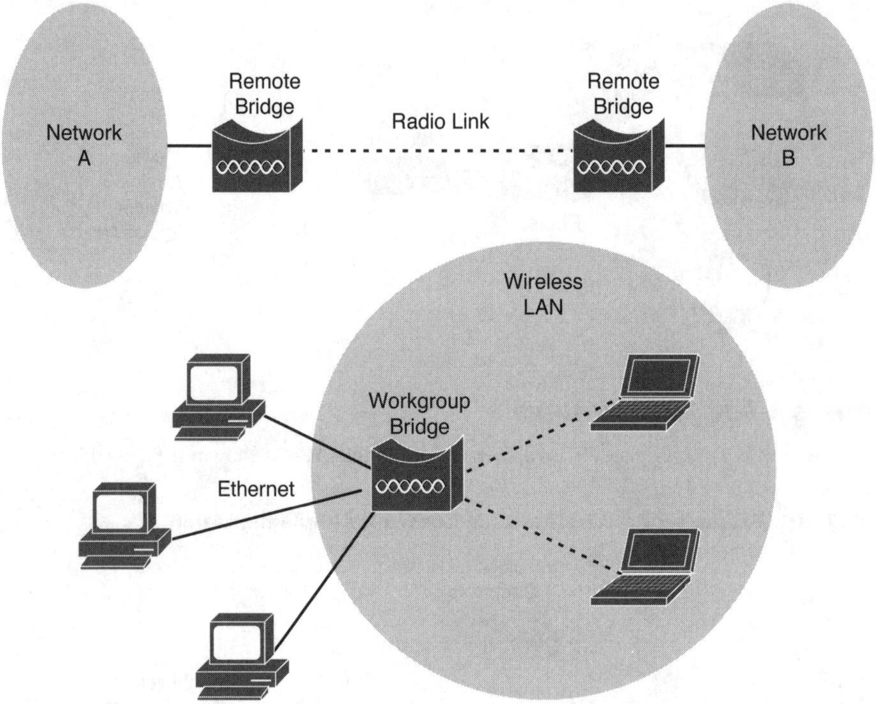

Video: Wireless Topologies and Devices

Refer to the Digital Study Guide to view this video.

Wireless Installation

In a home or small office, a wireless router should be installed in a central location that will provide the best coverage from its omnidirectional antenna. WLANs with more than one AP need to be carefully designed and configured so that the coverage is sufficient while minimizing interference.

Channels and Frequency Bands

For the 2.4GHz frequency, adjacent APs should be configured to operate on channels that do not overlap, as shown in Figure 17-12.

Figure 17-12   Using Three Channels in a WLAN 2.4GHz Implementation

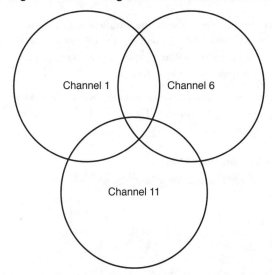

With three non-overlapping channels to choose from, an administrator can use a hexagonal pattern, such as the one shown in Figure 17-13, to determine the most effective placement of APs. Each of the APs should be configured with the same service set identifier (SSID) so that users can seamlessly roam from one AP to another.

Figure 17-13   Design Pattern for Installing APs Using the 2.4GHz Frequency

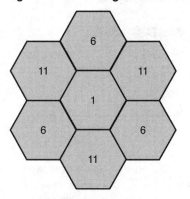

For the 5GHz band, there should be two cells between APs that are configured to use the same channel.

Most wireless routers and APs on the market today are dual-band. They support both 2.4GHz and 5GHz frequencies. The newest models use 802.11ac for the 5GHz band and are backward compatible with 802.11n. To improve performance in environments in which the density of wireless devices is a concern, consider using the 5GHz band whenever possible.

Wireless Site Surveys

For a home or small office WLAN with a handful of wireless clients, there is no need to perform a wireless site survey. For larger implementations with multiple APs configured to operate on different channels and frequency bands, a site survey is necessary. Without a survey, users often end up with inadequate coverage and suffer from low performance in some areas.

Site survey tools are designed to measure the signal strength and signal-to-noise ratio of AP beacons and 802.11 frames. These tools can generate a heat map, as shown in Figure 17-14, that the administrator can then use to quickly locate problem areas.

Figure 17-14   Cisco Wireless Control System Heat Map

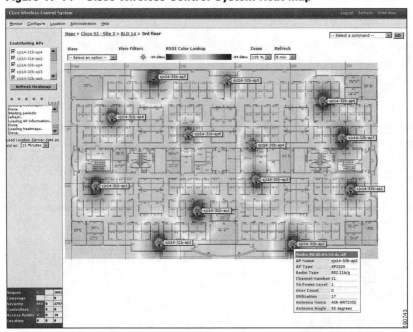

Wireless Router Configuration

For the Network+ exam, you should be familiar with the basic tasks necessary to configure a wireless router. The interface for each manufacturer will be different. However, the configuration tasks are the same. The following steps are demonstrated using the Netgear Nighthawk R7000 dual-band wireless router:

Step 1.   Log in to the device.

Many older home and small office wireless routers came with a default IP address, user-name, and password that anyone could use to access the device. These defaults are easily found on the Internet with a quick search. To address these security weaknesses, most newer models ask you to create a username and password during installation.

Step 2.   Configure administrative access.

Change the default administrative password, as shown in Figure 17-15. Some wireless routers will also allow you to change the default administrator username.

Figure 17-15   Changing the Administrator Password

Step 3.   Modify the DHCP settings.

Change the DHCP settings for the LAN interfaces to something other than the default. For example, many wireless routers use the 192.168.0.0/24 network. You should change this to something different—for example, another private network, as shown in Figure 17-16.

Figure 17-16   Modifying the DHCP Settings for LAN and WLAN Access

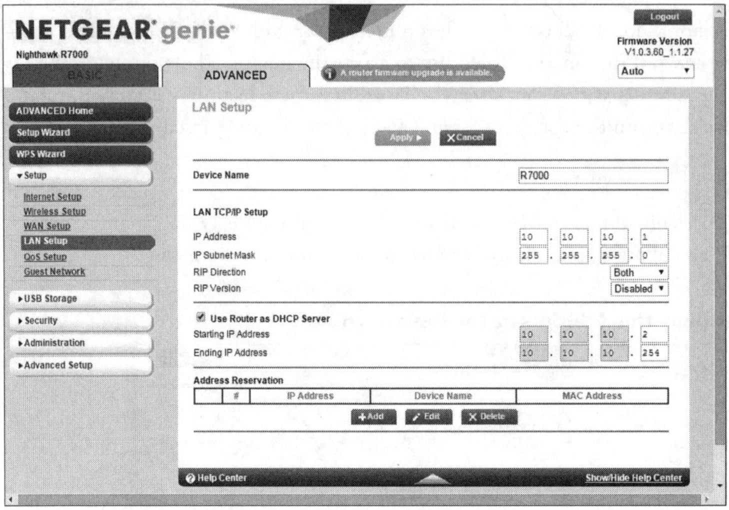

Step 4.   Configure the wireless settings.

Each band will need an SSID, a security option, and a password. WPA2 with AES is configured in Figure 17-17. Note in the figure that SSID broadcast is enabled so that users can easily find the "netplus123" WLAN when attempting to connect. Disabling the SSID broadcast is a security best practice. However, users must then manually configure it, which may not be ideal in some circumstances.

Figure 17-17   Configuring the Wireless Settings

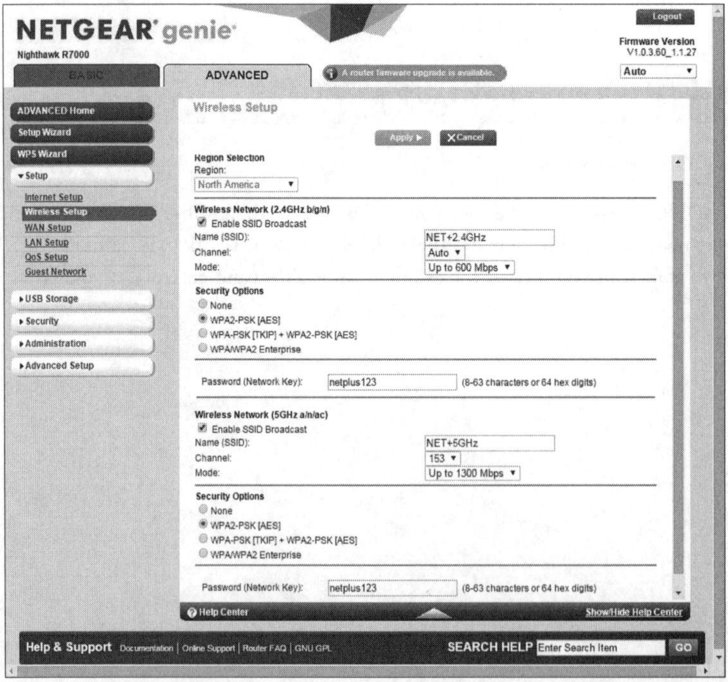

Step 5.   Test a wireless client connection.

Many different devices can be used to test the WLAN configuration, including smartphones, laptops, tablets, gaming devices, and media devices, such as smart televisions. Each device will have its own configuration interface. Usually, you will find it in a Settings menu, such as the iPhone shown in Figure 17-18.

Figure 17-18   Testing an iPhone's Wireless Connection to the 5GHz Band

 Activity: Identify the Wireless Association Parameters

Refer to the Digital Study Guide to complete this activity.

Study Resources

For today's exam topics, refer to the following resources for more study.

NOTE: For a deep dive into any particular WLAN technology, I suggest referring to Jim Geier's excellent book *Designing and Deploying 802.11 Wireless Networks: A Practical Guide to Implementing 802.11n and 802.11ac Wireless Networks*, Second Edition, which you can access through your Safari Books Online account.

Resource	Location	Topic
Primary Resources		
Certification Guide	8	Introducing Wireless LANs
		Deploying Wireless LANs
Video Course	9	Wireless LAN Configuration
Exam Cram	8	Understanding Wireless Basics
Supplemental Resources		
Lab Simulator	6	Configuring Small Office/Home Office Router-Network User Security Settings
	8	Wireless Antenna Placement
		Manually Configuring Wireless Signals on a Small Office/Home Office Router
Flash Cards	15	Implementing a Wireless LAN
Quick Reference	15	Implementing a Wireless LAN

 Check Your Understanding

Refer to the Digital Study Guide to take a 10-question quiz covering the content of this day.

Risks, Threats, and Vulnerabilities

CompTIA Network+ N10-006 Exam Topics

- 3.1 Compare and contrast risk-related concepts
- 3.2 Compare and contrast common network vulnerabilities and threats

Key Topics

Today's review focuses on the types of risk, threats, and vulnerabilities inherent in computer networks. A wide variety of denial of service (DoS) attacks must be defended against, and wireless networks are vulnerable to a number of unique threats. Therefore, network administrators must be vigilant in maintaining strong risk management procedures.

Denial of Service

The primary objective of a DoS attack is to overwhelm the ability of computer systems to adequately respond to legitimate user requests. For example, the attacker in Figure 16-1 is using a spoofed IP address to flood the server with requests. The spike in traffic could be enough to overwhelm the server.

Figure 16-1   Denial of Service Example

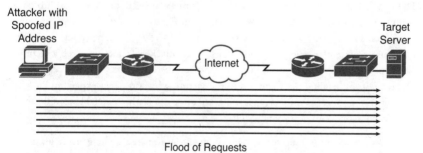

Attacker with
Spoofed IP
Address

Target
Server

Internet

Flood of Requests

Two unique types of DoS attacks include

- **Friendly DoS**—DoS attacks can be caused unintentionally by a friendly source, such as an internal system with a faulty NIC that is flooding the LAN or a compromised system that is under the control of a remote attacker.

- **Permanent DoS**—Instead of lasting only a short period of time, a permanent DoS attack never stops. This causes the network administrator to respond by changing routing, IP addressing, or other configurations.

Distributed DoS

Today's DoS attacks are almost always distributed, meaning that there are many sources of the attack. A distributed DoS (DDoS) attack uses botnets, which are large collections of compromised systems called zombies. These zombies are geographically dispersed, hard to trace, and are under the control and coordination of one attacker.

There are three basic varieties of DDoS attacks: directed, reflected, and amplified. Examples of directed DDoS attacks include the following:

- **Ping of Death**—Attacker sends ICMP packets that are too big.

- **TCP SYN flood**—The attacker sends multiple TCP SYN packets to initiate a TCP session but never finishes the synchronization. The sessions stay open until they time out, leaving the server unable to respond to legitimate user TCP initiation requests.

- **Buffer overflow**—Some programs may only be allotted a certain amount of memory on the server. Attackers can exploit this vulnerability by filling up the memory buffer, potentially causing the program to crash.

- **Fraggle attack**—The attacker sends spoofed UDP packets to a network's broadcast address attempting to flood the system.

Reflected and Amplified Attacks

A reflected DDoS attack is similar to a fraggle attack in that the attacker floods a network's broadcast address with spoofed source IP addresses. For example, in Figure 16-2, the attacker is spoofing the server's IP address and requesting that all devices on the 172.16.0.0/16 subnet reply to a ping. A smurf attack is an example of a reflected DDoS attack. If an attacker decides to attack a victim, the attacker sends packets to a source who thinks these packets are legitimate. The source then responds to the requests by sending the responses to the victim, who was never expecting these response packets from the source. Protocols that use UDP are particularly vulnerable to reflected attacks, such as the Network Time Protocol (NTP).

Amplification attacks are a form of reflected attacks in which the response traffic is made up of packets that are much larger than those initially sent by the attacker. Domain Name Service (DNS) is a popular protocol for amplified attacks. The attacker can use a source to reflect an attack to a DNS server requesting that the server respond with domain records. The attacker sends a DNS request for a site that has many DNS A records. This causes the server to respond with a much larger packet than a normal DNS reply, thus amplifying the reflected attack.

Figure 16-2   Smurf Attack

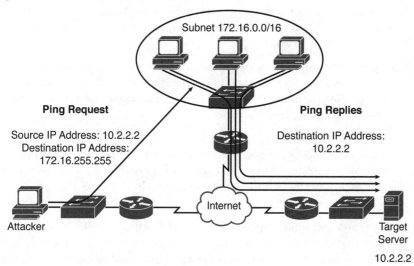

 Video: Distributed DoS Attacks

Refer to the Digital Study Guide to view this video.

Other Attack and Threat Terminology

The following is a list of other attacks and threats you should be familiar with for the Network+ exam:

- **Packet/protocol abuse**—Packet abuse refers to the ability of an attacker to manipulate the bits in a packet to take advantage of inherent weaknesses. Similarly, protocol weaknesses can be abused, such as with the TCP SYN flood attack previously discussed.

- **Spoofing**—The attacker replaces the real source information for a transmission, file, or email with a fake source, such that the destination will respond to the attacker instead of the authentic source.

- **Brute force**—The attacker continuously attempts to gain access to a system by continuously guessing the username and/or password.

- **Man-in-the-middle**—The attacker uses techniques to convince another system that the attacker's system is a legitimate source for traffic. ARP cache poisoning is an example of a man-in-the-middle attack. The source sends out an ARP request for a destination. The attacking system responds with a spoofed ARP reply. All systems that receive the reply update their ARP cache with the attacker's MAC address. All traffic for the destination is now sent to the attacker.

- **Session hijacking**—A type of man-in-the-middle attack in which the attacker fakes the destination into thinking that it is still talking with the original source. For example, an attacker can use the source's cookie from a banking session to impersonate the source and continue to use the banking website.

- **Social engineering**—The attacker attempts to manipulate individuals into divulging secure information that compromises the security of a target system and the privacy of the individual. For example, pretexting is a tactic in which the attacker pretends to need personal information to verify the identity of the victim.

- **VLAN hopping**—The attacker connects to a switch and imitates another switch by sending automatic trunking messages, such as Cisco's proprietary Dynamic Trunking Protocol (DTP). If successful in establishing a trunk with the switch, the attacker can send and receive traffic for all the VLANs configured on the remote switch.

- **Zero-day attacks**—These attacks involve viruses and worms that can spread across the network or Internet in a matter of minutes, beginning on day zero as a previously unknown vulnerability is exploited. Zero-day attacks take advantage of a window that exists between the time a threat is released and the time the security vendor releases a fix or security-related patch to address the vulnerability.

- **Insider threats and malicious employees**—Disgruntled or former employees, contractors, or even current employees who have inside information can pose a threat to the privacy and security of an organization. Security policies and best practices should be implemented to protect from malicious insider threats.

Wireless Attacks

Wireless devices are susceptible to the attacks and threats previously reviewed. However, they are also vulnerable to some unique attacks and threats, as listed in Table 16-1.

Table 16-1   Wireless Attacks

Wireless Attack	Description
Rogue AP	A wireless access point that is not authorized to be part of the WLAN. For example, an employee attaches a home router to the network in an attempt to extend wireless service into an area.
Evil twin	A rogue AP that intentionally poses as a legitimate AP in an attempt to intercept WLAN user traffic.
War driving	Attackers drive around looking for unsecure WLANs.
War chalking	The drawing of symbols in public areas to identify or advertise open or unsecured Wi-Fi networks. Attackers record authentication information on a wall or nearby structure to let others know how to access the WLAN.
Bluejacking	The sending of unauthorized or unsolicited messages over a Bluetooth connection to a device.
Bluesnarfing	The unauthorized access of data from a wireless device through a Bluetooth connection.
WEP/WPA attacks	WEP and WPA are no longer considered secure wireless authentication protocols because of weak encryption. WLANs that use WEP and WPA are susceptible to attacks.
WPS attacks	Wi-Fi Protected Setup (WPS) is a feature that some home devices use to simplify the wireless configuration of devices. However, the technology is susceptible to brute-force attacks.

Vulnerabilities

Computer systems have a wide variety of vulnerabilities that must be addressed. Vulnerabilities that are specific to the Network+ exam include the following:

- **Unnecessary running services**—A primary step in implementing a security solution is device hardening, which we will review tomorrow. Part of the hardening process is to disable unnecessary services. For example, if no programs rely on Windows sharing features, turn them off or disable these services.

- **Open ports**—Attackers use reconnaissance tools to scan systems for open ports. However, even a response refusing a port connection tells the attacker that the computer exists. Free tools are available, such as *ShieldsUP!!* at http://www.grc.com, that can help you determine if a system's ports are open.

- **Patches and updates**—Software such as Windows operating systems are patched and updated regularly. The administrator should establish a policy for downloading and installing patches and updates. Legacy systems that are still in use to maintain business continuity should be secured as much as possible. If necessary, place legacy systems on an isolated network to limit their exposure to known vulnerabilities.

- **Unencrypted channels**—Communications across networks should be encrypted whenever possible. Virtual private networks (VPNs) should be configured when using the Internet to establish a connection to a remote site.

- **Unsecure protocols**—At a minimum, an administrator should ban all protocols that send clear-text messages. An attacker can capture packets using a variety of protocol sniffer software, such as Wireshark, and read the unencrypted data, including usernames and passwords. Unsecure protocols include Telnet, Hypertext Transfer Protocol (HTTP), Serial Line Internet Protocol (SLIP), File Transfer Protocol (FTP), Trivial FTP (TFTP), and Simple Network Management Protocol versions 1 and 2 (SNMPv1 and SNMPv2). Whenever possible, use Secure Shell (SSH), SNMPv3, Transport Layer Security/Secure Socket Layer (TLS/SSL), Secure FTP (SFTP), Secure Copy (SCP), Secure HTTP (HTTPS), and Internet Protocol Security (IPsec).

- **TEMPEST/RF emanation**—An attacker could be motivated to use a sniffer to pick up the emanations from equipment and cabling. The Telecommunications Electronics Material Protected from Emanating Spurious Transmissions (TEMPEST) standard specifies methods for reducing the exposure of data through leaking emanations, including radio frequency (RF) signals, electrical signals, sounds, and vibrations. For a device to be approved as a TEMPEST, it must undergo extensive testing, done to exacting standards that the U.S. government dictates. Today, control zones and white noise are used to accomplish the shielding. TEMPEST-certified equipment often costs twice as much as non-TEMPEST equipment.

Risk Management

A standard mantra in the security community about the inevitability of attack is "not if, but when." Administrators implement security measures to protect networks, not if, but when an attack occurs. A primary security goal is to ensure business continuity. Managing the risk of an attack includes the following tasks:

- **Vulnerability assessment**—Administrators should have a full inventory of all network assets. Each asset should be quantified as to its value and importance. The vulnerabilities of each asset should be identified.

- **Vulnerability scanning**—A technician on staff can quickly use a tool that will scan systems for known vulnerabilities and report back any potential exposures. For example, Tenable Network Security offers the Nessus product line of vulnerability scanners. Nessus Home version, shown in Figure 16-3, is a free download. Vulnerability scans should be run continuously or at least once a month.

Figure 16-3   Nessus Home Vulnerability Scanner

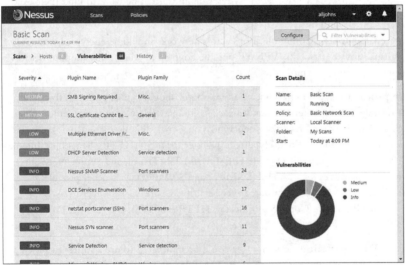

- **Penetration testing**—If your network is particularly sensitive to attacks, such as a financial institution or large corporation, hire expert security specialists at least once a year to conduct a penetration test. Penetration testing looks to exploit known weaknesses in the architecture of certain systems and protocols. For example, the weaknesses of the TCP/IP protocol suite are well documented. An expert will know exactly how to test your systems for these vulnerabilities.

- **End-user awareness and training**—The weakest security link in any network is the users. A user can be susceptible to social engineering techniques, revealing sensitive information in order to be helpful. Security policies should be developed and enforced for user access, including authentication, authorization, and auditing (referred to as "triple A"). AAA tools ensure administrators know who accesses what information and what the user did (or does) while accessing the information. Adherence to the security policy should be periodically verified and deviations from the policy addressed.

- **Single point of failure**—A single point of failure is a device in a network that, if offline, interrupts normal network operations for users. Most networks have several single points of failure. For example, your home router is a single point of failure. If it is down, your entire home network will be down. As part of the vulnerability assessment in a business, the administrator should determine which devices and assets are considered critical to business continuity. Further, because implementing redundant devices is complex and expensive, the administrator should evaluate what amount of downtime is acceptable. Some businesses require the "five nines" of uptime, meaning that the network should be up 99.999% of the time or has no more than 5 minutes of downtime a year. If the "five nines" are required, the administrator should implement a fully redundant network design, including backups for routers, switches, servers, power supplies, hard drives, interface cards, and universal power supplies.

- **Disaster recovery**—Every disaster recovery plan should address procedures for preserving and recovering data. This is only possible by using a consistent backup schedule that includes full, differential, and incremental backups. Backups should be stored offsite, possibly with a cloud service provider. When there is a data breach, system failure, or disaster, such as a fire, the disaster recovery plan should immediately go into effect. First responders should be alerted so that they can begin the data recovery process.

- **Business continuity**—Encompasses a structured and defined set of perpetrations and detailed plans that ensure the continued flow of critical business operations should a disaster occur. Business continuity planning is directly related to risk management and contingency planning. Risk management is the identification and assessment of potential risks. Contingency planning details the organization's readiness to deal with disasters or incidents.

 Activity: Identify the Security Terminology

Refer to the Digital Study Guide to complete this activity.

Study Resources

For today's exam topics, refer to the following resources for more study.

NOTE: The Study Resources for today list the CCNA Security 210-260 Official Cert Guide. I highly recommend that you use your Safari Books Online account to read the first two chapters.

Resource	Location	Topic
Primary Resources		
Certification Guide	12	Security Fundamentals
		Categories of Network Attacks
Video Course	14	Network Security
Exam Cram	11	Disaster Recovery
		Managing Common Security Threats
Supplemental Resources		
CCNA Security Cert Guide	1	Networking Security Concepts
	2	Common Security Threats
Lab Simulator	12	Network Vulnerabilities—the Hacker and Network Admin Perspectives
		Secure Protocols vs. Unsecure Protocols
		Types of Network Threats and Attacks
Flash Cards	16	Network Security Overview
Quick Reference	16	Network Security Overview

 Check Your Understanding

Refer to the Digital Study Guide to take a 10-question quiz covering the content of this day.

Hardening Devices

CompTIA Network+ N10-006 Exam Topics

- 3.3 Given a scenario, implement network hardening techniques

Key Topics

Today, we review the methods an administrator uses to harden devices in the network. All devices should use the latest anti-malware protection. Switches and routers should be hardened using a variety of techniques. User authentication should be appropriate for the security requirements of the network. Wireless LANs (WLANs) should use the latest authentication and encryption standards.

Anti-malware Software

Anti-malware software is specifically designed to defend against malware. Anti-malware products usually include antivirus and anti-spyware, as well as other products, such as, rootkit removal and scanning tools. Anti-malware can be deployed in the following ways:

- **As host-based anti-malware**—This type of anti-malware is installed on individual end devices. Examples include Symantec's Norton Security and McAfee's Total Protection, although many other reputable and excellent host-based anti-malware options are available.

- **As network-based anti-malware**—This type of anti-malware is installed on a device connected to the network that monitors all traffic, such as an intrusion detection system (IDS) or intrusion prevention system (IPS).

- **As cloud/server-based anti-malware**—This type of anti-malware offloads most of the heavy-duty data analysis and signature definitions to a cloud-based provider. End devices have lightweight client software installed that communicates with the server in the cloud. Most cloud-based anti-malware offerings are simply enhancements to vendors' existing anti-malware, such as Symantec Insight and McAfee Global Threat Intelligence.

Device Hardening

Device hardening includes several important tasks that the administrator should complete, including disabling unused services, using secure protocols, configuring switch port security, and implementing strong user authentication techniques.

Disable Unused Network Services

Networking devices, such as switches and routers, often come with many network services enabled by default. Services that are running, but are not needed, present a security risk. An attacker can search for these services and use them to gain additional access into the network. When a network service is not being used, it should be disabled. The following are some examples of services you might want to disable on a Cisco router: BOOTPD, CDP, FTP, TFTP, PAD, TCP and UDP minor services, SNMP, HTTP, DNS, ICMP redirects, and IP source routing.

Use Secure Protocols

The security policy for the network should specify that only secure protocols be used for data transmission and communication. Table 15-1 lists the secure protocols you should know for the Network+ exam.

Table 15-1   Secure Protocols

Acronym	Name	Purpose
SSH	Secure Shell	SSH is used for secure remote access (for example, accessing a router). SSH should always be used instead of Telnet, which sends all messages in clear text.
SNMPv3	Simple Network Management Protocol version 3	SNMP is used by administrators to gather information from network devices. Prior versions of SNMP are not secure because the GET and SET messages are not authenticated or encrypted.
TLS/SSL	Transport Layer Security/Secure Sockets Layer	TLS is the preferred protocol to use in client-server applications when data is sent over an unsecure network, such as the Internet. TLS is often listed with SSL, its predecessor. However, the latest version of SSL, which is 3.0, is no longer secure.
SFTP	Secure File Transfer Protocol	SFTP should always be used instead of the older, unsecure FTP. SFTP uses SSH to establish a secure connection for file transfers.
HTTPS	Hypertext Transfer Protocol Secure	This web browser protocol should be used instead of HTTP, to securely retrieve content from a web server.
IPsec	IP Security	IPsec is set of security protocols and methodologies used to establish, maintain, and terminate secure connections over virtual private networks.

Configure Switch Port Security

The switch is the first network device that wired end devices connect to in order to access other areas of the network or the default gateway to access remote networks and the Internet. Therefore, a variety of port security measures should be implemented. Figure 15-1 is a sample topology we will use to review these measures.

Figure 15-1   Port Security Topology

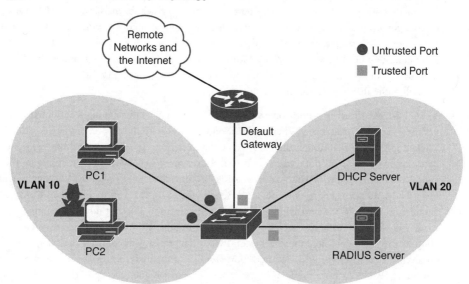

- **DHCP snooping**—The attacker on PC2 could spoof a DHCP server, answering all DHCP requests and establishing a connection with PC1 to carry out further attacks. DHCP snooping is a security feature you configure on switches to detect the presence of DHCP spoofing. The administrator determines which ports are trusted and untrusted. Trusted ports are those you would expect to send and receive a lot of DHCP messages, such as the port connected to the legitimate DHCP server in Figure 15-1. Untrusted ports are usually access ports connected to end clients. These ports should not send or receive many DHCP messages. For example, the Cisco IOS command **ip dhcp snooping limit rate 5** configured on an access port would limit the number of DHCP packets to 5 per second.

- **ARP inspection**—Similar to DHCP, ARP replies can be spoofed. For example, the attacker on PC2 can respond to ARP requests from PC1. This poisons the MAC address tables on the switch and PC1. Each will now associate the intended destination MAC address with the attacker's IP address. Dynamic ARP inspection (DAI) mitigates these attacks by not relaying invalid ARP replies out other ports on the same VLAN. On a Cisco switch, DAI requires DHCP snooping to be configured. Then, by default, DAI is enabled on the ports that are untrusted for DHCP snooping. Ports connected to trusted devices, such as the default gateway or servers in Figure 15-1, should be configured with the **ip arp inspection trust** command.

- **VLAN assignments**—VLANs are not only great for segmenting network broadcast domains, but are also useful tools for separating user groups. Ports on the switch are assigned to specific VLANs. For example, you can configure one VLAN for servers and another VLAN for users, as shown in Figure 15-1. Access between the two VLANs can then be tightly controlled through the use of access control lists (ACLs) configured on the router.

- **Access control lists (ACL)**—The default setting on ports is to allow all traffic. ACLs are commonly configured on ports to filter traffic between areas within the network. ACLs can be configured for a variety of traffic features, including source address, destination address, and application. For example, an ACL could be configured to only allow devices on VLAN 10 to communicate with devices on VLAN 20 for specific services, such as DHCP and authentication messages to the servers. Once configured and applied to a port, an ACL will implicitly deny all traffic that is not explicitly permitted.

- **MAC address filtering**—Ports on a switch can be statically or dynamically configured with specific MAC addresses. When enabled, only devices with those MAC addresses are allowed to send traffic through the port. To configure a Cisco switch to learn MAC addresses dynamically on an access port, you enable **switchport port-security** and then configure the **switchport port-security mac-address sticky** command. Once configured, the switch will learn the MAC address of the first device to send traffic to on the port. If any other device connects to the port, the port will log a port security violation and shut down. An administrator will need to manually re-enable the port after investigating the violation. For example, consider the situation where the attacker on PC2 in Figure 15-1 disconnects the cable and connects it to a wireless router. Without port security configured, the wireless router would receive an IP address from the DHCP server and serve as a rogue access point.

NOTE: You can also configure static MAC addresses on most wireless routers, which would then allow only those devices specified to connect to the wireless LAN (WLAN).

- **IEEE 802.1X**—This standard provides better security than MAC address filtering. 802.1X is a port-based access control and authentication mechanism that uses a RADIUS server to authorize a device to send traffic through the port. 802.1X uses the Extensible Authentication Protocol (EAP). On Cisco switches, configure ports with the **authentication port-control auto** command to enable 802.1X authentication.

 Video: Hardening a Cisco Switch

Refer to the Digital Study Guide to view this video.

User Authentication

For the Network+ exam, you are responsible for knowing a variety of user authentication methods and terminology, as summarized in Table 15-2.

Table 15-2   User Authentication Terminology

Acronym	Name	Description
PAP	Password Authentication Protocol	PAP sends authentication information in clear text. Today, PAP is only used to access older servers that do not support stronger authentication protocols.

Acronym	Name	Description
CHAP	Challenge Handshake Authentication Protocol	CHAP is one-way authentication that is performed through a three-way handshake (challenge, response, and acceptance messages) between a server and a client. CHAP does not send login credentials across the network. Instead, it uses a hashing algorithm, such as Message Digest version 5 (MD5), to create a secret phrase that only the server and client can decipher.
MSCHAP	Microsoft Challenge Handshake Authentication Protocol	MSCHAP extends the capabilities of CHAP with additional features, including the ability to do two-way authentication.
EAP	Extensible Authentication Protocol	EAP is an authentication method that is implemented in a variety of situations, such as for 802.1X, WLAN authentication, and VPNs.
Kerberos	—	Like CHAP, Kerberos does not send username and password combinations across the network. Instead, a trusted third party issues tickets to the client and server to use in the authentication process.
Two-factor authentication	—	Instead of just using a username and password combination to authenticate, two-factor authentication adds an additional factor. Usually, the factor is physical, such as the user's fingerprint or a security code generated on security key fob.
Multifactor authentication	—	Similar to two-factor authentication, but adds two or more types of successful authentication before access is granted.
Single sign-on	—	Single sign-on allows a user to authenticate only once to gain access to all the authorized network resources. For example, once a remote user authenticates through a VPN to the corporate network, that user will be able to access email, file servers, and other resources without authenticating again.

Data Integrity and Hashing

Secure authentication methods use encryption to ensure a message has not been modified in transit. Hashing is one approach used to provide message integrity. For the Network+ exam, you should be familiar with two common hashing algorithms:

- **Message Digest 5 (MD5)**—Creates 128-bit hash digests

- **Secure Hash Algorithm 1 (SHA-1)**—Creates 160-bit hash digests

However, both of these versions are no longer considered secure. An attacker can intercept these messages, manipulate them, and then recalculate the hash, sending it on to the destination. The destination would consider it a valid message.

To counteract this, additional secret keys are used to calculate the hash value, such as with hash-based message authentication code (HMAC). In addition, newer versions of encryption algorithms, such as SHA-256, use longer digests.

Wireless Security

On Day 17, "WLAN Implementation," we reviewed WLAN implementation, which included configuring WPA2 authentication. Today, we compare authentication and encryption methods.

Wired Equivalent Privacy (WEP) was part of the original 802.11 standard introduced in 1997. By 2001, researchers had discovered a number of flaws in the WEP algorithm. For the Network+ exam, you should know to avoid implementing WEP in WLANs.

Wi-Fi Protected Access (WPA) was created to address the flaws in WEP. In addition, the Temporal Key Integral Protocol (TKIP) was developed as an interim encryption solution. TKIP protected against the most common WEP attacks at that time. The major benefit of WPA with TKIP was that existing WEP equipment could be upgraded to support it with a firmware upgrade. WPA comes in two versions:

- **WPA Personal**—Uses a pre-shared key (PSK) to associate with clients. The key can be 8 to 63 characters.

- **WPA Enterprise**—Authenticates clients using a RADIUS server and 802.1X. Recall that 802.1X uses EAP to encrypt messages.

In the final IEEE 802.11i publication, WPA2 replaced WPA's TKIP encryption algorithm with the mandatory Counter Mode Cipher Block Chaining Message Authentication Code Protocol (CCMP). CCMP uses the Advanced Encryption Standard (AES) to encrypt wireless traffic.

However, WPA and WPA2 are vulnerable to dictionary, brute-force attacks if a short passphrase is used. Therefore, it is recommended that the passphrase be at least 14 characters or five random words.

Activity: Identify the Device Hardening Terminology

Refer to the Digital Study Guide to complete this activity.

Study Resources

For today's exam topics, refer to the following resources for more study.

Resource	Location	Topic
Primary Resources		
Certification Guide	12	Defending Against Attacks
Exam Cram	8	Securing Wireless Networks
	11	Authentication, Authorization, and Accounting (AAA)
Video Course	14	Network Security

Resource	Location	Topic
Supplemental Resources		
Lab Simulator	4	Configuring Port Security
Flash Cards	17	Network Hardening
Quick Reference	17	Network Hardening

 Check Your Understanding

Refer to the Digital Study Guide to take a 10-question quiz covering the content of this day.

Physical Security, Firewalls, Access Control, and Forensics

CompTIA Network+ N10-006 Exam Topics

- 3.4 Compare and contrast physical security controls
- 3.5 Given a scenario, install and configure a basic firewall
- 3.6 Explain the purpose of various network access control models
- 3.7 Summarize basic forensic concepts

Key Topics

Today, we review a variety of security topics, including physical security, firewalls, access control, and forensics.

Physical Security

If an attacker can gain physical access to devices on your network, then no amount of network security you implement will protect you. Various physical security controls are available that range from simple locked cages or closets to the sophisticated security measures implemented at large data centers. In general, physical access to your networking devices should be protected by a two- or three-layer security model:

- **Perimeter security**—Controls access to the building
- **Computer room security**—Controls access to the computer room
- **Wiring closet**—Controls access to the closet or cage within the computer room where the networking devices are stored

Many business networks do not need all three layers, but every business should consider the accessibility of networking devices. At least two of these three layers should be implemented.

The following list summarizes the physical security controls you should be familiar with for the Network+ exam:

- **Network closets**—At a minimum, a small office or small business network should lock networking devices and servers in a cage or closet. Access to the closet should be strictly limited. Also, use security cables to lock down workstations and other user equipment that are not meant to be mobile.

- **Video monitoring**—Closed-circuit TVs (CCTVs) can be placed strategically to record activity in the area. However, IP cameras are cheaper and can send the video feeds across the network.

- **Mantraps**—A mantrap is usually placed inside a building to secure access between a low-security area and a high-security area. It consists of a series of doors—an entrance and an exit—creating a space in which there is room for only one person. The purpose is to provide an additional level of authentication.

- **Door access controls**—Mantraps are justifiable in situations that demand a high level of security, such as in a data center. However, some type of access control should be used to prevent unauthorized access to networking devices. Door access beyond a simple lock and key include the following:

  - **Keypad/cipher locks**—The user is required to know a key code to gain access.

  - **Proximity readers/key fob**—The user must have a card or key fob that uses near field communication (NFC) technology to communicate with the access device.

  - **Biometrics**—Refers to an identifiable body part of the user, such as a fingerprint, a retina pattern, or a handprint.

  - **Security guard**—Armed or unarmed, a security guard can provide an additional level of access control.

Firewalls

On Day 31, "Network Devices," we reviewed network devices, including firewalls and IDS/IPS devices. Remember that a firewall is a networking device, either hardware or software based, that controls access to your organization's network. This controlled access is designed to protect data and resources from an outside threat. For the Network+ exam, you should be able to choose the right firewall for the given situation. The firewall icon in Figure 14-1 could be a router or a specialized hardware firewall, such as a Cisco Adaptive Security Appliance.

Figure 14-1   Simplified Firewall Topology

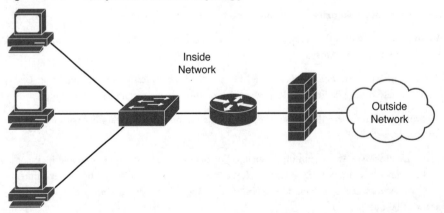

Although firewalls began as a corporate security measure, home and small office networks now regularly include one or more firewalls to protect against threats from the Internet. For example, most home routers today include a stateful packet inspection (SPI) firewall. In addition, PCs running a Windows OS include Windows Firewall. Furthermore, many home antivirus and anti-spyware packages include some type of firewall. You should be able to classify a firewall based on the following characteristics:

- **Host-based and network-based firewalls**—Host-based firewalls are implemented in software on end devices, such as computers and servers. Network-based firewalls are inline on the network, meaning they control traffic crossing the network. A network-based firewall can be a physical device or it can be software installed on a virtual machine running in another device.

- **Software and hardware firewalls**—Software firewalls are loaded into RAM for a given device, such as a PC or a gateway router. Therefore, they are processor-intensive. Hardware firewalls also run software, but are optimized for firewall purposes. Some hardware firewalls embed much of the traffic filtering and decision making into application-specific integrated circuits (ASICs), which can provide line speed performance that does not degrade the network's throughput.

- **Stateless and stateful inspection firewalls**—Stateless firewalls work at Layer 2 and Layer 3, inspecting each frame or packet in isolation. They have no way of knowing if the frame or packet is part of a conversation. Stateful firewalls, as called stateful packet inspection (SPI) firewalls use Layer 4 connection information in a state table for each source-destination data flow. However, stateful firewalls provide no application layer inspection. They cannot track UDP or ICMP traffic flows, nor can they defend against applications that use dynamic port negotiation.

- **Application-aware and context-aware firewalls**—These firewalls go beyond Layer 4 packet inspection, which only looks at the TCP or UDP port numbers. They also consider the context in which a certain application is accessed, evaluating whether the type of access conforms to expected behavior.

- **Unified Threat Management (UTM) firewalls**—A UTM is an all-inclusive firewall solution providing multiple security functions within the same product, such as the following:

    - NAT, VPN, and SPI

    - Inline intrusion prevention system (IPS)

    - Application inspection and behavior control

    - Policy enforcement based on user and device profiles

    - Website reputation monitoring and URL blocking

    - Gateway antivirus and anti-spam

Video: Types of Firewalls

Refer to the Digital Study Guide to view this video.

Activity: Identify the Firewall Terminology

Refer to the Digital Study Guide to complete this activity.

Firewall Placement and Configuration

Firewalls and many other devices can be configured with access control lists (ACLs) for traffic inspection. An ACL is made up of one or more access control entries (ACEs). Each ACE is a line of code in the ACL. An ACE normally permits or denies traffic based on specific criteria, such as IP address, protocol, or port number. The ACL can then be placed to evaluate inbound and/or outbound traffic. Each packet is evaluated against the ACEs in the ACL, beginning with the first ACE. If the packet matches the ACE criteria, then the action is taken, either permit or deny. If there is no match, the next ACE in the ACL is evaluated. If the packet does not match any of the ACEs in the ACL, then the packet is implicitly denied access. Firewalls, therefore, should be carefully placed in order to evaluate traffic as intended.

For example, Figure 14-2 shows a simple topology with a firewall placed between an inside, trusted network (labeled INSIDE Zone); an outside, untrusted network (labeled OUTSIDE Zone); and a demilitarized zone (DMZ).

Figure 14-2   Firewall Placement Between Zones

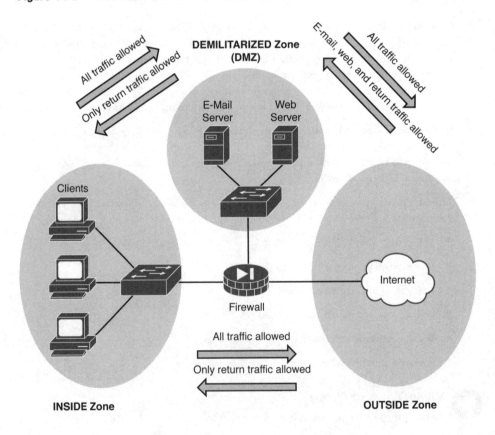

Notice that the proper placement of the firewall allows the implementation of the following policy:

■ INSIDE zone devices are allowed access to the DMZ and OUTSIDE zones.

■ DMZ devices are allowed to access the OUTSIDE zone but are only allowed to reply to sessions initiated by INSIDE zone devices.

■ OUTSIDE zone devices are allowed to initiate email and web sessions with DMZ devices and reply to sessions initiated by INSIDE zone or DMZ devices.

 Video: Firewall Configuration

Refer to the Digital Study Guide to view this video.

Access Control Models

Access control methods include a variety of tools and terminology you should be familiar with, such as the following:

■ **IEEE 802.1X**—Switch port access control and authentication mechanism that uses a RADIUS server to authorize a device to send traffic through the port. There are three roles in the 802.1X authenticating process, as shown in Figure 14-3: supplicant, authenticator, and authentication server. Clients that request access must be running software that complies with the 802.1X standard.

Figure 14-3   802.1X Roles

■ **Posture assessment**—The main purpose of a posture assessment is to evaluate whether a device connecting to the network is compliant with the network's security policy. This can be done by a variety of devices, such as Cisco's Network Access Control appliance.

■ **Persistent and non-persistent agents**—The posture assessment agent running on the client could be a persistent agent that is running all the time or a temporary one that is run only during an attempt by the client computer to connect to the network.

■ **Quarantine network**—If a client fails the posture assessment, it can be placed in a special quarantined network where remediation procedures can occur. For example, maybe the client only needs to be updated with the latest virus signature definitions. The process might be transparent to the end user as the update only takes a few additional seconds.

- **Guest network**—Most organizations will want to provide visitors and guests free access to the Internet. This should be done only through special guest networks, preferably with an access code given to the guest for a limited-time use. The guest network should be considered untrusted and not allowed to access trusted network assets. Guest networks may also be an appropriate holding place for clients that fail a posture assessment.

- **Edge and access control**—802.1X and posture assessment are examples of controlling access at the edge of the network. After the user has been authenticated and connected to the network, you can further control access with ACLs and various permissions.

Forensic Concepts

Procedures should be established in case of a security breach. The procedures may include the following:

- **First responder**—This is the person or persons designated to initially respond to a security event. Most likely, this person is the security administrator.

- **Secure the area**—Maintain custody of evidence as well as contain the damage to data assets by securing the area. Escalate the incident and bring in other parties, when necessary.

- **Document the scene**—Document a detailed description of the state of the system or network. Record all the steps taken to identify, detect, and repair the impacted systems or network.

- **Evidence, data collection, and ediscovery**—Data and evidence that would be valuable for potential litigation is called ediscovery or e-discovery. This data must be handled with extreme care.

- **Chain of custody**—Part of documenting the scene and gathering evidence is making sure that chain of custody is always maintained. Documentation must include who has the evidence, who has seen the evidence, and where it is located.

- **Data transport**—Once the data is documented and collected, secure the data for transport (for example, to a lab, attorney, or third-party secure holding facility). This may be necessary to comply with legal hold requirements, which may necessitate keeping the data for a very long time.

- **Forensics report**—After the incident is over, compile a detailed report that analyzes the incident, describes what could have been done differently, and makes recommendations for how to handle a similar situation in the future.

Study Resources

For today's exam topics, refer to the following resources for more study.

Resource	Location	Topic
Primary Resources		
Certification Guide	12	Firewalls
Video Course	2	Firewalls
		Intrusion Detection Devices
Exam Cram	11	Firewalls, Appliances, and Physical Security
Supplemental Resources		
Lab Simulator	12	Security Terminology and Descriptions
		Security Appliance Terminology and Methods
Flash Cards	17	Network Hardening
Quick Reference	17	Network Hardening

Check Your Understanding

Refer to the Digital Study Guide to take a 10-question quiz covering the content of this day.

Network Models

CompTIA Network+ N10-006 Exam Topics

- 5.1 Analyze a scenario and determine the corresponding OSI layer

Key Points

As a new student to networking, one of the very first topics you probably learned was the layers of the OSI and TCP/IP models. Now that you have completed your studies and are reviewing for your certification exam, you more than likely can see the benefit of using these models. Each helps our understanding of networks in its own way.

NOTE: Understanding the basics the TCP/IP model is part of tomorrow's exam topic. However, we are reviewing the TCP/IP model and encapsulation today because it makes sense to compare it with the OSI model.

The OSI and TCP/IP Models

Network models provide a variety of benefits:

- Reduce complexity
- Standardize interfaces
- Assist understanding
- Promote rapid product development
- Support interoperability
- Facilitate modular engineering

Initially, networks were built on proprietary standards and hardware. Layered models, such as the TCP/IP and OSI models, support interoperability between competing vendor product lines.

Today, we use the OSI model principally as a tool for explaining networking concepts. However, the protocols of the TCP/IP suite are the rules by which networks now operate. Because both models are important, you should be well versed in each model's layers as well as how the models map to each other. Figure 13-1 summarizes the two models.

Figure 13-1   The OSI and TCP/IP Models

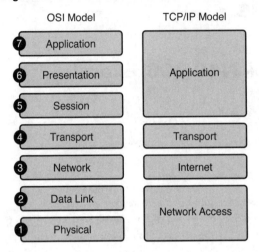

It can be confusing using two models; however, these simple guidelines might help:

- When discussing layers of a model, we are usually referring to the OSI model.

- When discussing protocols, we are usually referring to the TCP/IP model.

OSI Layers

Table 13-1 summarizes the layers of the OSI model and provides a brief functional description of each.

Table 13-1   The OSI Model Layers and Functions

Layer	Functional Description
Application (7)	Refers to interfaces between the network and application software. Also includes authentication services.
Presentation (6)	Defines the format and organization of data. Includes encryption.
Session (5)	Establishes and maintains end-to-end bidirectional flows between endpoints. Includes managing transaction flows.
Transport (4)	Provides a variety of services between two host computers, including connection establishment and termination, flow control, error recovery, and segmentation of large data blocks into smaller parts for transmission.
Network (3)	Refers to logical addressing, routing, and path determination.
Data link (2)	Formats data into frames appropriate for transmission onto some physical medium. Defines rules for when the medium can be used. Defines the means by which to recognize transmission errors.
Physical (1)	Defines the electrical, optical, cabling, connectors, and procedural details required for transmitting bits, represented as some form of energy passing over a physical medium.

The following mnemonic phrase where the first letter represents the layer ("A" stands for "Application") can be helpful to memorize the name and order of the layers from top to bottom:

All **P**eople **S**eem **T**o **N**eed **D**ata **P**rocessing

TCP/IP Layers and Protocols

The TCP/IP model defines four categories of functions that must occur for communications to be successful. Most protocol models describe a vendor-specific protocol stack. However, because the TCP/IP model is an open standard, one company does not control the definition of the model.

Table 13-2 summarizes the TCP/IP layers, their functions, and the most common protocols.

Table 13-2   The TCP/IP Layer Functions

TCP/IP Layer	Function	Example Protocols
Application	Represents data to the user and controls dialog	DNS, Telnet, SMTP, POP3, IMAP, DHCP, HTTP, FTP, SNMP
Transport	Supports communication between diverse devices across diverse networks	TCP, UDP
Internet	Determines the best path through the network	IP, ARP, ICMP
Network access	Controls the hardware devices and media that make up the network	Ethernet, Wireless standards

Video: Data Encapsulation and Decapsulation Overview

Refer to the Digital Study Guide to view this video.

Data Flow Through the Layers

We will review protocols and the encapsulation process in more detail tomorrow. For now, let's summarize how data is encapsulated through the layers of the TCP/IP model.

Each layer of the TCP/IP model adds its own header information. As the data travels down through the layers, it is encapsulated with a new header. At the network access layer, a trailer is also added. This encapsulation process can be described in five steps:

Step 1.   Create and encapsulate the application data with any required application layer headers. For example, the HTTP OK message can be returned in an HTTP header, followed by part of the contents of a web page.

Step 2.   Encapsulate the data supplied by the application layer inside a transport layer header. For end-user applications, a TCP or UDP header is typically used.

Step 3.   Encapsulate the data supplied by the transport layer inside an Internet layer (IP) header. IP is the only protocol available in the TCP/IP network model at the Internet layer.

Step 4. Encapsulate the data supplied by the Internet layer inside a network access layer header and trailer. This is the only layer that uses both a header and a trailer.

Step 5. Transmit the bits. The physical layer encodes a signal onto the medium to transmit the frame.

The numbers in Figure 13-2 correspond to the five steps in the list, graphically showing the same encapsulation process.

Figure 13-2 Five Steps of Data Encapsulation

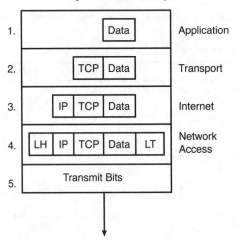

NOTE: The letters LH and LT stand for link header and link trailer, respectively, and refer to the data link layer header and trailer.

 Video: Data Encapsulation Summary
Refer to the Digital Study Guide to view this video.

 Activity: Identify the Encapsulation Layer
Refer to the Digital Study Guide to complete this activity.

Study Resources

For today's exam topics, refer to the following resources for more study.

Resource	Location	Topic
Primary Resources		
Certification Guide	2	All
Exam Cram	2	The Networking Models
Video Course	1	Protocol Reference Models

Resource	Location	Topic
Supplemental Resources		
Lab Simulator	2	OSI Model Layer and Network Devices
		OSI Model Layer Functions
Flash Cards	22	The OSI Model
Quick Reference	22	The OSI Model

 ## Check Your Understanding

Refer to the Digital Study Guide to take a 10-question quiz covering the content of this day.

Network Theory

CompTIA Network+ N10-006 Exam Topics

- 5.2 Explain the basics of network theory and concepts

Key Topics

Today's exam topic includes details about the layers of the TCP/IP protocol suite as well as network theory and concepts. Therefore, our review will progress through the layers.

The TCP/IP Application Layer

The application layer of the TCP/IP model provides an interface between software, such as a web browser, and the network itself. The process of requesting and receiving a web page works like this:

1. An HTTP request is sent, including an instruction to "get" a file, which is often a website's home page.

2. An HTTP response is sent from the web server with a code in the header. This is usually either 200 (request succeeded and information is returned in response) or 404 (page not found).

The HTTP request and the HTTP response are encapsulated in headers. The content of headers allows the application layers on each end device to communicate. Regardless of the application layer protocol (HTTP, FTP, DNS, and so on), all use the same general process for communicating between application layers on the end devices.

The TCP/IP Transport Layer

The transport layer, through TCP, provides a mechanism to guarantee delivery of data across the network. TCP supports error recovery to the application layer through the use of basic acknowledgment logic. Adding to the process for requesting a web page, TCP operation works like this:

1. The web client sends an HTTP request for a specific web server down to the transport layer.

2. TCP encapsulates the HTTP request with a TCP header and includes the destination port number for HTTP.

3. Lower layers process and send the request to the web server.

4. The web server receives HTTP requests and sends a TCP acknowledgement back to the requesting web client.

5. The web server sends the HTTP response down to the transport layer.

6. TCP encapsulates the HTTP data with a TCP header.

7. Lower layers process and send the response to the requesting web client.

8. The requesting web client sends acknowledgement back to the web server.

If data is lost at any point during this process, it is TCP's job to recover the data. HTTP at the application layer does not get involved in error recovery. UDP, the other transport layer protocol, is connectionless. Therefore, it provides no mechanism for error recovery. On Day 8, "Implement Ports and Protocols," we will compare TCP and UDP.

The TCP/IP Internet Layer

The Internet layer of the TCP/IP model uses the Internet Protocol (IP) to label each packet with a logical source and destination address. In addition, the Internet layer defines the process of routing so that routers can determine the best path to send these packets to the destination. Continuing with the web page example, IP addresses the data as it passes from the transport layer to the Internet layer:

1. A web client sends an HTTP request.

2. TCP encapsulates the HTTP request.

3. IP encapsulates the transport segment into a packet, adding source and destination addresses.

4. Lower layers process and send the request to the web server.

5. The web server receives HTTP requests and sends a TCP acknowledgement back to the requesting web client.

6. The web server sends the HTTP response down to the transport layer.

7. TCP encapsulates the HTTP data.

8. IP encapsulates the transport segment into a packet, adding source and destination addresses.

9. Lower layers process and send the response to the requesting web client.

10. The requesting web client sends acknowledgement back to the web server.

The TCP/IP Network Access Layer

IP depends on the network access layer to deliver IP packets across a physical network. Therefore, the network access layer defines the protocols and hardware required to deliver data across some physical network by specifying exactly how to physically connect a networked device to the physical media over which data can be transmitted.

The network access layer includes a large number of standards to deal with the different types of media that data can cross on its way from source device to the destination device.

Collisions

Ethernet and wireless both use shared media, which means that other devices on the local network can send data at the same time. Therefore, both network access methods require a way to resolve potential collisions. Although collisions in Ethernet are rare because modern devices support full-duplex transmission, wireless networks have no equivalent full-duplex method.

In Ethernet, the method for resolving collisions is called Carrier Sense Multiple Access with Collision Detection (CSMA/CD). The CSMA/CD algorithm works like this:

1. A device with a frame to send listens until the Ethernet is not busy.

2. When the Ethernet is not busy, the sender(s) begin(s) sending the frame.

3. The sender(s) listen(s) to make sure that no collision occurred.

4. If a collision occurs, the devices that had been sending a frame each send a jamming signal to ensure that all stations recognize the collision.

5. After the jamming is complete, each sender randomizes a timer and waits that long before trying to resend the collided frame.

6. When each random timer expires, the process starts again from the beginning.

Wireless networks use a similar algorithm called Carrier Sense Multiple Access with Collision Avoidance (CSMA/CA). A WLAN device listens for a transmission on a wireless channel to determine whether it is safe to transmit. The collision avoidance part of the CSMA/CA algorithm causes wireless devices to wait for a random back-off time before transmitting.

 Video: CSMA/CD and CSMA/CA Overview
Refer to the Digital Study Guide to view this video.

Transmission Techniques

The exam topic for today lists several physical layer transmission techniques, which includes the following terminology:

- **Modulation**—The process of sending a signal within another signal. This is accomplished through multiplexing and is the sending of multiple streams over the same medium. For example, voice and data packets can be interleaved. The receiving end de-multiplexes the transmission into its separate streams. Encoding can be digital or analog, depending on the media.

- **Time-division multiplexing (TDM)**—TDM is a modulation technique used to share the bandwidth on a leased line between one or more applications or services that need use of that bandwidth. Another feature called statistical TDM can leverage the fact that not all the applications or services might need all the bandwidth that they are allocated all the time. As a result, statistical TDM allocates more time slots to applications or services that need them if at the same time the other services do not.

- **Broadband and baseband**—The two fundamental approaches to bandwidth usage on a network are broadband and baseband. Broadband uses frequency-division multiplexing (FDM) to divide the signal into separate channels. For example, a cable modem divides the signal coming from the cable company into separate frequencies for voice, data, and all the various TV channels. Baseband technologies, in contrast, use all the available frequencies on a medium to transmit data. Ethernet is an example of a networking technology that uses baseband.

- **Bit rate and baud rate**—The bit rate is the number of data bits transmitted in 1 second. Baud rates are normally associated with modems and refer to the number of times a signal in a communications channel changes. The baud rate, which represents data being communicated, is less than the bit rate.

- **Sampling size**—When data is being encoded on a network, the specifications include details about sampling size. This enables both the sending and the receiving devices to correctly encode and decode the signals off of the network by using the same standard. The key thing to know is that you can often configure the sampling size, and the more sampling you do, the more you can slow the system down.

- **Wavelength**—This is the distance between identical points in a waveform signal between two adjacent cycles of that waveform. In fiber optics, different groupings of wavelengths are divided into individual channels to send multiple sessions of data over a single fiber-optic cable.

End-to-End Communication

With the network access layer, we can now finalize our web page example. The following reviews all the basic concepts of network theory while using the example of requesting and sending a web page:

1. A web client sends an HTTP request.

2. TCP encapsulates the HTTP request.

3. IP encapsulates the transport segment into a packet, adding source and destination addresses.

4. The network access layer encapsulates the packet in a frame, addressing it for the local link.

5. The network access layer sends the frame out as bits on the media.

6. Intermediary devices process the bits at the network access and Internet layers and then forward the data toward the destination.

7. The web server receives the bits on the physical interface and sends them up through the network access and Internet layers.

8. The web server sends a TCP acknowledgement back to the requesting web client.

9. The web server sends the HTTP response down to the transport layer.

10. TCP encapsulates the HTTP data.

11. IP encapsulates the transport segment into a packet, adding source and destination addresses.

12. The network access layer encapsulates the packet in a frame, addressing it for the local link.

13. The network access layer sends the frame out as bits using a transmission technique appropriate for the media.

14. Lower layers process and send the response to the requesting web client.

15. The response travels back to the source over multiple data links.

16. The requesting web client receives a response on the physical interface and sends the data up through the network access and Internet layers.

17. The requesting web client sends a TCP acknowledgement back to the web server.

18. The web page is displayed in requesting device's browser.

 Video: Data Encapsulation and Decapsulation Overview

Refer to the Digital Study Guide to view this video.

 Activity: Identify Network Theory Terminology

Refer to the Digital Study Guide to complete this activity.

Numbering Systems

As a final topic for today, we'll review numbering systems. The base10 numbering system is referred to as decimal because it uses 10 numbers, 0 through 9. The base2 numbering system is referred to as binary because it uses two numbers, 0 and 1. The base16 numbering system is referred to as hexadecimal because it user 16 characters, 0 through 9 and A through F (in decimal, A equals 10, B equals 11, and so on). Finally, the base8 numbering system is referred to as octal because it uses eight numbers, 0 through 7.

Computers communicate in binary—a series of 1s and 0s. Humans are most familiar with the decimal numbering system. Therefore, we prefer to convert binary to decimal, as in the dotted decimal format of an IPv4 address or decimal port numbers. In some cases, we convert binary to hexadecimal, as in MAC addresses and IPv6 addresses.

Octal numbering systems may still be used in some legacy computing systems that use 12-bit, 24-bit, or 36-bit words because these could be abbreviated using 3-bit octal characters. However, modern computer systems use 16-, 32-, or 64-bit words. Therefore, hexadecimal's 4-bit representation is now used.

NOTE: We are not reviewing the process of converting between binary and decimal. At this point in your studies, you should be very comfortable moving between the two numbering systems. If not, take some time to practice this necessary skill. You can search the Internet for binary conversion tricks, tips, and games to help you practice.

 Video:Compare Numbering Systems

Refer to the Digital Study Guide to view this video.

Study Resources

For today's exam topics, refer to the following resources for more study.

Resource	Location	Topic
Primary Resources		
Certification Guide	2	The TCP/IP Stack
Exam Cram	2	The TCP/IP Four-Layer Model
	7	General Media Considerations
		Comparing and Contrasting LAN Technologies
Video Course	2	Network Devices and Theory
Secondary Resources		
Flash Cards	22	Network Theory
Quick Reference	22	Network Theory

Check Your Understanding

Refer to the Digital Study Guide to take a 10-question quiz covering the content of this day.

Wired and Wireless Standards

CompTIA Network+ N10-006 Exam Topics

- 5.4 Given a scenario, deploy the appropriate wired connectivity standard
- 5.3 Given a scenario, deploy the appropriate wireless standard

Key Topics

Today's review focuses on the physical layer media standards for wired and wireless networks. In addition, we do a basic review of Ethernet.

Ethernet Standards

802.3 is the IEEE standard for Ethernet, and both terms are commonly used interchangeably. The terms Ethernet and 802.3 both refer to a family of standards that together define the physical and data link layers of the definitive LAN technology.

Ethernet separates the functions of the data link layer into two distinct sublayers:

- **Logical Link Control (LLC) sublayer**—Defined in the 802.2 standard
- **Media Access Control (MAC) sublayer**—Defined in the 802.3 standard

The LLC sublayer handles communication between the network layer and the MAC sublayer. In general, LLC provides a way to identify the protocol that is passed from the data link layer to the network layer. In this way, the fields of the MAC sublayer are not populated with protocol type information, as was the case in earlier Ethernet implementations.

The MAC sublayer has two primary responsibilities:

- **Data encapsulation**—Includes frame assembly before transmission, frame parsing upon reception of a frame, data link layer MAC addressing, and error detection.
- **Media Access Control**—Because Ethernet is a shared media and all devices can transmit at any time, media access is controlled by a method called Carrier Sense Multiple Access with Collision Detection (CSMA/CD) when operating in half-duplex mode.

Wired Standards

At the physical layer, Ethernet specifies and implements encoding and decoding schemes that enable frame bits to be carried as signals across coaxial copper cables (in legacy implementations), twisted-pair copper cables, and fiber-optic cables. As shown in Table 11-1, the bandwidth capacities of twisted-pair and fiber-optic cabling continue to increase as cabling and signaling technologies evolve.

Table 11-1   Ethernet Cabling Properties

Ethernet Standard	Media Type	Bandwidth Capacity	Distance Limitation
10BASE5	Coax (thicknet)	10Mbps	500 m
10BASE2	Coax (thinnet)	10Mbps	185 m
10BASE-T	Cat 3 (or higher) UTP	10Mbps	100 m
100BASE-TX	Cat 5 (or higher) UTP	100Mbps	100 m
100BASE-FX	MMF	100Mbps	2 km
1000BASE-T	Cat 5e (or higher) UTP	1Gbps	100 m
1000BASE-TX	Cat 6 (or higher) UTP	1Gbps	100 m
1000BASE-LX	MMF/SMF	1Gbps/1Gbps	5 km
1000BASE-LH	SMF	1Gbps	10 km
1000BASE-ZX	SMF	1Gbps	70 km
10GBASE-SR	MMF	10Gbps	26–82 m
10GBASE-LR	SMF	10Gbps	10 km
10GBASE-ER	SMF	10Gbps	40 km
10GBASE-SW	MMF	10Gbps	300 m
10GBASE-LW	SMF	10Gbps	10 km
10GBASE-EW	SMF	10Gbps	40 km
10GBASE-T	Cat 6a (or higher)	10Gbps	100 m
100GBASE-SR10	MMF	100Gbps	125 m
100GBASE-LR4	SMF	100Gbps	10 km
100GBASE-ER4	SMF	100Gbps	40 km

NOTE Additional and creative ways of using Ethernet technology include IEEE 1901.5-2013, which could be used for Ethernet over HDMI cables and Ethernet over existing power lines to avoid having to run a separate cabling just for networking.

TIA/EIA 568A and 568B Standards

The three most common Ethernet standards used today—10BASE-T (Ethernet), 100BASE-TX (Fast Ethernet, or FE), and 1000BASE-T (Gigabit Ethernet, or GE)—use UTP cabling. Some key differences exist, particularly with the number of wire pairs needed in each case and in the type (category) of cabling.

The UTP cabling used by popular Ethernet standards include either two or four pairs of wires. The cable ends typically use an RJ-45 connector. The RJ-45 connector has eight specific physical locations into which the eight wires in the cable can be inserted, called pin positions or, simply, pins.

The Telecommunications Industry Association (TIA) and the Electronics Industry Alliance (EIA) define standards for UTP cabling, color coding for wires, and standard pinouts on the cables. Figure 11-1 shows the pinouts for the 568A and 568B standards.

Figure 11-1   TIA/EIA Standard Ethernet Cabling Pinouts

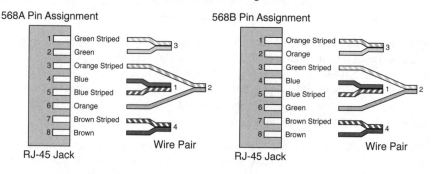

NOTE: For the Network+ exam, you should know that the Data Over Cable Service Interface Specification (DOCSIS) is an international standard that enables the transmission of high-bandwidth data over an existing coaxial cable TV system. Users who receive network services from their cable providers are likely using a DOCSIS cable modem as part of the delivery for the services. DOCSIS allows cable companies to use the existing hybrid fiber and coaxial (HFC) network to offer its customers Internet access.

 Video: Ethernet and Wired Standards Overview

Refer to the Digital Study Guide to view this video.

Wireless Standards

Like Ethernet, wireless network capabilities continue to improve with each iteration of the IEEE 802.11 standard. The 802.11 wireless standards can differ in terms of speed, transmission ranges, and frequency used, but in terms of actual implementation they are similar. All standards can use either an infrastructure or ad hoc network design. For the Network+ exam, you should know the following variants of the 802.11 standard:

- **802.11**—The original 802.11 standard was ratified in 1997. It supported a direct-sequence spread spectrum (DSSS) and a frequency-hopping spread spectrum (FHSS) implementation, both of which operated in the 2.4GHz band. However, with supported speeds of 1Mbps and 2Mbps, the original 802.11 standard lacks sufficient bandwidth to meet the needs of today's WLANs.

- **802.11a**—Ratified in 1999, 802.11a supports speeds as high as 54Mbps. Other supported data rates are 6, 9, 12, 18, 24, 36, and 48Mbps. The 802.11a standard uses the 5GHz band and uses the orthogonal frequency-division multiplexing (OFDM) transmission method. 802.11a is not backward-compatible with 802.11b.

- **802.11b**—Ratified in 1999, 802.11b supports speeds of 5.5 and 11Mbps. The 802.11b standard uses the 2.4GHz band and uses the DSSS transmission method.

- **802.11g**—Ratified in 2003, 802.11g supports speeds as high as 54Mbps. As with 802.11a, other supported data rates include 6, 9, 12, 18, 24, 36, and 48Mbps. 802.11g works in the 2.4GHz band, which enables it to offer backward compatibility to 802.11b devices. 802.11g can use either the OFDM or the DSSS transmission method.

- **802.11n**—Ratified in 2009, 802.11n supports a wide variety of speeds, depending on its implementation. The speed of an 802.11n network could exceed 300Mbps. 802.11n can operate in the 2.4GHz band and/or the 5GHz band. 802.11n uses the OFDM transmission method. 802.11n uses a technology called multiple input multiple output (MIMO) with multiple antennas. Channel bonding is also supported, which bonds two adjacent 20MHz bands into one 40MHz channel for higher throughput.

- **802.11ac**—Ratified in 2013, 802.11ac is a 5GHz-only technology that builds on 802.11n. It can use wider channels in the 5GHz band, more spatial streams, and multi-user MIMO (MU-MIMO). 802.11ac with an 80MHz channel width can support 433Mbps per stream and multiple simultaneous streams.

Table 11-2 summarizes the IEEE 802.11 variants.

Table 11-2   802.11 Characteristics

Standard	Band	Maximum Bandwidth	Transmission Method	Maximum Range
802.11	2.4GHz	1Mbps or 2Mbps	DSSS or FHSS	20 m indoors/ 100 m outdoors
802.11a	5GHz	54Mbps	OFDM	35 m indoors/ 120 m outdoors
802.11b	2.4GHz	11Mbps	DSSS	32 m indoors/ 140 m outdoors
802.11g	2.4GHz	54Mbps	OFDM or DSSS	32 m indoors/ 140 m outdoors
802.11n	2.4GHz or 5GHz (or both)	> 300Mbps (with channel bonding)	OFDM	70 m indoors/ 250 m outdoors
802.11ac	5GHz	> 3Gbps (with MU-MIMO and several antennas)	OFDM	Similar to 802.11n operating at 5GHz

Video: Wireless Standards Overview

Refer to the Digital Study Guide to view this video.

Activity: Compare 802.3 and 802.11 Networks

Refer to the Digital Study Guide to complete this activity.

Study Resources

For today's exam topics, refer to the following resources for more study.

Resource	Location	Topic
Primary Resources		
Certification Guide	4	Principles of Ethernet
	8	WLAN Standards
Video Course	6	EIA/TIA 568 Standards
		Ethernet Standards
Exam Cram	7	General Media Considerations
		Comparing and Contrasting LAN Technologies
	8	802.11 Wireless Standards
Supplemental Resources		
Lab Simulator	8	Matching Wireless Standards and Terminology
		Wireless Security Terminology
Flash Cards	22	Wireless Standards
		Wired Standards
Quick Reference	22	Wireless Standards
		Wired Standards

 Check Your Understanding

Refer to the Digital Study Guide to take a 10-question quiz covering the content of this day.

Implement Policies, Procedures, and Safety Practices

CompTIA Network+ N10-006 Exam Topics

- 5.5 Given a scenario, implement the appropriate policies or procedures
- 5.6 Summarize safety practices

Key Topics

Today, we review the policies, procedures, and safety practices that are common to network monitoring, management, and maintenance.

Policies and Procedures

Policies and procedures are created by senior management. In smaller organizations, this could simply be the owner. Regardless the size of the organization, policies and procedures play an important role in networks. The following are the policies and procedures you should be aware of for the Network+ exam.

- **Security policies**—Drafting a solid security policy begins with a classification of business-critical assets. The policy should define what controls are necessary to maintain the security of systems, users, and networks. These assets include physical and intellectual property as well as the people who work for the organization. As an employment requirement, users should give consent to the company monitoring their actions and activities.

- **Acceptable use policies (AUP)**—Users should have a clear understanding of what activities are permitted or not allowed regarding network activity and system use. This includes policies for the installation and use of personal software or connecting devices, such as flash drives, to a company computer. Consequences for violation of the policy are clearly outlined.

- **Network policies**—Closely associated with AUPs are network policies, which specify the types of content and data that a particular user can access. Firewalls and authentication servers enforce the policy. In addition, bring-your-own-device (BYOD) policies define what employee-owned devices are allowed to connect to the organization's network. Mobile device management (MDM) and mobile application management (MAM) systems can be used to help organizations make sure those devices adhere to the network policy.

- **Standard business documents**—Standard business documents and their commonly used acronyms are listed next:

    - **Service level agreement (SLA)**—An SLA is a commitment between two parties to deliver a certain level of service. SLAs are common between ISPs and their WAN customers.

    - **Memorandum of understanding (MOU)**—An MOU can be used to establish an agreement between two or more parties prior to, or in lieu of, a formal agreement. It generally lacks one or more legal elements that would make it a binding contract.

    - **Master service agreement (MSA)**—An MSA is used when two or more parties agree that they will enter a relationship that will require additional, future transactions. Those future transactions are made easier by the MSA stipulations.

    - **Statement of work (SOW)**—An SOW is effectively the legal equivalent of a contract between an organization and a vendor. The SOW specifies the work to be done, a timeline for deliverables, and the price for the work.

Safety Policies

Network administrators and the companies they work for are responsible for implementing appropriate safety policies to protect people and equipment. The following are the safety policies you should be aware of for the Network+ exam:

- **Electrical safety**—Electrical systems should have proper grounding, and devices connecting into that electrical system should use the proper and approved cabling for the power. A dedicated ground, or isolated ground, has only the one outlet connected to it so that a spike sent to ground from one device does not adversely affect another device. In addition, surge protectors, uninterruptable power supplies (UPS), and power conditioners should be installed to guard against power outages that can damage or destroy computer equipment.

- **ESD (electrostatic discharge)**—ESD will permanently damage integrated circuitry. You should always wear a properly grounded ESD wrist strap whenever you open a computer case or networking device.

- **Installation safety**—Safety should be the number-one priority when network devices, equipment, or systems are installed. Policies should be in place to protect both the people and the equipment. Place equipment in appropriate spaces and follow all the manufacturer's installation guidelines. If lifting heavy boxes or equipment, be sure to bend at the hips when lifting and get enough people to assist to keep from anyone getting hurt. Rack installation should be done in such a way that the racks will not tip over. The placement of network devices, cables, and systems should be done in such a way that they don't pose a hazard, including tripping issues. Proper training should be done to ensure safety when any of these tools are being used.

- **MSDS (material safety data sheet)**—Any material and chemical that has the potential to harm the environment or people is required by the Environmental Protection Agency (EPA) to have an MSDS. MSDS information includes such things as boiling point, melting point, flash point, potential health risks, disposal recommendations, and the procedures to follow in the case of a spill or leak. MSDSs are prepared by vendors and delivered with the substance when it is received by the organization.

- **Emergency procedures**—Emergency procedures should be documented, periodically reviewed, and practiced. Some of the details might include an up-to-date building layout, fire escape plans, safety and emergency exits, emergency alert systems, and doors that either fail-open or fail-close in the event of a power failure. For example, an exit door should fail-open and fire doors should fail-close.

- **HVAC**—Procedures must be in place so that the heating, ventilation, and air-conditioning (HVAC) systems do not provide a conduit for the spread of contaminated air or fire throughout the rest of the building. In addition, the servicing of an HVAC unit might involve chemicals, gas, and electricity. Proper safety practices should be followed when servicing any portion of the HVAC.

- **Fire suppression**—Fire suppression is the act of extinguishing a fire as opposed to preventing the fire from happening. Fire suppression should not involve the use of water in wiring closets, data centers, or rooms with a lot of computing equipment. Water can damage the equipment and would probably be ineffective in suppressing an electrical fire. There are two types of fire-suppression systems:

  - **Fire extinguishers** are portable systems. They are classified as A, B, C, and D. Typically, a fire extinguisher will be multipurpose, meaning that it can satisfy more than one classification, as shown in Table 10-1. Personnel should be certified in the use of fire extinguishers, which includes the ability to demonstrate the PASS procedure. PASS is an acronym that stands for pull, aim, squeeze, and sweep.

Table 10-1   Fire Extinguisher Classifications

Type	Use	Retardant Composition
A	Wood and paper	Largely water or chemical
B	Flammable liquids	Fire-retardant chemicals
C	Electrical	Nonconductive chemicals
D	Flammable metals	Varies, type specific

  - **Fixed systems** are part of the building infrastructure and usually include fire detectors that trigger fire suppression systems. These systems use either water sprinklers or fire-suppressing gas. Data centers commonly use FM200 gas, which can displace the oxygen in the room, thereby smothering the fire.

Video: Policies, Procedures, and Safety Practices Overview

Refer to the Digital Study Guide to view this video.

Activity: Identify the Policy, Procedure, or Safety Practice

Refer to the Digital Study Guide to complete this activity.

Study Resources

For today's exam topics, refer to the following resources for more study.

Resource	Location	Topic
Primary Resources		
Certification Guide	11	Configuration Management
Exam Cram	6	Safety Practices
	11	Disaster Recovery
Video Course	16	Security and Compliance Requirements
	17	Safety Procedures
Supplemental Resources		
Flash Cards	22	Policies and Procedures
		Safety Practices
Quick Reference	22	Policies and Procedures
		Safety Practices

Check Your Understanding

Refer to the Digital Study Guide to take a 10-question quiz covering the content of this day.

Best Practices and Change Management

CompTIA Network+ N10-006 Exam Topics

- 5.7 Given a scenario, install and configure equipment in the appropriate location using best practices

- 5.8 Explain the basics of change management procedures

Key Topics

Today, we review best practices for installing and configuring equipment. Once the equipment is installed, changes to the equipment location or configuration should be managed through the use of documented procedures.

Best Practices

There are established best practices for operating networks. The following summarizes the best practices you should be aware of for the Network+ exam:

- **Wiring closets**—Networking equipment, servers, and cable management devices should be appropriately placed in a room that can be secured. In larger organizations with multiple floors or buildings, wiring closets are classified as intermediate distribution frames (IDFs) and the main distribution frame (MDF). IDFs normally contain patch panels, cable trays, and access layer switches. The patch panels terminate horizontal cable runs from end-user computer devices. Cable trays are used to keep the cables neat and organized as they enter and exit the IDF. Access layer switches provide user access to the rest of the internal network or connection to the MDF. The MDF is how an IDF connects to other IDFs. The MDF is also typically the place where outside telecommunication connections enter the building. Care should be taken to place devices in such a way as to provide adequate air flow and access to power.

- **Cable management**—Designing and troubleshooting large networks requires documentation about a network's existing cable infrastructure. Using cable trays, patch panels, and proper labeling can assist in troubleshooting when problems arise with physical connectivity. This documentation might include a physical network topology that indicates the location of patch panels as well as the sources and destinations of all cable runs. Cables should be clearly labeled with a consistent numbering system.

- **Power management**—Proper power management may include ensuring that you have some form of power redundancy. This could be as simple as an uninterruptable power supply (UPS) that provides power long enough to safely save data and power off systems. However, installing UPSs is only the beginning of a power management plan in larger organizations. These networks will mostly likely include power converters (which step the voltage down), power inverters (which step the power up), redundancy (should a circuit become unstable), and plenty of UPS devices.

- **Rack systems**—Even in small organizations, a 19-inch-wide rack system may be installed to support rack-mountable equipment. Rack monitoring systems and rack security systems can also be used to secure the devices that are being kept in the racks. The height of rack-mountable equipment is measured in rack units (U or RU). One rack unit is 1.75 inches. Access layer switches are typically 1U. The four main components of rack systems are as follows:

    - **Server rail racks**—These are the rails that hold the servers within the rack.

    - **Two-post racks**—As the name implies, the servers are attached to the rack system at two locations (one on each side).

    - **Four-post racks**—The servers are attached to the rack system at four locations (two on each side).

    - **Free-standing racks**—These can stand on their own and support the servers within, as opposed to being mounted to a wall.

- **Labeling**—The importance of accurate labeling becomes immediately clear when a network technician is attempting to troubleshoot a problem and cannot determine which cable is connected to a device. But labeling does not stop at cables. All important networking equipment and systems should be appropriately and accurately labeled. Be sure to label systems, ports, circuits, and patch panels and follow standard naming conventions.

Change Management

Change, especially in networking technology, is inevitable. For example, operating systems need to be regularly updated to protect against the latest threats as well as to take advantage of newer technologies. A network administrator should not simply download the latest updates and install them. Instead, a systematic method of change management should be employed. Change management is the process of identifying what needs to be done, obtaining authorization for the change, and documenting the change after it happens. For the Network+ exam, you should be aware of the following steps to effectively manage a change to the network:

Step 1.   **Document the reason for a change.**

This step requires justifying to those in charge (and to yourself) why you think a change is necessary. The process of documenting the reason will help you to think carefully about the benefits and costs associated with the change as well as provide the primary information for the next step.

Step 2.   **Change request.**

The change request formally documents the recommendation and could include one of more of the following: the reason for the change (documented in Step 1); potential impacts; cost estimations; a preliminary schedule recommendation; rollback procedures for configured equipment in case the change fails; and a list of those who need to be notified.

Step 3.   **Approval process.**

The change request is then evaluated by a senior staff to determine whether and when the request will be granted. The approval can come from a single person, such as the network administrator, or from a formal committee based on the size of the company and the scope of the change being requested.

Step 4.   **Maintenance window.**

The approval process will probably include a timeframe in which you are authorized to make the change. For example, an upgrade to routers would probably be done during the off-peak hours, such as at night when most of the workforce is away from their desks. Once the maintenance window is firmly established, make the change according to plan.

Step 5.   **Notification of change.**

Those affected by a change should be notified after the change has taken place. For example, network technicians should know that a router's operating system has been updated. The notification should include resources for training, if necessary, and who to contact with any questions.

Step 6.   **Document the changes made.**

The last step is to document what was done. Documentation should include the physical location of the equipment impacted by the change as well as any updates to device configurations. For major upgrades or installations, this might include a "lessons learned" document that will provide guidance for future, similar changes. If necessary, update the change management procedures as required to address any unforeseen or unique circumstance encountered during the change process.

 Video: Best Practices and Change Management Overview

Refer to the Digital Study Guide to view this video.

 Activity: Order the Steps in the CompTIA Change Management Process

Refer to the Digital Study Guide to complete this activity.

Study Resources

For today's exam topics, refer to the following resources for more study.

Resource	Location	Topic
Primary Resources		
Certification Guide	11	Configuration Management
Exam Cram	6	Installing and Configuring Equipment
	7	Components of Wiring Distribution
	9	Documentation Management
Video Course	17	Network Best Practices
Supplemental Resources		
Flash Cards	22	General Best Practices
Quick Reference	22	General Best Practices

Check Your Understanding

Refer to the Digital Study Guide to take a 10-question quiz covering the content of this day.

Implement Ports and Protocols

CompTIA Network+ N10-006 Exam Topics

- 5.9 Compare and contrast the following ports and protocols
- 5.10 Given a scenario, configure and apply the appropriate ports and protocols

Key Topics

Today, we spend some time on the transport protocols: TCP and UDP. Then we review the ports and protocols called out in the Network+ exam topics.

Transport Protocols: TCP and UDP

Recall that the Transmission Control Protocol (TCP) is a connection-oriented protocol, meaning it provides methods to reliably deliver data across a network. In contrast, the User Datagram Protocol (UDP) is an connectionless, unreliable protocol used to send data that does not require or need error recovery. Table 8-1 lists the main features supported by the transport protocols. The first item is supported by TCP and UDP. The remaining items are supported only by TCP.

Table 8-1   TCP/IP Transport Layer Features

Function	Description
Multiplexing using ports	Function that allows receiving hosts to choose the correct application for which the data is destined, based on the destination port number.
Error recovery (reliability)	Process of numbering and acknowledging data with Sequence and Acknowledgment header fields.
Flow control using windowing	Process that uses a sliding window size that is dynamically agreed upon by the two end devices at various points during the virtual connection. The window size, represented in bytes, is the maximum amount of data the source will send before receiving an acknowledgement from the destination.
Connection establishment and termination	Process used to initialize port numbers and Sequence and Acknowledgment fields.
Ordered data transfer and data segmentation	Continuous stream of bytes from an upper-layer process that is "segmented" for transmission and delivered to upper-layer processes at the receiving device, with the bytes in the same order.

TCP and UDP Headers

TCP provides error recovery, but to do so, it consumes more bandwidth and uses more processing cycles than UDP. TCP and UDP rely on IP for end-to-end delivery. TCP is concerned with providing services to the applications of the sending and receiving computers. To provide all these services, TCP uses a variety of fields in its header. Figure 8-1 shows the fields of the TCP header.

Figure 8-1   TCP Header

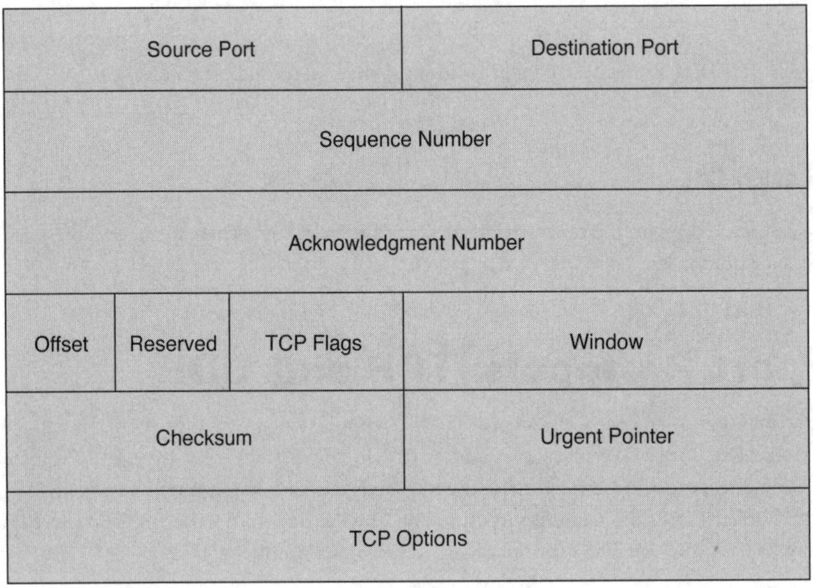

Source Port		Destination Port	
Sequence Number			
Acknowledgment Number			
Offset	Reserved	TCP Flags	Window
Checksum		Urgent Pointer	
TCP Options			

UDP is a connectionless, unreliable protocol because it provides no mechanisms for managing data streams. The UDP segment's header simply contains source and destination port numbers, a UDP checksum, and the segment length, as shown in Figure 8-2.

Figure 8-2   UDP Header

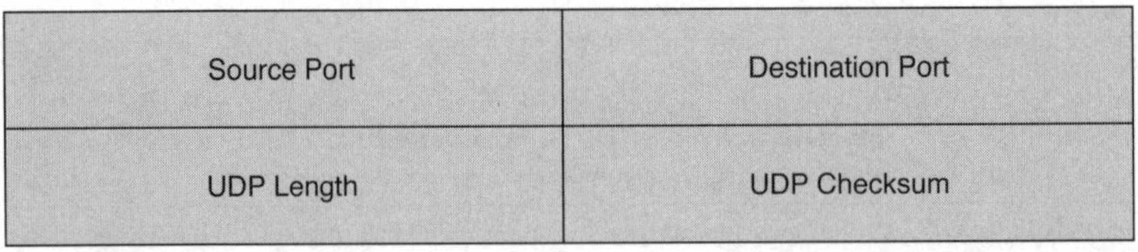

Source Port	Destination Port
UDP Length	UDP Checksum

Error Recovery

Also known as reliability, error recovery is provided by TCP during data transfer sessions between two end devices that have established a connection. The Sequence and Acknowledgment fields in the TCP header are used to track every byte of data transferred and ensure that missing bytes are retransmitted.

In Figure 8-3, the Acknowledgment field sent by the web client (4000) implies the next byte to be received; this is called *positive acknowledgement*.

Figure 8-3   TCP Acknowledgment Without Errors

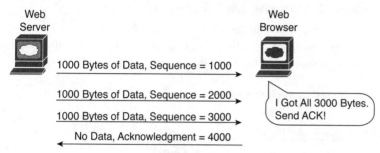

Figure 8-4 depicts the same scenario, except now we have some errors. The second TCP segment was lost in transmission. Therefore, the web client replies with an ACK field set to 2000. This is called a positive acknowledgement with retransmission (PAR), because the web client is requesting some of the data be retransmitted. The web server will now resend data starting at segment 2000. In this way, lost data is recovered.

Figure 8-4   TCP Acknowledgment with Errors

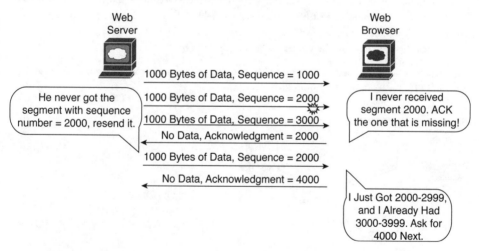

Although not shown, the web server also sets a retransmission timer, awaiting acknowledgment, just in case the acknowledgment is lost or all transmitted segments are lost. If that timer expires, the web server sends all segments again.

Flow Control

Flow control is handled by TCP through a process called *windowing*. The two end devices negotiate the window size when initially establishing the connection; then they dynamically renegotiate window size during the life of the connection, increasing its size until it reaches the maximum window size of 65,535 bytes or until errors occur. Window size is specified in the Window field of the TCP header. After sending the amount of data specified in the window size, the source must receive an acknowledgment before sending the next window size of data.

Connection Establishment and Termination

Connection establishment is the process of initializing Sequence and Acknowledgment fields and agreeing on port numbers and window size. The three-way connection-establishment phase shown in Figure 8-5 must occur before data transfer can proceed.

Figure 8-5   TCP Connection Establishment

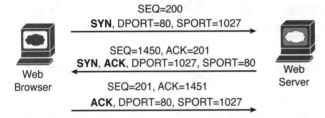

In the figure, DPORT and SPORT are the destination and source ports. SEQ is the sequence number. In bold are SYN and ACK, which each represent a 8-bit flag in the TCP header used to signal connection establishment. TCP initializes the Sequence Number and Acknowledgment Number fields to any number that fits into the 4-byte fields. The initial sequence number is a random 32-bit number generated with each new transmission. The acknowledgment number is received back and increments the sender's sequence number by 1.

After data transfer is complete, a four-way termination sequence occurs that uses an additional flag, called the FIN bit, as shown in Figure 8-6.

Figure 8-6   TCP Connection Termination

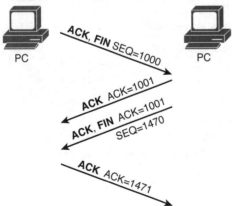

UDP

TCP establishes and terminates connections between endpoints, whereas UDP does not. Therefore, UDP is called a *connectionless protocol*. It provides no reliability, no windowing, and no reordering of the data. However, UDP does provide data transfer and multiplexing using port numbers, and it does so with fewer bytes of overhead and less processing than TCP. Applications that use UDP are ones that can trade the possibility of some data loss for less delay, such as VoIP. Figure 8-7 compares the length and content of the TCP and UDP headers.

Figure 8-7   TCP and UDP Headers

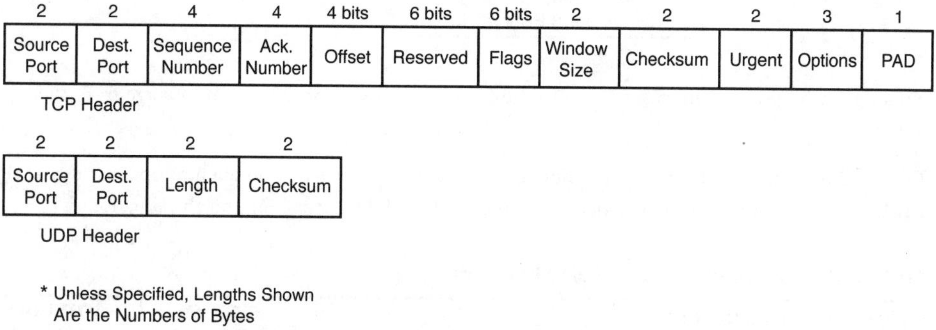

2	2	4	4	4 bits	6 bits	6 bits	2	2	2	3	1
Source Port	Dest. Port	Sequence Number	Ack. Number	Offset	Reserved	Flags	Window Size	Checksum	Urgent	Options	PAD

TCP Header

2	2	2	2
Source Port	Dest. Port	Length	Checksum

UDP Header

* Unless Specified, Lengths Shown
 Are the Numbers of Bytes

Video: TCP Connection Establishment and Termination

Refer to the Digital Study Guide to view this video.

Port Numbers

Notice in Figure 8-7 that the first two fields of the TCP and UDP headers are the source and destination ports. Port numbers provide TCP and UDP a way to multiplex multiple applications on the same computer.

Source ports are usually dynamically assigned by TCP and UDP from the range starting with 1024 and going up to a maximum of 65535. Port numbers below 1024 are reserved for well-known applications. For example, Hypertext Transfer Protocol (HTTP) commonly uses port 80. Figure 8-8 shows an example of source and destination ports.

Figure 8-8   Source and Destination Port Numbers Example

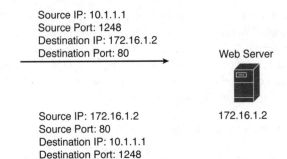

Client

10.1.1.1

Source IP: 10.1.1.1
Source Port: 1248
Destination IP: 172.16.1.2
Destination Port: 80

Source IP: 172.16.1.2
Source Port: 80
Destination IP: 10.1.1.1
Destination Port: 1248

Web Server

172.16.1.2

Notice that the port numbers switch from source to destination for the return message from the web server.

Table 8-2 lists some of the more common application layer protocols and applications that use TCP and UPD for transport. Some protocols may use TCP or UDP depending on the situation.

Table 8-2   Protocols and Port Numbers

Protocol	Description	TCP Port	UDP Port
FTP	File Transfer Protocol: Transfers files with a remote host (typically requires authentication of user credentials)	20 and 21	
SFTP	Secure FTP: Provides FTP file-transfer service over a SSH connection	22	
SCP	Secure Copy: Provides a secure file-transfer service over a SSH connection and offers a file's original date and time information, which is not available with FTP	22	
SSH	Secure Shell: Used to securely connect to a remote host (typically via a terminal emulator)	22	
Telnet	Telnet: Used to connect to a remote host (typically via a terminal emulator)	23	
rsh	Remote Shell: Allows commands to be executed on a computer from a remote user	514	
DNS	Domain Name System: Resolves domain names to corresponding IP addresses	53	53
NetBIOS	Network Basic Input/Output System: Provides network communication services for LANs that use NetBIOS	139	137, 138
SMB	Server Message Block: Used to share files, printers, and other network resources	445	
TFTP	Trivial File Transfer Protocol: Transfers files with a remote host (does not require authentication of user credentials)		69

Protocol	Description	TCP Port	UDP Port
DHCP	Dynamic Host Configuration Protocol: Dynamically assigns IP address information (for example, IP address, subnet mask, DNS server's IP address, and default gateway's IP address) to a network device		67, 68
HTTP	Hypertext Transfer Protocol: Retrieves content from a web server	80	
HTTPS	Hypertext Transfer Protocol Secure: Used to securely retrieve content from a web server	443	
SMTP	Simple Mail Transfer Protocol: Used for sending email	25	
POP3	Post Office Protocol Version 3: Retrieves email from an email server	110	
IMAP	Internet Message Access Protocol: Retrieves email from an email server	143	
NNTP	Network News Transport Protocol: Supports the posting and reading of articles on Usenet news servers	119	
NTP	Network Time Protocol: Used by a network device to synchronize its clock with a time server (NTP server)		123
SNTP	Simple Network Time Protocol: Supports time synchronization among network devices, similar to Network Time Protocol (NTP), although SNTP uses a less complex algorithm in its calculation and is slightly less accurate than NTP		123
LDAP	Lightweight Directory Access Protocol: Provides directory services (for example, a user directory including username, password, email, and phone number information) to network clients	389	
RTSP	Real-Time Streaming Protocol: Communicates with a media server (for example, a video server) and controls the playback of the server's media files	554	554
RDP	Remote Desktop Protocol: A Microsoft protocol that allows a user to view and control the desktop of a remote computer	3389	
SNMP	Simple Network Management Protocol: Used to monitor and manage network devices		161
SNMP Trap	Simple Network Management Protocol Trap: A notification sent from an SNMP agent to an SNMP manager	162	162
SIP	Session Initiation Protocol: Used to create and end sessions for one or more media connections, including Voice over IP calls	5061	5060
MGCP	Media Gateway Control Protocol: Used as a call control and communication protocol for Voice over IP networks		2427, 2727
H.323	H.323: A signaling protocol that provides multimedia communications over a network	1720	
RTP	Real-time Transport Protocol: Used for delivering media-based data over networks, such as Voice over IP	5004, 5005	5004, 5005

Video: Ports, Protocols, and Applications Overview

Refer to the Digital Study Guide to view this video.

Activity: Identify the Protocol

Refer to the Digital Study Guide to complete this activity.

Study Resources

For today's exam topics, refer to the following resources for more study.

Resource	Location	Topic
Primary Resources		
Certification Guide	2	Common Application Protocols in the TCP/IP Stack
Exam Cram	2	Protocols
Video Course	1	IP, ICMP, UDP, and TCP
		Ports and Protocols
Supplemental Resources		
Lab Simulator	2	Matching Well-Known Port Numbers
		TCP/IP Protocols and Their Functions
		Application Layer Network Server Descriptions
Flash Cards	22	Ports and Protocols
Quick Reference	22	Ports and Protocols

Check Your Understanding

Refer to the Digital Study Guide to take a 10-question quiz covering the content of this day.

Troubleshooting Methodology

CompTIA Network+ N10-006 Exam Topics

- 4.1 Given a scenario, implement the following network troubleshooting methodology

Key Topics

Troubleshooting is one of the five domains in the Network+ exam. At 24 percent exam coverage, it is the largest domain. Therefore, we will spend the last week reviewing troubleshooting. Today, we review CompTIA's seven-step troubleshooting methodology, which is as follows:

1. Identify the problem.

2. Establish a theory of probable cause.

3. Test the theory to determine cause.

4. Establish a plan of action to resolve the problem and identify potential effects.

5. Implement the solution or escalate as necessary.

6. Verify full system functionality and if applicable implement preventative measures.

7. Document findings, actions, and outcomes.

Identify the Problem

The first step in troubleshooting is to identify the problem, which includes the following list of substeps. Let's use a scenario to provide an example of questions an administrator might ask.

Scenario: A user calls the help desk complaining of network connectivity issues.

- **Test connectivity**—Test connectivity to the loopback address on your system by pinging the reserved loopback IPv4 address 127.0.0.1 or the local IPv6 address ::1. This tests the TCP/IP protocol stack installed on your device.

- **Gather information**—Ask the user if he changed anything on his device since the last time he was able to connect. For example, did he change any settings? Update any software? Install new software?

- **Duplicate the problem, if possible**—Can you repeat the connectivity issue from the user's device?

- **Question users**—Are other users with similar access rights and in the same location having the same problem? If so, you know the problem is not isolated to the user.

- **Identify symptoms**—What services are the user able to access, if any? Can the user open and work in standalone applications that do not require network connectivity?

- **Determine whether anything has changed**—Have any configuration or device changes occurred over the past couple of days?

- **Approach multiple problems individually**—When questioning other users, do they report additional issues that are unrelated to the incident you are investigating? Create separate tickets for these issues to be pursued separately from the issue currently under investigation.

Establish a Theory

If you have a lot of experience troubleshooting, the cause of the problem might be obvious. Be sure to take a moment and question that assumption. Could anything else be causing the issue?

Consider multiple approaches to establishing a theory:

- **Top-down approach**—You could start from the top of the OSI model at the application layer. Open a web browser and see what happens. Open several web browsers. Check other applications that depend on the network.

- **Bottom-up approach**—You could start from the bottom of the OSI model at the physical or data link layer. Check the link lights on the computer's NIC or at the switch port.

- **Divide-and-conquer approach**—You could start right in the middle of the OSI model. Open a command prompt and investigate the PC's setting with **ipconfig** and verify the IP addressing information is accurate. Ping a website to test Layer 3 connectivity and DNS services.

Test the Theory

Once you have an idea of what caused the problem, determine the next steps that are necessary to resolve it. Does a NIC need to be replaced? Is there a setting that needs to be adjusted?

If your theory can't be supported with evidence, return to the previous step and attempt to establish another theory. The issue may be beyond your capabilities. Or you may not have rights to investigate certain network devices. If so, escalate the issue to someone who can help you.

Establish a Plan of Action

In some situations, it may seem that the plan of action is simple. For example, maybe the port that the PC connects to is disabled. The action plan is to re-enable the port. However, why did the setting get changed? A plan of action should include steps to prevent the issue from reoccurring. Maybe you discovered during your investigation that the PC's network cable was used temporarily to connect a personal laptop to the network.

Implement the Solution or Escalate

With a plan of action in hand, you should be able to either implement the solution or escalate the issue to someone with the appropriate rights. For example, although you know that the issue was caused by a rogue device being attached to the switch port, you may not have the administrative rights to log in to the switch and re-enable the port.

Verify the Solution and Implement Preventative Measures

After the plan of action has been executed, verify that the solution resolved the problem. For example, can the user now get back on the Internet or access other network resources? Preventive measures might include educating the user on company security policies.

Document Findings, Actions, and Outcomes

Normally, you will be using some type of ticketing system to document all the steps taken to address the issues. Once the issue is resolved and verified, document your findings and the actions in the help ticket. Depending on the issue, additional reports may be required. For example, if a security violation is considered serious enough by your organization, you may be required to fill out a report for human resources.

Video: CompTIA Troubleshooting Methodology

Refer to the Digital Study Guide to view this video.

Activity: Order the Steps in the CompTIA Troubleshooting Methodology

Refer to the Digital Study Guide to complete this activity.

Study Resources

For today's exam topics, refer to the following resources for more study.

Resource	Location	Topic
Primary Resources		
Certification Guide	13	Troubleshooting Basics
Video Course	18	7-Step Troubleshooting Methodology
Exam Cram	12	Troubleshooting Steps and Procedures

Resource	Location	Topic
Supplemental Resources		
Lab Simulator	13	Reordering Troubleshooting Steps
Flash Cards	18	Network Troubleshooting Methodologies
Quick Reference	18	Network Troubleshooting Methodologies

 ## Check Your Understanding

Refer to the Digital Study Guide to take a 10-question quiz covering the content of this day.

Troubleshooting Tools

CompTIA Network+ N10-006 Exam Topics

- 4.2 Given a scenario, analyze and interpret the output of troubleshooting tools

Key Topics

Today, we focus on the tools commonly used to troubleshoot network issues. These tools include command-line tools, hardware tools, and software tools. For command-line tools, I encourage you to review these commands, whenever possible, on your own computer. Review the different command switches and be able to interpret the output. The Lab Simulator in the "Study Resources" section is particularly useful today because there are several activities that review important tools.

Command-Line Tools

There are a handful of very useful commands you can enter at the command line for various operating systems. Table 6-1 lists each command you should know for the Network+ exam.

Table 6-1   **Command-Line Tools**

Tool	Description
ipconfig	Used to view and renew TCP/IP configuration on a Windows system.
ifconfig	Used to view TCP/IP configuration on a UNIX, Linux, or Mac OS X system.
tracert traceroute	Used to track the path a packet takes as it travels across a network. Whereas **tracert** is used on Windows systems, **traceroute** is used on UNIX, Linux, and Mac OS X systems.
tracert -6 traceroute6 traceroute -6	Performs the same function as **tracert** and **traceroute**, but using the IPv6 protocol in place of IPv4.
ping	Used to test connectivity between two devices on a network with IPv4.
ping6 ping -6	Used to test connectivity between two devices on a network using the IPv6 protocol in place of IPv4.
pathping	A Windows-based utility that combines the functionality of **ping** and **tracert** to test connectivity between two devices on a network.
arp	Used to view and work with the IP address to MAC address resolution cache.
netstat	Used to view the current TCP/IP connections on a system.
nbtstat	Used to view statistics related to NetBIOS name resolution and to see information about current NetBIOS over TCP/IP (NBT) connections.

Tool	Description
nslookup dig	Used to perform manual DNS lookups. **nslookup** can be used on Windows, UNIX, Mac OS X, and Linux systems. **dig** can be used on UNIX, Linux, and Mac OS X systems.
show mac-address- table	A Cisco-specific command used to show the MAC address lookup table.

The ipconfig **Command**

The **ipconfig** or **ifconfig** command can be used to view the TCP/IP configuration settings on a device. For the Windows version, use the **/all** switch to view a full listing of the information, as shown in Example 6-1.

Example 6-1   Sample ipconfig /all **Output**

```
C:\> ipconfig /all
<some output omitted>


Windows IP Configuration

    Host Name . . . . . . . . . . . . : Allan-PC
    Primary Dns Suffix  . . . . . . . :
    Node Type . . . . . . . . . . . . : Hybrid
    IP Routing Enabled. . . . . . . . : No
    WINS Proxy Enabled. . . . . . . . : No


Ethernet adapter Local Area Connection:

    Connection-specific DNS Suffix  . :
    Description . . . . . . . . . . . : Realtek PCIe GBE Family Controller
    Physical Address. . . . . . . . . : F0-4D-A2-DD-A7-B2
    DHCP Enabled. . . . . . . . . . . : Yes
    Autoconfiguration Enabled . . . . : Yes
    Link-local IPv6 Address . . . . . : fe80::449f:c2:de06:ebad%10(Preferred)
    IPv4 Address. . . . . . . . . . . : 10.10.10.10(Preferred)
    Subnet Mask . . . . . . . . . . . : 255.255.255.0
    Lease Obtained. . . . . . . . . . : Wednesday, September 30, 2015 10:11:47 PM
    Lease Expires . . . . . . . . . . : Monday, October 05, 2015 10:11:53 AM
    Default Gateway . . . . . . . . . : 10.10.10.1
    DHCP Server . . . . . . . . . . . : 10.10.10.1
    DHCPv6 IAID . . . . . . . . . . . : 250629538
    DHCPv6 Client DUID. . . . . . . . : 00-01-00-01-15-77-3B-02-F0-4D-A2-DD-A7-B2
    DNS Servers . . . . . . . . . . . : 10.10.10.1
    NetBIOS over Tcpip. . . . . . . . : Enabled
```

```
Ethernet adapter VirtualBox Host-Only Network:

   Connection-specific DNS Suffix  . :
   Description . . . . . . . . . . : VirtualBox Host-Only Ethernet Adapter
   Physical Address. . . . . . . . : 08-00-27-00-70-A1
   DHCP Enabled. . . . . . . . . . : No
   Autoconfiguration Enabled . . . . : Yes
   Link-local IPv6 Address . . . . . : fe80::3158:9cf2:76cf:edd4%15(Preferred)
   IPv4 Address. . . . . . . . . . : 192.168.56.1(Preferred)
   Subnet Mask . . . . . . . . . . : 255.255.255.0
   Default Gateway . . . . . . . . :
   DHCPv6 IAID . . . . . . . . . . : 419954727
   DHCPv6 Client DUID. . . . . . . : 00-01-00-01-15-77-3B-02-F0-4D-A2-DD-A7-B2
   DNS Servers . . . . . . . . . . : fec0:0:0:ffff::1%1
                                     fec0:0:0:ffff::2%1
                                     fec0:0:0:ffff::3%1
   NetBIOS over Tcpip. . . . . . . : Enabled

C:\>
```

The tracert Command

The trace utility uses ICMP echo packets to report back information at each hop in the router. The first three packets sent have a hop count of one. The first Layer 3 device in the path to the destination decrements the hop count to zero and sends back a "time exceeded" message. The originating device displays the milliseconds it took to receive each response, which is called the round trip timer (RTT). Then the source sends out three more packets, this time with a hop count of two. The second Layer 3 device in the path responds like the first device. The process continues until the final destination responds or the trace utility times out. Example 6-2 shows sample output for successfully tracing the route to comptia.org on a Windows system.

Example 6-2   Sample tracert Output

```
C:\> tracert -d comptia.org

Tracing route to comptia.org [198.134.5.6]
over a maximum of 30 hops:

  1    32 ms    33 ms    33 ms   10.101.9.2
  2    33 ms    43 ms    32 ms   72.163.16.185
  3    33 ms    31 ms    32 ms   72.163.16.50
  4    33 ms    33 ms    34 ms   72.163.0.78
  5    34 ms    34 ms    34 ms   72.163.0.26
  6    33 ms    35 ms    34 ms   157.130.134.189
  7     *        *        *      Request timed out.
  8    35 ms    34 ms    36 ms   204.255.168.202
```

```
  9    64 ms    63 ms    63 ms  207.88.14.238
 10    59 ms    59 ms    60 ms  216.156.0.162
 11    61 ms    62 ms    62 ms  216.55.11.62
 12    61 ms    59 ms    60 ms  198.134.5.6

Trace complete.

C:\>
```

Notice that the device at the seventh hop timed out. This could be for any number of reasons. Most likely, the device is configured to not reply to ICMP echo requests. Also notice that the **-d** switch was used to generate output that does not include the host name of the devices. All the command switches for the Windows **tracert** command are shown in Example 6-3.

Example 6-3   Windows tracert **Command Switches**

```
C:\> tracert /?

Usage: tracert [-d] [-h maximum_hops] [-j host-list] [-w timeout]
               [-R] [-S srcaddr] [-4] [-6] target_name

Options:
    -d                      Do not resolve addresses to hostnames.
    -h maximum_hops         Maximum number of hops to search for target.
    -j host-list            Loose source route along host-list (IPv4-only).
    -w timeout              Wait timeout milliseconds for each reply.
    -R                      Trace round-trip path (IPv6-only).
    -S srcaddr              Source address to use (IPv6-only).
    -4                      Force using IPv4.
    -6                      Force using IPv6.

C:\>
```

The ping **Command**

By now, you should be very familiar with the **ping** utility, shown in Example 6-4. The **ping** command tests Layer 3 connectivity between the source and destination.

Example 6-4   Sample ping **Output**

```
C:\> ping comptia.org

Pinging comptia.org [198.134.5.6] with 32 bytes of data:
Reply from 198.134.5.6: bytes=32 time=102ms TTL=112
Reply from 198.134.5.6: bytes=32 time=60ms TTL=112
Reply from 198.134.5.6: bytes=32 time=62ms TTL=112
```

```
Reply from 198.134.5.6: bytes=32 time=60ms TTL=112


Ping statistics for 198.134.5.6:
    Packets: Sent = 4, Received = 4, Lost = 0 (0% loss),
Approximate round trip times in milli-seconds:
    Minimum = 60ms, Maximum = 102ms, Average = 71ms


C:\>
```

You should also be familiar with the more common **ping** command switches, which are shown for the Windows operating system in Example 6-5.

Example 6-5   Windows ping **Command Switches**

```
C:\> ping /?
<some output omitted>


Options:
    -t              Ping the specified host until stopped.
                    To see statistics and continue - type Control-Break;
                    To stop - type Control-C.
    -a              Resolve addresses to hostnames.
    -n count        Number of echo requests to send.
    -r count        Record route for count hops (IPv4-only).
    -s count        Timestamp for count hops (IPv4-only).
    -w timeout      in milliseconds to wait for each reply.
    -6              Force using IPv6.


C:\>
```

The **ping** command is an important tool for verifying and troubleshooting connectivity. If you do not have connectivity to a certain destination, you can use the following method to test connectivity starting with your device:

1. Test connectivity to the loopback address on your system by pinging the reserved loopback IPv4 address 127.0.0.1 or the local IPv6 address ::1. This tests the TCP/IP protocol stack installed on your device.

2. Test connectivity to the IP address assigned to your NIC. This tests the functionality of your NIC.

3. Test connectivity to the default gateway. The IP address is found using the **ipconfig** command. This tests connectivity within your local network.

4. Finally, test connectivity to a well-known website such as google.com, cisco.com, or comptia.org. This will test connectivity to remote networks.

Windows pathping Command

Although useful, the **tracert** and **traceroute** commands do not necessarily convey latency in the path from source to destination. For example, suppose the fourth hop in the path reports an unusually high RTT value. This does not mean that the fourth device is responsible. Any of the other devices in the path to the fourth device could be experiencing a temporary high load. In addition, the fourth device could be configured with a policy or quality of service (QoS) prioritization that gives ICMP messages a lower priority.

Windows, therefore, provides the **pathping** command as a tool to better diagnose latency in the path. First, it quickly traces the route to the destination. Then, it sends 100 ICMP echo request packets (pings) to each hop in the path. As shown in Example 6-6, this can take several minutes depending on how many hops are in the path. However, the result is a much more accurate estimation of the RTT to each hop.

Example 6-6   Sample pathping Output

```
C:\> pathping -n google.com


Tracing route to google.com [2607:f8b0:4000:801::200e]
over a maximum of 30 hops:
  0   2001:420:c0cc:1001::116
  1   2001:420:c0cc::1
  2   2001:420:1000:2c::
  3   2001:420:1000:f::
  4   2001:420:1100:11::6
  5   2001:420:1100:a::
  6   2001:504:0:5:0:1:5169:1
  7   2001:4860::1:0:dd7
  8   2001:4860:0:1::15d9
  9   2607:f8b0:4000:801::200e


Computing statistics for 225 seconds...
            Source to Here   This Node/Link
Hop   RTT   Lost/Sent = Pct  Lost/Sent = Pct  Address
  0                                           2001:420:c0cc:1001::116
                             0/ 100 =   0%   |
  1   36ms  0/ 100 =   0%    0/ 100 =   0%    2001:420:c0cc::1
                             0/ 100 =   0%   |
  2   34ms  0/ 100 =   0%    0/ 100 =   0%    2001:420:1000:2c::
                             0/ 100 =   0%   |
  3   36ms  0/ 100 =   0%    0/ 100 =   0%    2001:420:1000:f::
                             0/ 100 =   0%   |
  4   41ms  0/ 100 =   0%    0/ 100 =   0%    2001:420:1100:11::6
                             0/ 100 =   0%   |
  5   34ms  0/ 100 =   0%    0/ 100 =   0%    2001:420:1100:a::
                             0/ 100 =   0%   |
```

```
6    37ms     0/ 100 =  0%     0/ 100 =  0%  2001:504:0:5:0:1:5169:1
                                0/ 100 =  0%  |
7    38ms     0/ 100 =  0%     0/ 100 =  0%  2001:4860::1:0:dd7
                                0/ 100 =  0%  |
8    37ms     0/ 100 =  0%     0/ 100 =  0%  2001:4860:0:1::15d9
                                0/ 100 =  0%  |
9    39ms     0/ 100 =  0%     0/ 100 =  0%  2607:f8b0:4000:801::200e

Trace complete.

C:\>
```

In Example 6-6, the **-n** command switch was used to display only the IP addresses. The rest of the **pathping** command switches are shown in Example 6-7.

Example 6-7   Windows pathping **Command Switches**

```
C:\> pathping

Usage: pathping [-g host-list] [-h maximum_hops] [-i address] [-n]
                [-p period] [-q num_queries] [-w timeout]
                [-4] [-6] target_name

Options:
    -g host-list     Loose source route along host-list.
    -h maximum_hops  Maximum number of hops to search for target.
    -i address       Use the specified source address.
    -n               Do not resolve addresses to hostnames.
    -p period        Wait period milliseconds between pings.
    -q num_queries   Number of queries per hop.
    -w timeout       Wait timeout milliseconds for each reply.
    -4               Force using IPv4.
    -6               Force using IPv6.

C:\>
```

The arp **Command**

The Address Resolution Protocol (ARP) is used by IPv4 devices to discover and map Layer 2 MAC addresses to Layer 3 IP addresses. In today's networks, devices are almost always attempting to communicate with a destination located on a remote network. Therefore, the device uses the local default gateway's MAC address for the next hop to the destination. However, if the device is looking for another device on the same network, such as a printer or a server, then it must send out an ARP request. ARP replies are stored in the ARP table. In Windows, you can view the current entries in the ARP table using the **arp -a** command, as shown in Example 6-8.

Example 6-8   Sample arp -a Output

```
C:\> arp -a


Interface: 10.10.10.10 --- 0xa
  Internet Address      Physical Address       Type
  10.10.10.1            e4-f4-c6-12-82-21      dynamic
  10.10.10.3            6c-ad-f8-17-25-32      dynamic
  10.10.10.4            c4-17-fe-8e-e3-fb      dynamic
  10.10.10.5            00-18-fe-2c-40-ca      dynamic
  10.10.10.255          ff-ff-ff-ff-ff-ff      static
  224.0.0.2             01-00-5e-00-00-02      static
  224.0.0.22            01-00-5e-00-00-16      static
  224.0.0.251           01-00-5e-00-00-fb      static
  224.0.0.252           01-00-5e-00-00-fc      static
  224.0.1.60            01-00-5e-00-01-3c      static
  239.255.255.250       01-00-5e-7f-ff-fa      static
  255.255.255.255       ff-ff-ff-ff-ff-ff      static


C:\>
```

Dynamic entries are added to the table automatically and can expire unless refreshed. Static entries never expire. Common Windows command switches for the **arp** command are shown in Example 6-9.

Example 6-9   Windows arp Command Switches

```
C:\> arp /?


Displays and modifies the IP-to-Physical address translation tables used by
address resolution protocol (ARP).

ARP -s inet_addr eth_addr [if_addr]
ARP -d inet_addr [if_addr]
ARP -a [inet_addr] [-N if_addr] [-v]


   -a          Displays current ARP entries by interrogating the current
               protocol data.  If inet_addr is specified, the IP and Physical
               addresses for only the specified computer are displayed.  If
               more than one network interface uses ARP, entries for each ARP
               table are displayed.
   -g          Same as -a.
   -v          Displays current ARP entries in verbose mode.  All invalid
               entries and entries on the loop-back interface will be shown.
   inet_addr   Specifies an internet address.
```

```
  -N if_addr      Displays the ARP entries for the network interface specified
                  by if_addr.
  -d              Deletes the host specified by inet_addr. inet_addr may be
                  wildcarded with * to delete all hosts.
  -s              Adds the host and associates the Internet address inet_addr
                  with the Physical address eth_addr.  The Physical address is
                  given as 6 hexadecimal bytes separated by hyphens. The entry
                  is permanent.
  eth_addr        Specifies a physical address.
  if_addr         If present, this specifies the Internet address of the
                  interface whose address translation table should be modified.
                  If not present, the first applicable interface will be used.
Example:
  > arp -s 157.55.85.212    00-aa-00-62-c6-09  .... Adds a static entry.
  > arp -a                                     .... Displays the arp table.

C:\>
```

The netstat Command

On Day 21, "Network Monitoring and Metrics," we briefly reviewed the **netstat -a** command, which is used to show open ports. Today, we look more closely at the various **netstat** command switches. One of the primary purposes of the **netstat** command is to display information about TCP connections. However, it can do more than that, as you shall see. The switches for the Windows **netstat** command are shown in Example 6-10.

Example 6-10 Windows netstat **Command Switches**

```
C:\> netstat /?

Displays protocol statistics and current TCP/IP network connections.

NETSTAT [-a] [-b] [-e] [-f] [-n] [-o] [-p proto] [-r] [-s] [-t] [interval]

  -a              Displays all connections and listening ports.
  -b              Displays the executable involved in creating each connection or
                  listening port. In some cases well-known executables host
                  multiple independent components, and in these cases the
                  sequence of components involved in creating the connection
                  or listening port is displayed. In this case the executable
                  name is in [] at the bottom, on top is the component it called,
                  and so forth until TCP/IP was reached. Note that this option
                  can be time-consuming and will fail unless you have sufficient
                  permissions.
  -e              Displays Ethernet statistics. This may be combined with the -s
                  option.
```

```
-f              Displays Fully Qualified Domain Names (FQDN) for foreign
                addresses.
-n              Displays addresses and port numbers in numerical form.
-o              Displays the owning process ID associated with each connection.
-p proto        Shows connections for the protocol specified by proto; proto
                may be any of: TCP, UDP, TCPv6, or UDPv6.  If used with the -s
                option to display per-protocol statistics, proto may be any of:
                IP, IPv6, ICMP, ICMPv6, TCP, TCPv6, UDP, or UDPv6.
-r              Displays the routing table.
-s              Displays per-protocol statistics.  By default, statistics are
                shown for IP, IPv6, ICMP, ICMPv6, TCP, TCPv6, UDP, and UDPv6;
                the -p option may be used to specify a subset of the default.
-t              Displays the current connection offload state.
interval        Redisplays selected statistics, pausing interval seconds
                between each display.  Press CTRL+C to stop redisplaying
                statistics.  If omitted, netstat will print the current
                configuration information once.


C:\>
```

Use the **-n** switch, as shown in Example 6-11, to display only the destination (foreign) IP addresses for current active TCP connections.

Example 6-11 Sample netstat -n **Output**

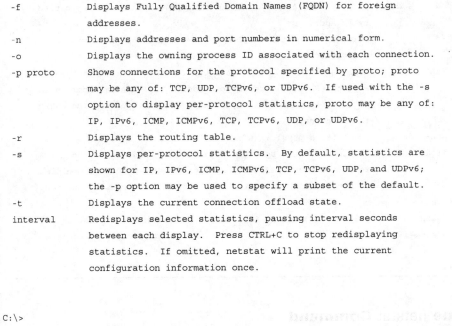

```
C:\> netstat -n
<some output omitted>
Active Connections

  Proto  Local Address          Foreign Address         State
  TCP    10.10.10.2:64479       72.163.19.133:443       ESTABLISHED
  TCP    10.89.1.137:53770      173.36.12.72:36611      ESTABLISHED
  TCP    10.89.1.137:53845      184.173.90.195:80       ESTABLISHED
  TCP    10.89.1.137:56984      173.36.12.72:36611      ESTABLISHED
  TCP    10.89.1.137:58794      173.36.12.72:6855       ESTABLISHED
  TCP    10.89.1.137:59246      173.36.9.135:10123      ESTABLISHED
  TCP    10.89.1.137:59447      107.21.210.221:443      CLOSE_WAIT
  TCP    10.89.1.137:59462      54.192.142.226:443      CLOSE_WAIT
  TCP    10.89.1.137:60338      74.112.184.85:443       CLOSE_WAIT
  TCP    10.89.1.137:60340      74.112.185.182:443      CLOSE_WAIT
  TCP    10.89.1.137:60341      74.112.185.182:443      CLOSE_WAIT
  TCP    127.0.0.1:19872        127.0.0.1:50694         ESTABLISHED
  TCP    127.0.0.1:50694        127.0.0.1:19872         ESTABLISHED
  TCP    127.0.0.1:50701        127.0.0.1:50702         ESTABLISHED
```

```
TCP    127.0.0.1:58445         127.0.0.1:62522         ESTABLISHED
TCP    127.0.0.1:62522         127.0.0.1:58445         ESTABLISHED

C:\>
```

Use the **-e** switch, as shown in Example 6-12, to display NIC statistics. A high error count could indicate that the NIC or cable connection is faulty.

Example 6-12 Sample netstat -e **Output**

```
C:\> netstat -e
Interface Statistics

                              Received              Sent

Bytes                       1550357356         240009539
Unicast packets               68209734          32904708
Non-unicast packets            1415070            460337
Discards                          7830              7830
Errors                               0                 0
Unknown protocols                    0

C:\>
```

Use the **-r** switch to show the routing table for a Windows PC, as shown in Example 6-13. The **route print** command generates the same output.

Example 6-13 Sample netstat -r **Output**

```
C:\> netstat -r
<some output omitted>

IPv4 Route Table
===========================================================================
Active Routes:
Network Destination        Netmask          Gateway       Interface  Metric
          0.0.0.0          0.0.0.0      10.10.10.1      10.10.10.10     10
       10.10.10.0    255.255.255.0       On-link       10.10.10.10    266
      10.10.10.10  255.255.255.255       On-link       10.10.10.10    266
     10.10.10.255  255.255.255.255       On-link       10.10.10.10    266
        127.0.0.0        255.0.0.0       On-link         127.0.0.1    306
        127.0.0.1  255.255.255.255       On-link         127.0.0.1    306
  127.255.255.255  255.255.255.255       On-link         127.0.0.1    306
     192.168.56.0    255.255.255.0       On-link      192.168.56.1    276
     192.168.56.1  255.255.255.255       On-link      192.168.56.1    276
```

```
    192.168.56.255  255.255.255.255           On-link       192.168.56.1   276
         224.0.0.0        240.0.0.0           On-link          127.0.0.1   306
         224.0.0.0        240.0.0.0           On-link       192.168.56.1   276
         224.0.0.0        240.0.0.0           On-link        10.10.10.10   266
   255.255.255.255  255.255.255.255           On-link          127.0.0.1   306
   255.255.255.255  255.255.255.255           On-link       192.168.56.1   276
   255.255.255.255  255.255.255.255           On-link        10.10.10.10   266
===============================================================================

C:\>
```

The nbtstat Command

The Windows **nbtstat** command can be used to view NetBIOS statistics. For example, to view NetBIOS names of other Windows PCs on the local network, use the **nbtstat -r** command, as shown in Example 6-14.

Example 6-14 Sample nbtstat -r **Output**

```
C:\> nbtstat -r
<some output omitted>


    NetBIOS Names Resolution and Registration Statistics
    ------------------------------------------------------


    Resolved By Broadcast     = 428
    Resolved By Name Server   = 0


    Registered By Broadcast   = 10
    Registered By Name Server = 0


    NetBIOS Names Resolved By Broadcast
---------------------------------------------
          BECKY-PC
          JAZMINE-PC
          VICTORIA-PC

C:\>
```

The nslookup Command

The **nslookup** command can be used to discover the IP address for a given domain name. You can enter the domain name as an argument to the **nslookup** command, such as **nslookup cisco.com**. Or you can enter the command by itself to begin a process to look up multiple IP addresses, as shown in Example 6-15.

Example 6-15 Sample nslookup **Output**

```
C:\> nslookup
Default Server:  UnKnown
Address:  10.10.10.1

> www.google.com
Server:  UnKnown
Address:  10.10.10.1

Non-authoritative answer:
Name:    www.google.com
Addresses:  2607:f8b0:4000:80a::2004
          24.155.92.51
          24.155.92.52
          24.155.92.49
          24.155.92.59
          24.155.92.56
          24.155.92.50
          24.155.92.58
          24.155.92.53
          24.155.92.48
          24.155.92.60
          24.155.92.61
          24.155.92.54
          24.155.92.57
          24.155.92.55
          24.155.92.47

> www.comptia.org
Server:  UnKnown
Address:  10.10.10.1

Non-authoritative answer:
Name:    www.comptia.org
Address:  198.134.5.6

> exit

C:\>
```

The Cisco show mac-address-table Command

Cisco switches use the **show mac-address-table** command to list all currently known MAC addresses for devices connected and the ports to which they are connected, as shown in Example 6-16.

Example 6-16 Sample show mac-address-table **Output**

```
S1# show mac-address-table
          Mac Address Table
-------------------------------------------

Vlan    Mac Address       Type       Ports
----    -----------       --------   -----

   1    0001.c933.9989    DYNAMIC    Fa0/2
   1    0002.4a4e.035b    DYNAMIC    Fa0/4
   1    0003.e43c.ae7a    DYNAMIC    Fa0/6
   1    0006.2a33.5402    DYNAMIC    Fa0/1
   1    000c.85cd.3c69    DYNAMIC    Fa0/1
   1    0060.5c90.2960    DYNAMIC    Fa0/3
   1    0090.21cc.522a    DYNAMIC    Fa0/5
S1#
```

 Video: Command-Line Tools Overview

Refer to the Digital Study Guide to view this video.

 Activity: Identify the Command-Line Tool

Refer to the Digital Study Guide to complete this activity.

Hardware and Software Tools

In addition to the command-line tools for gathering statistics, the network administrator is also armed with a variety of hardware and software tools for testing and tracking down the cause of issues. Table 6-2 summarizes these tools.

Table 6-2   Hardware and Software Tools

Tool	Description
Multimeter	A multimeter can check a variety of a cable's electrical characteristics, including resistance (in ohms), current (in amps), and voltage (in volts). A multimeter can be used in troubleshooting the power outlet in the user's office or to verify connectivity between pin 1 on one end of a patch cable and pin 1 on the other end.

Tool	Description
Cable tester	A cable tester can be used to test for shorts, improperly attached connectors, and other cable faults. Other similar tools include line testers and cable certifiers. A line tester can be used for any device that tests a media line. A cable certifier is a type of tester that enables you to certify cabling by testing it for speed and performance to see that the implementation will live up to the ratings.
Light meter	A light meter, such as an optical time domain reflectometer (OTDR), helps identify issues in a fiber-optic cable run. You can use a light meter to certify and troubleshoot fiber. A light source is placed on one end and the light meter is used at the opposite end to measure loss.
Toner probe	A toner probe allows you to place a tone generator at one end of a connection (for example, someone's office) and use a probe on a punch-down block to audibly detect to which pair of wires the tone generator is connected.
Speed test sites	There are many speed test services that can assist in verifying throughput from a local computer to an Internet site. One example is speedtest.net. Using sites such as this can assist when determining whether the overall connection to the Internet is slow or if it is just a specific site or server that is slow to respond.
Looking glass sites	Looking glass sites are servers that allow you to see routing information. The servers act as read-only portals allowing you to see information on ISP routers, including pings, traces, and Border Gateway Protocol (BGP) routing table information. To find a BGP looking glass site, use Google to search for "BGP looking glass."
Wi-Fi analyzer	This type of tool would be used as part of a wireless site survey after Wi-Fi has been implemented to create a heat map of the wireless airspace. Such devices can be used in the troubleshooting process to see where and how powerful RF signals are.
Protocol analyzer	A protocol analyzer can be a standalone device or software running on a laptop computer, such as Wireshark. You can use a protocol analyzer to capture traffic flowing through a network switch, using the port-mirroring feature of the switch. By examining the captured packets, you can discern the details of communication flows.

Study Resources

For today's exam topics, refer to the following resources for more study.

Resource	Location	Topic
Primary Resources		
Certification Guide	10	Command-Line Tools
	11	Maintenance Tools
Video Course	18	CLI Troubleshooting Utilities
Exam Cram	12	Working with Command-Line Utilities
		Networking Tools

Resource	Location	Topic
Supplemental Resources		
Lab Simulator	3	Using ARP to Discover a MAC Address
	5	Using ipconfig to Discover Network Settings
	13	Identifying Troubleshooting Commands to Use for Various Tasks
		Matching Command Output to Commands
		Verify a Data Link Connection from a Computer to a Network
		Using Extended ping (Command Switches) to Troubleshoot Connectivity
		Using NSLookup for DNS Troubleshooting
		Using ping to Troubleshoot Connectivity
		DNS Troubleshooting Simulation
Flash Cards	19	Network Troubleshooting Tools
Quick Reference	19	Network Troubleshooting Tools

Check Your Understanding

Refer to the Digital Study Guide to take a 10-question quiz covering the content of this day.

Troubleshoot Wireless Issues

CompTIA Network+ N10-006 Exam Topics

- 4.3 Given a scenario, troubleshoot and resolve common wireless issues

Key Topics

Today, our focus is to review the myriad issues that can occur in the implementation and operation of wireless LANs (WLANs). These issues are divided into two broad categories: transmission issues and configuration issues.

Wireless Transmission Issues

Wireless transmission issues can result from a variety of factors. Combining two or more of the factors together will compound the issue. Table 5-1 summarizes some of the more common factors that impact wireless transmission.

Table 5-1   Factors That Impact Wireless Transmission

Wireless Transmission Issue	Description
Signal loss	Can be caused by a variety of factors, including distance from the closest access point (AP), lack of sufficient power to the AP, and obstruction between the AP and the end user.
Interference	WLANs operate in either the 2.4GHz or 5GHz radio frequency band. Other devices, such as baby monitors and wireless telephones, also operate in the 2.4GHz range. The signals from these devices can interfere with WLAN transmissions if the channels are overlapping.
Overlapping channels	Devices that use the 2.4GHz range should be configured to use the non-overlapping channels 1, 6, and 11. If all the APs are configured correctly and there is still interference, use a Wi-Fi analyzer to determine if there are unknown devices overlapping with an AP.
Mismatched channels	Most end devices are set to auto-negotiate the wireless channel with the AP during the association process. However, if this setting is configured manually, this could cause a problem, especially if the device is mobile, such as a smartphone or tablet.
Signal-to-noise ratio	Noise is additional information that is present on the network but is not part of the desired signal. Signal-to-noise ratio can give the administrator a good indication of the level of interference in the WLAN.

Wireless Transmission Issue	Description
Device saturation	This can occur in public locations such as schools or businesses. If too many devices are using the services of one AP, consider adding additional APs to distribute the load.
Bandwidth saturation	Too many devices accessing one AP will cause bandwidth saturation. But older technologies will also experience this problem because they are no longer able to keep up with the bandwidth demands of today's user. For example, it is unlikely that an 802.11b wireless router will be able to stream movies to your TV.
Environmental factors	Interference can be caused by a variety of physical materials including concrete walls, window film, and metal studs. Be sure to consider these factors when attempting to troubleshoot why users are experiencing signal loss. See Table 5-2 for more details on environmental obstacles.
Wireless standards–related factors	These factors include attempting to send more data than possible regarding a specific technology, going farther than the distance supported, and using channels or frequencies outside the scope or specifications of a given technology. Also, most APs are backward compatible with previous standards. However, this may cause issues if, for example, a 802.11g WLAN has to transmit at 802.11n speeds because one user's wireless card doesn't support the later standard.

Homes and offices can contain a variety of environmental features that prove to be obstacles to effective wireless transmission. Some examples are shown in Table 5-2.

Table 5-2   Interior Environmental Obstacles to Wireless Transmissions

Obstacle	Severity	Example Use
Wood/wood paneling	Low	Inside a wall or hollow door
Drywall	Low	Inside walls
Furniture	Low	Couches or office partitions
Clear glass	Low	Windows
Tinted glass	Medium	Windows
People	Medium	High-volume traffic areas that have considerable pedestrian traffic
Ceramic tile	Medium	Walls
Concrete blocks	Medium/high	Outer wall construction
Mirrors	High	Mirror or reflective glass
Metals	High	Metal office partitions, doors, metal office furniture
Water	High	Aquariums, fountains

Wireless Configuration Issues

Consumer-grade wireless APs and routers are configured by the manufacturer to be "out-of-the-box" ready to install, minimizing the technical skills needed by the average consumer. However, in larger environments, such as businesses, schools, and other organizations, an AP installation must be properly configured to work with the existing network infrastructure and address the needs of the user. Table 5-3 summarizes the variety of configuration issues that can arise when installing a wireless router or AP.

Table 5-3   Wireless Configuration Issues

Wireless Configuration Issue	Description
Untested updates	Test updates in a nonproduction environment before applying them to live routers or APs.
Wrong SSID	The Service Set Identifier (SSID) used by clients must match the one configured on the AP. This could be a regular issue if users must manually enter the SSID because SSID broadcast is turned off.
Power levels	Some APs allow you to adjust the power level. The higher the power level, the wider area covered by the AP. In some cases, you might want to reduce the power level to prevent co-channel interference between two APs or avoid sending wireless signals into an unsecure area, such as outside or an adjacent office.
Open networks	WLAN access should be secured with the latest technology, currently WPA2. Users should know to avoid connecting devices to open networks, which can be a security risk.
Rogue access point	A rogue AP could be installed intentionally or unintentionally. Regardless, when users are connected to a rogue AP, confidentiality can be compromised. The person managing the rogue access point could have direct access to all network traffic that is then going to or from the clients' wireless computers.
Wrong antenna type	Better-quality antennas can be purchased for some APs, which can boost the distance the signal can go. Make sure you do not use the wrong antenna type or have other incompatibilities.
Incompatibilities	Any features that are required for network connectivity on the wireless network must be supported by both the client and the AP. For example, incompatible wireless standards, such 802.11a and 802.11g, cannot exist on the same WLAN.
Wrong encryption	If encryption is enabled on the connecting system, the encryption type must match what is set on the AP. For example, if the AP uses WPA2-AES, the connecting system must also use WPA2-AES.
Bounce	Wireless signals bounce off walls, ceilings, and other objects. Some technologies, such as 802.11n and 802.11ac, can leverage this tendency to some degree, but fewer obstructions between the access point and the client make for a better wireless connection.

Wireless Configuration Issue	Description
MIMO	802.11n and 802.11ac APs can leverage multiple-input and multiple-output (MIMO), which uses multiple antennas and channels simultaneously. If throughput is not as expected, confirm that the client and access point both support the technology that uses MIMO, or in the case of 802.11ac, the enhanced multi-user MIMO (MU-MIMO).
AP placement	If signal strength is low, try moving the AP to a new location. Moving it just a few feet can make a difference. Wireless site surveys tools can be used to assist with proper Wi-Fi AP placement as well as new Wi-Fi network planning.
AP configurations (LWAPP, thin vs. thick)	Autonomous APs, or thick APs, perform key functions, such as authentication, filtering, QoS enforcement, port forwarding, and so on. A thin AP relies on a wireless LAN controller (WLC) for these services. The AP and WLC typically use the Lightweight Access Point Protocol (LWAPP) to relay configuration parameters. If this is done wirelessly, then all the potential issues that impact AP-to-client connections can also impact AP-to-WLC connections.

Video: Wireless Troubleshooting Overview

Refer to the Digital Study Guide to view this video.

Activity: Identify the Wireless Issue

Refer to the Digital Study Guide to complete this activity.

Study Resources

For today's exam topics, refer to the following resources for more study.

Resource	Location	Topic
Primary Resources		
Certification Guide	8	Wireless LANs
	13	Wireless Troubleshooting
Video Course	18	Wireless LAN Issues
Exam Cram	8	Wireless Troubleshooting Checklist
Supplemental Resources		
Flash Cards	20	Wireless Troubleshooting
Quick Reference	20	Wireless Troubleshooting

Check Your Understanding

Refer to the Digital Study Guide to take a 10-question quiz covering the content of this day.

Troubleshoot Copper and Fiber Cabling Issues

CompTIA Network+ N10-006 Exam Topics

- 4.4 Given a scenario, troubleshoot and resolve common copper cable issues
- 4.5 Given a scenario, troubleshoot and resolve common fiber cable issues

Key Topics

Today, we review the common types of issues that occur with copper and fiber cabling. For the Network+ exam, you are not expected to be an expert cable installer. However, you should be aware of the types of problems network technicians run into during day-to-day operation, how to test for them, and what steps will need to be taken to resolve the issue. If the issue is with the cabling, you would most likely escalate the issue to the appropriate person to resolve the problem—especially if the issue is in a fiber installation.

Common Copper Cable Issues

Several issues can arise due to improper cable terminations or connections. Most of these issues can be easily detected using a multifunction cable tester. In addition, there are issues that are caused by going beyond the physical limitations of the copper cable. The following list details the common copper cable issues you should be aware of for the Network+ exam:

- **Bad wiring**–Straight-through cables should be terminated using the same standard on both ends. Crossover cables should be terminated with TIA-568A on one end and TIA-568B on the other end.

- **Tx/Rx reverse**–Although many NICs now support medium dependent interface crossover (MDIX) and can auto-detect the cable type connected, some older device connections may require you to connect the correct cable type to avoid reversing the transmit and receive pairs.

- **Short**–One or more pins incorrectly connect to the wrong pin or pins on the other end of the cable. For example, in a straight-through cable the 1 pin should connect to the 1 pin on the far side–not the 2 pin.

- **Open**–One or more pins do not have connectivity to the pin or pins on the other end of the cable. This can happen when the installer does not correctly trim the wires and sufficiently push the wires all the way into the RJ-45 connector.

- **Split pairs**–This occurs when, according to the standard, the incorrect wires are used for the transmit or receive pairs. Although this may work if both ends of the cable are similarly terminated, a cable tester will register a split pair.

- **Bad connections**–The physical connection where the cable connects to a device can cause issues. For example, although rare, the installer may have used a defective RJ-45 connector. Also, some connections are achieved using an adapter that converts from one cable type to another, such as small form-factor pluggable (SFP) and gigabit interface converter (GBIC) adapters. If the incorrect type of SFP, GBIC, cable, or cable termination is used, it could cause a failure. A faulty or bad SFP, GBIC, cable, or cable termination can also cause a problem.

- **Crosstalk**–Crosstalk happens when the signal in one cable interferes with the signal in another cable. There are two types of crosstalk: near-end (NEXT) and far-end crosstalk (FEXT). NEXT refers to interference between adjacent wire pairs within the twisted-pair cable at the near end of the link. FEXT is the same interference, but is detected to be originating at the far end of the cable. The result is that a portion of the outgoing signal is coupled back into the received signal. Crosstalk can be minimized by using a higher category of cabling because higher categories of cables better limit the radiation of electromagnetic waves.

- **Distance limitations**–All cable runs have a distance limitation before the signal begins to attenuate or weaken to a decibel level that cannot be interpreted at the far end. When cable lengths have to be run farther than the recommended lengths, signal repeaters can be used to boost the signal as it travels.

- **Cable placement**–Cabling should be placed in areas to avoid being near sources of electromagnetic interference (EMI) and radio frequency interference (RFI). Cable management, including the use of cable trays, protects the cables from physical abuse as well, such as being stepped on, tripped over, or stressed due to pulling. Appropriate cable placement along with proper labeling and documentation of patch panels and wiring closet connections improve the ability to troubleshoot if a connectivity issue is found.

Common Fiber Cable Issues

Fiber cables are susceptible to some of the same kinds of issues as copper cables. A single-mode fiber run can extend up to 2 kilometers without the need to repeat the signal, whereas multimode fiber runs are typically limited to 550 meters. Although fiber cable runs can go farther than copper, fiber still suffers from attenuation and decibel loss if the distance limit is exceeded.

In addition, the connectors and adapters used in fiber installation must be the correct type and in proper working order. The SFP/GBIC connectors and cabling all must support the type of frequencies used over a fiber cable. If there is a mismatch among the module type, the cabling, and the termination being used, that could cause a failure.

Clean fiber optic components are necessary to ensure that the light connections are as clear as possible. A 9-micrometer speck of dust is enough to completely block a single-mode fiber's ability to transmit light. A fiberscope that can provide at least 200× magnification is used to inspect the ends of fiber cables. Cleaning the ends is done using special dry cleaning tools and lint-free wipes or swabs.

Finally, fiber has limits on the amount of bend the cable can have before the light transmission is impeded or disrupted. The TIA-568B.3 standard specifies the bend radius for various fiber cable types and installation scenarios. For example, a horizontal cable run requires a no less than 25mm bend radius after installation. But during installation, that should be twice as much because you are applying tension to the cable.

Video: Cabling Issues Overview

Refer to the Digital Study Guide to view this video.

Activity: Identify the Cabling Issue

Refer to the Digital Study Guide to complete this activity.

Study Resources

For today's exam topics, refer to the following resources for more study.

Resource	Location	Topic
Primary Resource		
Certification Guide	13	Physical Layer Troubleshooting
Video Course	18	Layer 1 Troubleshooting
Exam Cram	12	Troubleshooting the Network
Supplemental Resource		
Lab Simulator	13	Identify Common Cat5 Wiring Problems
Flash Cards	20	Copper Troubleshooting
	21	Fiber Troubleshooting
Quick Reference	20	Copper Troubleshooting
	21	Fiber Troubleshooting

Check Your Understanding

Refer to the Digital Study Guide to take a 10-question quiz covering the content of this day.

Troubleshoot Network Issues

CompTIA Network+ N10-006 Exam Topics

- 4.6 Given a scenario, troubleshoot and resolve common network issues

Key Topics

Network issues typically involve one or more of the first three layers of the OSI model. Today, we review common network issues at the physical, data link, and network layers, which you should be familiar with for the Network+ exam.

Physical Layer Issues

Nothing can happen on the network without a solid physical layer implementation. That is why I would tell my students to check the physical layer whenever they had a problem with a lab configuration. More often than not, they had incorrectly wired the equipment, had not powered on a device, or had missed some other physical layer issue that was causing the problem.

For the Network+ exam you should be familiar with the following physical layer issues:

- **Cable placement**—Recall from yesterday's review that cabling should be placed in areas to avoid being near sources of electromagnetic interference (EMI) and radio frequency interference (RFI). Use cable management techniques and products to avoid cable stress and to keep them orderly.

- **Hardware failure**—If the cabling has been verified, the issue could be hardware failure, such as the NIC on the client computer or the switch to which the client connects. Identify where the failure is occurring and replace that hardware component. If the hardware component is integrated, it might require replacing an entire motherboard or device. Another alternative is to simply use a different port when possible; for example, a user on a laptop could employ a network adapter that you can add to the system via USB.

- **Power failure/power anomalies**—To protect against power failures and anomalies, such as brownouts or dips in current, use power conditioners with uninterruptible power supplies (UPS). For longer-term protection against power loss, use power generators.

- **Interface errors**—The operating systems on switches and routers typically gather statistics on each interface, including interface errors, resets, and dropped packets. Use monitoring tools such as SNMPv3 to securely allow events such as excessive interface errors to be reported to an SNMP management station.

- **Simultaneous wired/wireless connections**—Many laptops have a wired and a wireless NIC. If both interfaces are active and are connected to different networks, the operating system might not handle that situation successfully. One resolution for this is to disable one of the network interface cards.

- **MTU/MTU black hole**—The maximum transmission unit (MTU) is the maximum packet size that a particular interface will transmit. If a packet is too big, it must be fragmented. If a network device has been configured to fragment packets and to not reply to the sender to indicate that there is a problem, an MTU black hole will result. To resolve this issue, use an application that discovers the smallest MTU in the path. Once this is discovered, the application will make sure that the MTU never exceeds the smallest MTU during the network session.

Data Link Layer Issues

Networks rely on Ethernet switches that operate at the data link layer. Data link issues include the following:

- **Broadcast storms/switching loop**—Theoretically, modern networks should not have a broadcast storm or switching loop because the Spanning Tree Protocol (STP) takes care of making sure redundant paths are blocked. However, a bad interface module can break STP and cause issues.

- **Speed and duplex mismatch**—A duplex mismatch could result in slow communication. A speed mismatch could cause no communication. Whenever possible, and to avoid this issue, make sure that all interfaces are auto-negotiating speed and duplex settings.

- **Incorrect VLAN assignment**—Several issues could result from a VLAN misconfiguration, including the inability to connect to other devices that should be in the same VLAN. Keep in mind that all devices belonging to the same VLAN should be assigned IP addresses in the same subnet. Also, if you want traffic to flow between VLANs, that traffic has to be routed.

- **Discovering neighbors**—Neighbor discovery processes such as the open standard Link Layer Discovery Protocol (LLDP) and the Cisco proprietary Cisco Discovery Protocol (CDP) can help a network technician gather information about other devices on the network. Using **show** commands, such as **show cdp neighbors detail** on Cisco switches, can reveal important information about directly connected devices. However, LLDP and CDP are also a security concern. These protocols should be disabled on interfaces that connect to end users to avoid revealing sensitive information.

- **NIC teaming misconfiguration**—NIC teaming is the process of combining multiple NICs so that the operating system sees the NICs as one virtual NIC. For example, in Windows Server 2012, you can configure up to 32 NICs as part of the same team. The server would then see the team as one virtual NIC. Using all the physical NICs at the same time is called an active-active configuration. Placing one or more NICs in standby mode is called an active-passive configuration. On the switch, you can employ aggregation techniques, such as using the Link Aggregation Control Protocol (LACP), to bond multiple ports into one port channel. Therefore, issues can occur on one or both ends of this configuration. If the throughput of the server is not performing at acceptable levels, you will need to check both the server's NIC teaming configuration and the switch's port aggregation configuration.

Network Layer Issues

Many configurations, if done incorrectly, could cause a network failure for a device or an entire network. The misconfiguration of an interface, or applying a configuration for the wrong interface, could cause problems. Network layer issues are usually the result of either an IP addressing or routing protocol misconfiguration. The IP addressing issues could be on some device in the path that is hindering end-to-end connectivity. Or it could a DHCP or DNS server misconfiguration. The following list summarizes the types of network layer issues you should be able to identify and resolve for the Network+ exam:

- **Misconfigured IP addressing**—End devices must be configured with appropriate addressing in order to communicate with devices on the network. At least three addressing parameters need to be configured: the IP address, the subnet mask, and the default gateway. If any one of these is misconfigured, the device may not be able to communicate with other devices on the network. Misconfigured IP addressing issues normally occur because the device was statically configured. To avoid these types of issues, using dynamic addressing whenever possible.

- **Misconfigured DHCP**—Dynamic Host Configuration Protocol is commonly used in networks to ease the process of assigning addressing information to end devices. A pool of IP addresses, a default gateway, and a DNS server address are typical configurations for DHCP servers. One or more misconfigured parameters on the DHCP server could cause connectivity issues for end devices.

- **Misconfigured DNS**—The Domain Name System (DNS) resolves names to IP addresses so that when a user types in a web address, the computer can get the corresponding IP address. If the DNS server is not reachable, or the DNS server IP address is incorrect and does not point to a real DNS server, that could cause a failure of name resolution on the computer. You can use the **nslookup** tool to test the DNS resolution process on the computer.

- **Missing IP routes**—Similar to end-device configurations, routes to remote networks can be statically or dynamically configured on routers. Most stub routers are statically configured with one route pointing to another router to reach remote networks. Routers that have more than one way to get to a remote network are typically configured with a dynamic routing protocol. In either case (static or dynamic configurations), a router can have a missing route. Using **traceroute**, as well as displaying the routing table, helps identify a missing IP route. The correction to this problem is to either add a static route or to correctly configure the dynamic routing protocol so that the route appears in the table.

Video: Network Issues Overview

Refer to the Digital Study Guide to view this video.

Activity: Identify the Network Issue

Refer to the Digital Study Guide to complete this activity.

Study Resources

For today's exam topics, refer to the following resources for more study.

Resource	Location	Topic
Primary Resources		
Certification Guide	13	Physical Layer Troubleshooting
		Data Link Layer Troubleshooting
		Network Layer Troubleshooting
Video Course	18	Layer 1 Troubleshooting
		Layer 2 Troubleshooting
		Layer 3 Troubleshooting
Exam Cram	12	Troubleshooting the Network
Supplemental Resources		
Lab Simulator	6	Verifying a Router-to-Router Connection with Cisco Discovery Protocol
	10	Using ipconfig, ping, arp, and tracert Together to Troubleshoot Connectivity
		Using netstat to Troubleshoot Connectivity
		Using Basic Linux Troubleshooting Commands
	13	Troubleshooting Practice
Flash Cards	21	Common Network Issues
Quick Reference	21	Common Network Issues

Check Your Understanding

Refer to the Digital Study Guide to take a 10-question quiz covering the content of this day.

Troubleshoot Security Issues

CompTIA Network+ N10-006 Exam Topics

- 4.7 Given a scenario, troubleshoot and resolve common security issues

Key Topics

Some of the common security issues we review today were reviewed on Day 16, "Risks, Threats, and Vulnerabilities." However, today we focus on the security issues listed by CompTIA for this Network+ exam objective.

Security Configuration Issues

The devices and applications that secure our networks need to be configured properly if they are to do their jobs effectively. In addition, security must be monitored continuously and configurations updated to address emerging threats. The following are common security configuration issues you should be aware of for the Network+ exam:

- **Misconfigured firewall**—Firewall configurations can be somewhat complex. Therefore, it is not uncommon to allow unauthorized access through open ports or the wrong IP addresses. Conversely, the firewall may deny a legitimate user with the right IP address access because a port is closed. A firewall should be thoroughly tested in a lab environment before deployment in a production network. After deployment, the firewall must be vigilantly monitored to ensure that it is filtering traffic according to the company's security policy.

- **Misconfigured ACLs/applications**—Similar to firewall configurations, an ACL configured on a router, switch, or server could be too permissive and allow traffic that should otherwise be denied. Or it may be denying traffic that should be permitted. Recall that ACLs are evaluated from the top down. If an entry toward the top of the list is denying a user who is permitted later in the list, then you need to reorder the statements. Also, remember that ACLs have an implicit deny statement at the end of the list. If traffic is not explicitly permitted, it will be denied. Some applications also include security features that, if misconfigured, can allow users who should not have access to applications to gain it (or achieve elevated privileges).

- **Domain/local group configurations**—A popular way of managing Microsoft Active Directory domains and local groups is through group management. Providing a group access to network resources, and then associating multiple user accounts with that group, simplifies administration. If the permissions granted in either the domain or the local groups are incorrect or are too lenient, this poses a security risk. Periodic auditing should look for user accounts that have not been used for an extended period, which can then be disabled or deleted.

- **Authentication issues**—Misconfigured Terminal Access Controller Access-Control System (TACACS) and Remote Authentication Dial-In User Service (RADIUS) servers can leave devices vulnerable to security attacks. It is recommended that you run a vulnerability scanner, such as Nessus, against your own system to look for authentication problems. Authentication issues can result in users unintentionally or maliciously obtaining improper access. In addition, if a network device is unable to use a configured TACACS AAA server, troubleshooting might involve verifying that the password configured on both the AAA server and the network device that is trying to use the AAA server is correctly configured. For end-user authentication and authorization, it is common to use 802.1x and a centralized AAA server using RADIUS. Troubleshooting might involve verifying network connectivity between the switch attached to the user and the AAA server using **ping** or **traceroute**. Many vendors have equipment with a default password, which if not changed could be a vulnerability because an attacker could attempt to use that password for access to the network device.

- **Backdoor access**—Applications under development often contain backdoors so that programmers can quickly access areas they are working on. After the application is developed, any backdoor access should be removed for overall security purposes.

Other Security Issues

In addition to security configuration issues, you should be aware of the following additional security issues for the Network+ exam:

- **Malware**—Viruses, Trojans, and worms are types of malicious software, or malware. Malware is usually downloaded or installed as a result of a user opening an email attachment or visiting a website. Users should be trained on security awareness, and anti-malware software should be running on all user devices. Intrusion prevention systems (IPS) and unified threat management (UTM) systems can also help protect against malware.

- **Unpatched firmware/OSs**—Malware is usually coded to look for known vulnerabilities in firmware and operating systems. Therefore, a method for preventing malware is to apply updates as soon as a new security patch is released. If there is a known security flaw and a security patch is available, it should be implemented as quickly as it can be tested and verified.

- **Malicious users**—A malicious user is one who is either trusted (meaning the person has a user account and been granted access to the network at some level) or untrusted. In either case, the user could launch attacks against the network to discover confidential information or cause damage. Methods employed by malicious users for discovery and reconnaissance attacks sometimes include using network scans and packet-sniffing tools. One of the simplest defenses against reconnaissance and packet sniffing is to encrypt your network traffic.

- **Denial of service (DoS)**—DoS attacks keep systems so busy responding to non-legitimate requests that the ability to respond to legitimate requests is hampered. Although the ping of death is called out in the exam objectives, this threat has largely been mitigated by current operating systems and devices. However, DoS attacks continue to use more sophisticated methods, such as amplification and reflection attacks on specific protocol vulnerabilities. A DoS attack does not have to originate from outside the organization. For example, an attacker can use ARP cache poisoning techniques to trick devices on the LAN to forward all traffic to the attacker instead of the default gateway. The attacker is denying default gateway services to local users. Some approaches to mitigating a DoS attack include hardening network devices by removing unneeded services and controlling what those devices are allowed to do. Approaches to specific attacks, such as ARP cache poisoning, may require specific configurations on the local switches.

- **Banner grabbing**—Banner grabbing is the process of learning information about end systems or servers by capturing their responses to specific requests. For example, using tools such as Nmap, you can learn what version of Apache and Linux is running on a web server as well as what ports are open. Although an administrator might need to query a remote server to determine this information, attackers should be blocked from initiating the same type of requests.

- **MAC address OUI**—Banner grabbing can also reveal a device's MAC address. MAC addresses contain two parts: a Organizationally Unique Identifier (OUI) and a vendor code. As part of a reconnaissance attack, an attacker can use the OUI to look up the manufacturer and possibly the type of NIC that the MAC was assigned to. This type of information can help the attacker launch additional attacks. Firewall rules and policies should be implemented to restrict the revealing of MAC address information.

- **Jamming**—Normally associated with wireless networks, jamming is a type of DoS attack that uses specialized software to send out a stream of data (usually broadcasts) in one or more wireless channels. The result is that legitimate users cannot access the WLAN. To reduce this risk, a wireless LAN controller that is managing a group of access points can report on both rogue access points and malicious activity. Some vendors can also implement jamming as a preventive measure to stop rogue access points from successfully connecting to the corporate network.

Video: Security Issues Overview

Refer to the Digital Study Guide to view this video.

Activity: Identify the Security Issue

Refer to the Digital Study Guide to complete this activity.

Study Resources

For today's exam topics, refer to the following resources for more study.

Resource	Location	Topic
Primary Resources		
Certification Guide	12	All
Exam Cram	12	Managing Common Security Threats
Video Course	14	Network Security
Supplemental Resources		
Flash Cards	21	Security Issues
Quick Reference	21	Security Issues

Check Your Understanding

Refer to the Digital Study Guide to take a 10-question quiz covering the content of this day.

Troubleshoot WAN Issues

CompTIA Network+ N10-006 Exam Topics

- 4.8 Given a scenario, troubleshoot and resolve common WAN issues

Key Topics

In this final day before your Network+ exam, we review the common issues that can arise with WANs.

Common WAN Issues

In many circumstances, a WAN issue could be beyond your organization's control. However, sometimes it is the customer premises equipment (CPE) that is the cause of the issue. Furthermore, you could have ISP-facing configuration issues or policies that are causing the problem. The following list details the common WAN issues you should know for the Network+ exam:

- **Loss of Internet connectivity**—The top of the list of WAN issues is loss of connectivity. Assuming the account with the WAN service provider is up to date and there are no issues with the CPE, then try to ping the other end of your WAN connection. If the ping fails, call your provider. If, on the other hand, you can ping the other side, but can't reach a specific location, such as corporate headquarters, then use tools such as **traceroute** to determine where the traffic is blocked. Most likely, the issue is on the remote end, such as a new policy implementation, bad interface card, or equipment failure.

- **Interface errors**—The vendor-specific **show** commands on the router can reveal the quantity of interface errors. Network monitoring tools can be configured to poll interfaces periodically for these same statistics. If an unacceptable threshold of errors is exceeded, an alert can be sent to the administrator. The errors could be due to a variety of factors, such as an interface starting to fail or poor cable connections.

- **Split horizon**—To avoid routing loops, a router does not advertise a network over the same interface that it learned about a network. However, in some WAN topologies, such as hub-and-spoke, where the hub router is using one physical interface to connect to multiple branch locations, it may be necessary to disable the split horizon rule. This will allow the headquarters router (the hub) to advertise routes learned from one branch to other branches.

- **DNS issues**—DNS issues regarding WAN connectivity relate specifically the DNS configurations on your border devices. In larger organizations, local DNS servers help alleviate demands for WAN bandwidth by replying to local DNS requests. However, if the local DNS server does not have a record for a domain name, it must request the record from another DNS server. If the configuration for that remote DNS server is wrong, there will be issues resolving domain names. If DNS issues arise, be sure that border devices and internal DNS servers are configured with a remote DNS server for name resolutions.

- **Interference**—Recall from Day 4, "Troubleshoot Copper and Fiber Cabling Issues," that several sources of interference can cause cabling issues. The same holds true for WAN cabling. Use cable management to avoid sources of electromagnetic interference. If problems occur, use tools such as cable testers to track down the source of the issue. Wireless connectivity on the WAN side can be impacted by a number of factors, which we review a bit later when discussing satellites.

- **Router configurations**—A border router sits between an organization's network and the WAN service provider's network. Changes to the router configuration should be done by authorized administrators using proper change-control procedures. Backups of router configurations should be stored periodically and available if the system needs to be restored due to a complete loss of a router.

- **Customer premises equipment**—CPE is equipment located at the WAN customer's site. Some of the equipment may be owned or leased from the service provider. Service level agreements (SLAs) establish who is responsible for which management tasks. Care should be taken to protect against unauthorized access and changes to this equipment. The following list of terms normally apply to CPE:

  - The **demarcation point**, or demarc or point of demarcation (POD), is the physical point where the customer's responsibility for the network begins. This interface between the service provider and the company receiving WAN services is also sometimes referred to as the network interface unit (NIU).

  - A **smart jack**, also known as an intelligent network interface device (INID), can be used as the demarc. Smart jacks can be configured to code the signaling to match the customer's equipment.

  - Smart jacks typically use **loopbacks** to send diagnostic information back to the WAN service provider to test functionality of the WAN circuit. This is how they might be able to determine that an issue is on their side of the connection.

  - A **channel service unit/data service unit (CSU/DSU)** is a device that converts the digital signals that are used by the customer's router interfaces to make the signals compatible with the signals used on the wide area network. In today's equipment, this functionality is built in to the router WAN interface card, which can directly connect to a WAN circuit such as a T1.

  - **Copper line drivers** are used when the distance of a specific cable run needs to be extended beyond its limitation. These WAN-side repeaters regenerate and amplify the signal to keep it at an acceptable level.

- **Company security policy**—For WAN implementations, the security policy could include the throttling or the limiting of certain types of traffic that could help protect against a DoS attack. A security policy also can indicate that certain types of websites should not be accessible from company computers. This type of URL filtering based on type is a form of blocking. Blocking can also be applied to certain types of inbound requests to public-facing servers to help protect against attacks targeting those servers. A corporate policy might also include details regarding fair access and utilization limits to protect against misuse of network resources and services, including Internet access.

- **Satellites**—These wireless connections are susceptible to the following unique issues:

  - **Rain fade**—The smaller the dish, the more susceptible it is to moisture interference.

  - **Latency**—The time lapse between sending and requesting information is high due to the distance it has to travel.

  - **Line of sight**—The path between the satellite dish and the satellite should be as unobstructed as possible.

Video: **Common WAN Issues**

Refer to the Digital Study Guide to view this video.

Activity: **Identify the WAN Terminology**

Refer to the Digital Study Guide to complete this activity.

Study Resources

For today's exam topics, refer to the following resources for more study.

Resource	Location	Topic
Primary Resource		
Certification Guide	7	All
Exam Cram	7	Troubleshooting Common Issues
Secondary Resource		
Flash Cards	21	WAN Issues
Quick Reference	21	WAN Issues

Check Your Understanding

Refer to the Digital Study Guide to take a 10-question quiz covering the content of this day.

Today is your opportunity to prove that you have what it takes to design, configure, manage, and troubleshoot wired and wireless networks. Just 90 minutes and up to 90 questions stand between you and your Network+ certification. Use the following information to focus on the process details for the day of your Network+ exam.

What You Need for the Exam

Write down the exam location, date, exam time, exam center phone number, and the proctor's name.

Remember the following items on exam day:

- You must have two forms of ID that include a photo and signature, such as a driver's license, passport, or military identification. In addition, the test center admission process requires the capture of a digital photo and digital signature.

- The test proctor will take you through the agreement and set up your testing station after you have signed the agreement.

- The test proctor will give you a sheet for scratch paper or a dry erase pad. Do not take these out of the room.

- The testing center will store any personal items while you take the exam. It is best to bring only what you will need.

- You will be monitored during the entire exam.

What You Should Receive After Completion

When you complete the exam, you will see an immediate electronic response as to whether you passed or failed. The proctor will give you a certified score report with the following important information:

- Your score report, including the minimum passing score and your score on the exam. The report will also include a breakout displaying your percentage for each general exam topic.

- Identification information that you will need to track your certification. *Do not lose your certified examination score report.*

Summary

Your state of mind is a key factor in your success on the Network+ exam. If you know the details of the exam topics and the details of the exam process, you can begin the exam with confidence and focus. Arrive early to the exam. Bring earplugs in the off chance that a testing neighbor has a bad cough or any loud nervous habits. Do not let an extremely difficult or specific question impede your progress. Answer each question confidently and move on.

Post-Exam Information

The accomplishment of signing up for and actually taking the Network+ exam is no small feat. Many network engineers have avoided certification exams for years. The following sections discuss your options after exam day.

Receiving Your Certificate

If you passed the exam, you will receive your official CompTIA certificate in about six weeks (eight weeks internationally) after exam day. Your certificate will be mailed to the address you provided when you registered for the exam.

When you receive your certificate, you may want to frame it and put it on a wall. A certificate hanging on a wall is much harder to lose than a certificate in a filing cabinet or random folder. You never know when an employer or academic institution could request a copy.

Your Network+ certification is valid for three years. To keep your certificate valid, you must either pass the Network+ exam again, pass a higher-level CompTIA certification, or complete 30 continuing education units (CEUs). You can track all your CompTIA certifications and register for CEUs at the following website:

https://www.certmetrics.com/comptia/login.aspx

Examining Certification Options

After passing the Network+ exam, you may wish to pursue a higher-level CompTIA certification. The hierarchy of exams, from high to low, are as follows:

1. CompTIA Advanced Security Practitioner (CASP)

2. Security+

3. Network+

4. A+

However, if you wish to pursue a career in networking, why not consider a vendor-specific certification? Cisco Systems is the leader in the networking field and their certification exams are among the most highly regarded in the industry.

Cisco has many certifications, but the starting place is definitely the routing and switching Interconnecting Cisco Networking Devices 1 (ICND1) exam. Successfully passing this exam gets you the right to call yourself a Cisco Certified Entry Networking Technician (CCENT). After that, you can choose several paths, including Cisco Certified Network Associate (CCNA) Routing and Switching, Cisco Certified Network Associate Security (CCNA Security), Cisco Certified Design Associate (CCDA), and several others.

Although passing one of the many CCNA exams is not an easy task, it is the starting point for more advanced Cisco certifications such as the Cisco Certified Network Professional exams. To learn more about Cisco certifications, visit The Cisco Learning Network at https://learningnetwork.cisco.com/community/certifications.

If You Failed the Exam

If you fail your first attempt at the Network+ exam, you must wait at least 5 calendar days after the day of the exam to retest. Stay motivated and sign up to take the exam again within a 30-day period of your first attempt. The score report outlines your weaknesses. Find a study group, use online resources, and obtain additional study materials to help you with those difficult topics.

If you are familiar with the general concepts, focus on taking practice exams and memorizing the small details that make the exam so difficult. Consider your first attempt as a formal practice exam and excellent preparation to pass the second attempt.

Summary

Whether you display your certificate and update your resume or prepare to conquer the exam on your second attempt, remember to marvel at the innovation and creativity behind each concept you learn. The ability of our society to continually improve communication will keep you learning, discovering, and employed for a lifetime.

Index

Symbols

2.4GHz band, 165

5GHz band, 165

6to4 tunneling, IPv6, 84

10BASE2, 214

10BASE5, 214

10BASE-T, 214

   limitations of, 141

10GBASE-ER, 214

10GBASE-EW, 214

10GBASE-LR, 214

10GBASE-LW, 214

10GBASE-SR, 214

10GBASE-SW, 214

10GBASE-T, 214

100BASE-FX, 214

100BASE-TX, 214

100GBASE-ER4, 214

100GBASE-LR4, 214

100GBASE-SR10, 214

802.1Q, 159

802.1Q tag inside an Ethernet frame, 159

802.11, 215

   characteristics of, 216

802.11a, 215

802.11ac, 216

802.11a-ht, 165

802.11b, 216

802.11g, 216

802.11g-ht, 165

802.11n, 216

1000BASE-LH, 214

1000BASE-LX, 214

1000BASE-T, 214

1000BASE-TX, 214

1000BASE-ZX, 214

A

AAA (authentication, authorization, and accounting), 13

AAA configuration, 145–146

AAA server, 268

acceptable use policies (AUP), 219

access control entries (ACEs), 196

access control lists (ACLs), 188, 196

access control models, 197–198

access points (APs), 2, 165

ACEs (access control entries), 196

ACLs (access control lists), 188, 196

   misconfigured, 267

active mode, LACP, 146

AD (administrative distance), routing, 93

ad hoc WLAN topologies, 167

Address Resolution Protocol (ARP), 245

address types

   IPv4 addressing, 66–67

   IPv6, 78

      global unicast addresses, 79

      link-local unicast addresses, 79-80

addressing

   classless addressing, 71-73

   IPv4 addressing, 64

      address types, 66-67

      private, 66

      public, 66

      structure, 64-65

   IPv6 addressing. *See* IPv6 addressing

   local addressing, 63

      collision and broadcast domains, 63-64

      MAC addresses, 63

   VLSM, 71-73

administrative distance (AD), routing, 93

ADSL (asymmetric DSL), 27

T

X-Y-Z

To receive your 10% off
Exam Voucher, register
your product at:

www.pearsonitcertification.com/register

and follow the instructions.